D1549872

·710 078719 −2

LEEDS POLYTECHNIC LIBRARY

To Renew give the date due and this No.

145005

Renewal may be made by personal application, in writing or by telephone

Books should be returned on or before the last date shown below

Date due	Date due	Date due	Date due
14. NOV. 1975			
16. JAN. 1976			
−7. DEC. 1979			
−3. JUN. 1983			
−1. JUL. 1983			

TOWN PLANNING

71 0078719 2   TELEPEN

Housing Act 1974

CHAPTER 44

ARRANGEMENT OF SECTIONS

PART I

THE HOUSING CORPORATION: EXTENDED FUNCTIONS

PART II

REGISTRATION OF HOUSING ASSOCIATIONS

A

PART III

FINANCIAL ASSISTANCE FOR HOUSING ASSOCIATIONS

PART IV   *Circ. 14/75*

HOUSING ACTION AREAS

LEEDS POLYTECHNIC

145005

TP V

51253

11. 3. 75

346. 043 HOU

A 2

PART VIII *Circ. 160/74*

COMPULSORY IMPROVEMENT OF DWELLINGS

Dwellings in general improvement areas and housing action areas

A 3

ELIZABETH II

Housing Act 1974

1974 CHAPTER 44

An Act to extend the functions of the Housing Corporation and provide for the registration of, and the giving
of financial assistance to, certain housing associations;
to make further provision in relation to clearance
areas and other areas in which living conditions are
unsatisfactory or otherwise in need of improvement;
to provide for the making of grants towards the
improvement, repair and provision of housing accommodation and for the compulsory improvement of
such accommodation; to amend the law relating to
assistance for house purchase and improvement and
expenditure in connection with the provision and
improvement of housing accommodation and of
hostels; to raise the rateable value limits under the
Leasehold Reform Act 1967; to amend the Housing
Finance Act 1972; to amend the law relating to the
rights and obligations of landlords and tenants and
the enforceability of certain covenants relating to the
development of land; and for purposes connected
therewith. [31st July 1974]

BE IT ENACTED by the Queen's most Excellent Majesty, by and
with the advice and consent of the Lords Spiritual and
Temporal, and Commons, in this present Parliament
assembled, and by the authority of the same, as follows:—

PART I

THE HOUSING CORPORATION: EXTENDED FUNCTIONS

1.—(1) There shall continue to be an authority called the
Housing Corporation and the provisions of Schedule 1 to the

Continuation
of Housing
Corporation with
extended functions.

1964 Act (constitution, proceedings and other matters relating to the Corporation) as amended by Schedule 1 to this Act shall continue to apply in relation to the Corporation.

(2) Without prejudice to any specific function conferred on the Corporation by or under the following provisions of this Act or any other enactment, the Corporation shall have the following general functions, namely,—

(*a*) to promote and assist the development of registered housing associations and of unregistered self-build societies ;

(*b*) to facilitate the proper exercise and performance of the functions, and to publicise the aims and principles, of registered housing associations and unregistered self-build societies ;

(*c*) to establish and maintain a register of housing associations, to exercise supervision and control over registered housing associations and, to such extent as the Secretary of State may require, to act as his agent with respect to the consideration of applications for and the payment of grants to registered housing associations ; and

(*d*) to undertake, to such extent as the Corporation consider necessary, the provision (by construction, acquisition, conversion, improvement or otherwise) of dwellings for letting or for sale and of hostels and the management of dwellings or hostels provided by the Corporation.

(3) The Corporation shall exercise their general functions subject to and in accordance with the provisions of this Part of this Act and Parts II and III thereof.

Control by
Corporation
of dispositions
of land by
housing
associations.

2.—(1) Subject to the following provisions of this section,—

(*a*) a registered housing association may not sell, lease, mortgage, charge or otherwise dispose of any land, and

(*b*) an unregistered housing association may not sell, lease, mortgage, charge or otherwise dispose of any grant-aided land, as defined in Schedule 2 to this Act,

except with the consent of the Corporation.

(2) Subsection (1) above shall not apply to a disposition by a housing association which is a registered charity if—

1960 c. 58.

(*a*) the disposition is one which, by virtue of subsection (1) or subsection (2) of section 29 of the Charities Act 1960 (certain disposals not to take place without an order of the court or of the Charity Commissioners), cannot be made without such an order as is mentioned in that section ; or

(*b*) the disposition is of land which is not grant-aided land, as defined in Schedule 2 to this Act, and is one for which the sanction of an order under the said section 29 is not required by virtue of subsection (3) thereof (certain dispositions excluded from the requirements of that section).

(3) The Charity Commissioners shall consult the Corporation before making any order under section 29 of the Charities 1960 c. 58. Act 1960 permitting a disposition which, apart from subsection (2) above, would be a disposition requiring the consent of the Corporation.

(4) Subsection (1) above shall not apply to the grant of a lease for a term ending within the period of 7 years and 3 months beginning on the date of the grant unless—

(*a*) there is conferred on the lessee (whether by the lease or otherwise) an option for renewal for a term which, together with the original term, would expire outside that period ; or

(*b*) the lease is granted wholly or partly in consideration of a fine.

(5) Without prejudice to the generality of the expression " dispose " in subsection (1) above, in subsection (4) above the expression " lease " includes an agreement for a lease and a licence to occupy and the expressions " grant " and " term " shall be construed accordingly.

(6) Any reference in this section to the consent of the Corporation is a reference to an order under the seal of the Corporation giving their consent.

3.—(1) The Corporation may acquire land, whether by way Acquisition of of purchase, lease, exchange or gift— land.

(*a*) for the purpose of selling or leasing it to a registered housing association or an unregistered self-build society ; or

(*b*) for the purpose of their general functions under section 1(2)(*d*) above.

(2) For the purpose of the purchase of land in Scotland by agreement by the Corporation, the Lands Clauses Acts (except so much thereof as relates to the acquisition of land otherwise than by agreement, and the provisions relating to access to the

special Act, and except sections 120 to 125 of the Lands Clauses
Consolidation (Scotland) Act 1845), and section 6 and sections
70 to 78 of the Railways Clauses Consolidation (Scotland) Act
1845 (as originally enacted and not as amended by section 15
of the Mines (Working Facilities and Support) Act 1923) are
hereby incorporated with this section, and, in construing those
Acts for the purposes of this section, this section shall be deemed
to be the special Act and the Corporation shall be deemed to
be the promoters of the undertaking or company, as the case
may require.

(3) The Corporation may be authorised by the Secretary of
State to purchase land compulsorily for any purpose for which
they could acquire it by agreement under subsection (1) above.

(4) The Acquisition of Land (Authorisation Procedure) Act
1946 or, as the case may be, the Acquisition of Land (Authorisation Procedure) (Scotland) Act 1947 shall apply in relation to
a compulsory purchase of land by the Corporation under subsection (3) above as if the Corporation were a local authority
and as if that subsection were contained in an Act in force
immediately before the commencement of that Act.

(5) In Scotland the Corporation (without prejudice to their
own power to acquire land compulsorily) may request the
Scottish Special Housing Association to acquire land compulsorily on their behalf for any purpose for which the Corporation
may purchase land compulsorily as provided in section 175(2)

of the Housing (Scotland) Act 1966.

(6) The powers of acquisition conferred by this section may
be exercised as respects any land notwithstanding that it is not
immediately required for selling or leasing as mentioned in subsection (1)(a) above or for the purpose of any of the Corporation's general functions under section 1(2)(d) above.

Provision of
dwellings or
hostels and
clearance,
management
and
development
of land.

4.—(1) The Corporation may undertake the provision or
improvement of dwellings or hostels on any land belonging to
them.

(2) The Corporation may clear any land belonging to them
and carry out any other work on the land to prepare it as
a building site or estate, including the laying out and construction of streets or roads and open spaces and the provision of
sewerage facilities and supplies of electricity, gas and water.

(3) The Corporation shall have power to repair, maintain
and insure any buildings or works for the time being on any
land belonging to them and generally to deal in the proper
course of management with any such land and any such buildings or works and to charge for the tenancy or occupation
thereof.

(4) Without prejudice to subsection (3) above, the Corporation may carry out such operations on, and do any other such things in relation to, land belonging to them as appear to them to be conducive to facilitating the provision or improvement of dwellings or hostels on the land, whether by the Corporation themselves, by a registered housing association or by an unregistered self-build society.

(5) In the exercise of their powers under subsection (4) above, the Corporation may carry out any development ancillary to or in connection with the provision of dwellings or hostels, including development which makes provision for any building or land intended for use for commercial, recreational or other nondomestic purposes.

5.—(1) The Corporation may not dispose of any land except in accordance with the provisions of this section.

Disposal of land.

(2) The Corporation may dispose of any land in respect of which they have not exercised their powers under subsection (1) of section 4 above and on which they have not carried out any such development as is mentioned in subsection (5) of that section to—

(*a*) a registered housing association ; or

(*b*) an unregistered self-build society ; or

(*c*) a subsidiary of the Corporation ; or

(*d*) any other body in which the Corporation hold an interest.

(3) The Corporation may dispose of any land on which dwellings or hostels have been provided or improved in exercise of their powers under section 4 above to—

(*a*) a registered housing association, or

(*b*) the council of a county, district or London borough, the Greater London Council or the Common Council of the City of London, or

(*c*) a housing authority as defined in section 78(1) of the Housing (Financial Provisions) (Scotland) Act 1972, or

1972 c. 46.

(*d*) the Commission for the New Towns or a development corporation within the meaning of the New Towns Act 1965, or

1965 c. 59.

(*e*) a subsidiary of the Corporation,

and may sell or lease individual dwellings to persons for their own occupation.

(4) The Corporation may dispose of any building or land intended for use for commercial, recreational or other nondomestic purposes in respect of which development has been

carried out by virtue of section 4(5) above ; but no such building or land may be disposed of for less than the best consideration it commands except with the consent in writing of the Secretary of State.

(5) The Corporation may dispose of any land which is not required for the purposes for which it was acquired but, subject to subsection (6) below, if the land—

(a) was acquired compulsorily by, or on behalf of, the Corporation or by a local authority who transferred the land to the Corporation, or

(b) is not disposed of for the best consideration it commands,

the Corporation shall not dispose of the land except with the consent in writing of the Secretary of State.

(6) The consent of the Secretary of State shall not be required under subsection (5) above to the disposal of land for less than the best consideration it commands if the land is to be used as, or in connection with, a highway or a street not being a highway.

(7) For the purposes of subsection (5) above " local authority ", in relation to England and Wales, means—

(a) the council of a district or, in the case of an acquisition before 1st April 1974, the council of a county borough or county district ; and

(b) the council of a London borough or the Common Council of the City of London.

Acquisition of securities and control of subsidiaries.

6.—(1) The Corporation may with the consent of the Secretary of State subscribe for or acquire any securities of a body corporate and promote or participate in the promotion of any such body.

(2) The Corporation shall exercise their control over any subsidiary of theirs so as to secure that the subsidiary does not—

(a) engage in any activity which the Corporation are not empowered to carry on ;

(b) engage in any activity in a manner in which the Corporation themselves could not engage, by reason of any direction given to the Corporation under section 1(2) of the 1964 Act ;

(c) except with the consent of the Secretary of State, borrow money from any person other than the Corporation ; or

(d) except with the consent of the Secretary of State, raise money by the issue of shares or stock to any person other than the Corporation.

(3) In this section "securities" means shares, stock, deben-   PART I
tures, debenture stock and any securities of a like nature.

7.—(1) Subject to subsection (9) below, the borrowing powers Borrowing
of the Corporation shall be those, and only those, conferred by powers.
subsections (2) to (4) below ; and the powers conferred by those
subsections are subject to subsection (5) below.

(2) The Corporation may borrow from the Secretary of State,
and the Secretary of State may lend to the Corporation, by way
of temporary loan or otherwise, such sums in sterling as the
Corporation may require.

(3) Without prejudice to subsection (2) above, the Corporation may, with the consent of the Secretary of State or in accordance with a general authorisation given by him, borrow tem-
porarily by overdraft or otherwise such sums in sterling as the
Corporation may require.

(4) The Corporation may, with the consent of the Secretary of
State, borrow on such terms as the Secretary of State may from
time to time specify,—

    (*a*) from such persons as he may so specify, sums in a
         currency other than sterling ; and

    (*b*) from the European Investment Bank or the Commission
         of the European Communities, sums in any currency.

(5) The aggregate amount outstanding by way of the principal
of—

    (*a*) advances made to the Corporation under section 9 of
         the 1964 Act before the day appointed for the coming
         into operation of this Part of this Act,

    (*b*) advances made to housing associations, before the day
         appointed for the coming into force of section 34 of
         this Act, under section 7 of the Housing Act 1961, 1961 c. 65.
         section 11 of the Housing (Scotland) Act 1962 and 1962 c. 28.
         section 23 of the Housing (Financial Provisions) (Scot- 1968 c. 31.
         land) Act 1968 (being advances in respect of which the
         functions of the Secretary of State are by the said
         section 34 transferred to the Corporation),

    (*c*) any money borrowed by the Corporation under this
         section, and

    (*d*) any money borrowed by a subsidiary of the Corporation,
         otherwise than from the Corporation,

shall not exceed £400 million or such greater sum not exceeding
£750 million as the Secretary of State may by order specify,
and no such order shall be made unless a draft of it has been
laid before and approved by the Commons House of Parliament.

(6) Any loan made by the Secretary of State in pursuance of this section shall be repaid to him at such times and by such methods, and interest on the loan shall be paid to him at such rates and at such times, as he may from time to time determine.

(7) References in the preceding provisions of this section to the Secretary of State are references to him acting with the approval of the Treasury.

(8) The Treasury may issue out of the National Loans Fund to the Secretary of State such sums as are necessary to enable him to make loans in pursuance of subsection (2) above and any sums received by the Secretary of State in pursuance of subsection (6) above shall be paid into that Fund.

(9) References in this section to borrowing do not include any borrowing from a subsidiary of the Corporation.

Treasury guarantees.

8.—(1) The Treasury may guarantee, in such manner and on such conditions as they think fit, the repayment of the principal of and the payment of interest on any sums which the Corporation borrow from a person other than the Secretary of State.

(2) Immediately after a guarantee is given under this section the Treasury shall lay a statement of the guarantee before each House of Parliament; and where any sum is issued for fulfilling the guarantee so given the Treasury shall, as soon as possible after the end of each financial year (beginning with that in which the sum is issued and ending with that in which all liability in respect of the principal of the sum and in respect of interest thereon is finally discharged), lay before each House of Parliament a statement relating to that sum.

(3) Any sums required by the Treasury for fulfilling a guarantee under this section shall be charged on and issued out of the Consolidated Fund.

(4) If any sums are issued in fulfilment of a guarantee given under this section, the Corporation shall make to the Treasury, at such times and in such manner as the Treasury may from time to time direct, payments of such amounts as the Treasury so direct in or towards repayment of the sums so issued and payments of interest, at such rate as the Treasury so direct, on what is outstanding for the time being in respect of sums so issued.

(5) Any sums received by the Treasury in pursuance of subsection (4) above shall be paid into the Consolidated Fund.

Lending powers.

9.—(1) The Corporation may, by way of temporary loan or otherwise, lend to—

(a) a registered housing association,

(b) an unregistered self-build society,

(c) a subsidiary of the Corporation, and

(d) any other body in which the Corporation hold an interest,

for the purpose of enabling any of those bodies to meet the whole or any part of any expenditure incurred or to be incurred by it in carrying out its objects.

(2) The Corporation may, by way of temporary loan or otherwise, lend to an individual for the purpose of assisting him to acquire from the Corporation or from any of the bodies specified in paragraphs (a) to (d) of subsection (1) above a legal estate or interest in a dwelling which he intends to occupy.

(3) Any directions given to the Corporation under section 1(2) of the 1964 Act with respect to the terms of any loan made under subsection (1) or subsection (2) above shall require the consent of the Treasury and, subject to any such directions and to subsection (4) below, the terms on which any such loan is made shall be such as the Corporation may determine, either generally or in any particular case.

(4) The terms of any loan made under subsection (1) above may, and the terms of any loan made under subsection (2) above may not, include terms for preventing repayment of the loan or any part of it before a specified date without the consent of the Corporation.

(5) In any case where—

(a) the Corporation make a loan to an unregistered self-build society under subsection (1)(b) above, and

(b) under a mortgage or heritable security entered into by the society to secure the loan the Corporation have an interest as mortgagee or, as the case may be, as creditor in any land belonging to the society,

the Corporation may, with the written consent of the Secretary of State, give to the society directions with respect to the disposal of that land, and it shall be the duty of the society to comply with the directions so long as the Corporation continue to have such an interest in that land ; and any directions given under this subsection with such consent may be varied or revoked by subsequent directions given thereunder with the like consent.

(6) Where the Corporation propose, under subsection (5) above, to give directions to an unregistered self-build society requiring it to transfer its interest in any land to the Corporation or any other person, the Secretary of State shall not consent to the giving of the directions unless he is satisfied that arrange-

ments have been made which, if the directions are given, will secure that the members of the society receive fair treatment in connection with the transfer.

Miscellaneous financial provisions.   **10.**—(1) With the consent of the Secretary of State, given with the approval of the Treasury, the Corporation may guarantee the repayment of the principal of and the payment of interest on any sums borrowed (otherwise than from the Corporation)—

(*a*) by registered housing associations,

(*b*) by unregistered self-build societies, and

(*c*) by other bodies in which the Corporation hold an interest,

and in any case where the Corporation give a guarantee under this subsection they may impose such terms and conditions as they think fit.

(2) The aggregate amount outstanding in respect of—

(*a*) loans for which the Corporation have given a guarantee under subsection (1) above, and

(*b*) any payments which have been made by the Corporation in meeting any obligation arising by virtue of such a guarantee and have not been repaid to the Corporation,

shall not exceed £100 million.

(3) The Corporation may turn their resources to account so far as they are not required for the exercise of the Corporation's functions.

(4) Any excess of the revenues of the Corporation for any accounting year over the total sums properly chargeable to revenue account for that year shall be applied by the Corporation in such manner as the Secretary of State may, after consultation with the Corporation and with the approval of the Treasury, direct ; and such a direction may require the whole or part of the excess to be paid to the Secretary of State.

(5) The Secretary of State may, with the approval of the Treasury, give to the Corporation directions as to any matter relating to the establishment or management of reserves or the carrying of sums to the credit of any reserves or the application of any reserves for the purposes of the Corporation's functions.

(6) The Secretary of State may, with the approval of the Treasury and after consultation with the Corporation, direct the Corporation to pay to the Secretary of State the whole or part of any sums for the time being standing to the credit of any reserves of the Corporation or being of a capital nature and not required for the exercise of the Corporation's functions.

11. After section 342 of the Income and Corporation Taxes Act 1970 there shall be inserted the following section:—

" Disposals by Housing Corporation and certain housing associations.

342A.—(1) In any case where—

(a) the Housing Corporation dispose of any land to a registered housing association, or

(b) a registered housing association disposes of any land to another registered housing association, or

(c) in pursuance of a direction of the Housing Corporation given under Part II of the Housing Act 1974 requiring it to do so, a registered housing association disposes of any of its property, other than land, to another registered housing association, or

(d) a registered housing association or an unregistered self-build society disposes of any land to the Housing Corporation,

both parties to the disposal shall be treated for the purposes of corporation tax in respect of chargeable gains or, as the case may require, capital gains tax as if the land or property disposed of were acquired from the Housing Corporation, registered housing association or unregistered self-build society making the disposal for a consideration of such an amount as would secure that on the disposal neither a gain nor a loss accrued to the Corporation or, as the case may be, that association or society.

(2) In this section ' registered housing association ' and ' unregistered self-build society ' have the same meanings as in Part I of the Housing Act 1974 ".

PART I
Exclusion of certain disposals of land from tax on chargeable gains.
1970 c. 10.

12. In this Part of this Act—

" heritable security " means a heritable security within the meaning of section 9(8)(a) of the Conveyancing and Feudal Reform (Scotland) Act 1970 ;

" highway ", in relation to Scotland, includes a public right of way ;

" land " includes any estate or interest in or right over land ;

" self-build society " means a housing association whose object is to provide, for sale to, or occupation by, its members, dwellings built or improved principally with the use of its members' own labour and " unregistered self-build society " means a self-build society which is not a registered housing association ;

Interpretation of Part I.
1970 c. 35.

PART I
1948 c. 38.

1964 c. 56.

" subsidiary " has the same meaning as in the Companies
Act 1948 ; and

" the 1964 Act " means the Housing Act 1964.

PART II
REGISTRATION OF HOUSING ASSOCIATIONS

The register
of housing
associations.

13.—(1) There shall be a register of housing associations
which shall be established and maintained by the Corporation
and in which the Corporation may register any housing
association which—

(*a*) is a registered charity and not an exempt charity ; or

1965 c. 12.

(*b*) is a society registered under the Industrial and
Provident Societies Act 1965 (in this Part of this Act
referred to as " the 1965 Act ") and fulfils the
conditions in subsection (2) below.

(2) The conditions referred to in subsection (1)(*b*) above are
that the housing association does not trade for profit and is
established for the purpose of, or has among its objects or
powers those of, providing, constructing, improving or
managing—

(*a*) houses to be kept available for letting, or

(*b*) where the rules of the association restrict membership
of the association to persons entitled or prospectively
entitled (whether as tenants or otherwise) to occupy a
house provided or managed by the association, houses
for occupation by members of the association, or

(*c*) hostels,

and that, if the association has any additional purposes or
objects, it has none which are not mentioned in subsection (3)
below.

(3) The additional purposes or objects referred to in subsection (2) above are those—

(*a*) of providing land or buildings for purposes connected
with the requirements of the persons occupying the
houses or hostels provided or managed by the
association ;

(*b*) of providing amenities or services for the benefit of
those persons, either exclusively or together with other
persons ;

(*c*) of encouraging and giving advice on the formation of
other housing associations which would be eligible for
registration by the Corporation ; and

(*d*) of providing services for, and giving advice on the running of, registered housing associations.

(4) The Corporation shall, after consultation with the committee established under section 14 below, establish criteria which should be satisfied by a housing association seeking registration, and may from time to time, after such consultation, vary those criteria.

(5) In deciding whether to register a housing association, the Corporation shall have regard—

(*a*) to any advice given to them by the committee established under section 14 below, and

(*b*) to the question whether the association satisfies the criteria established in accordance with subsection (4) above.

(6) For all purposes other than rectification of the register, a body shall be conclusively presumed to be a housing association falling within subsection (1) above at any time when it is or was on the register of housing associations.

(7) The register of housing associations shall be open to inspection at the head office of the Corporation at all reasonable times.

14.—(1) There shall be a committee which shall be called the Housing Associations Registration Advisory Committee and shall have the function of advising the Corporation—

The Housing Associations Registration Advisory Committee.

(*a*) generally on the exercise of the Corporation's powers with respect to the registration of housing associations; and

(*b*) when consulted in accordance with subsection (4) of section 13 above, on the establishment and variation of the criteria referred to in that subsection; and

(*c*) on the question whether any particular housing association whose application for registration is referred to the Committee by the Corporation should be registered.

(2) The Committee shall consist of a chairman appointed by the Secretary of State and such number of other members so appointed as the Secretary of State may from time to time determine; and every member shall hold and vacate office in accordance with the terms of his appointment.

(3) The Committee shall consist of persons whom the Secretary of State considers to be qualified to advise the Corporation on the matters referred to in subsection (1) above.

(4) The Secretary of State may, out of money provided by Parliament, pay to all or any of the members of the Committee such salaries or other remuneration as he may with the consent of the Minister for the Civil Service determine.

(5) The Corporation may pay,—

(a) to all or any of the members of the Committee, such travelling and other expenses, and

(b) to persons attending their meetings at the request of the Committee, such travelling and other allowances (including compensation for loss of remunerative time),

as the Secretary of State may with the consent of the Minister for the Civil Service determine.

Removal of bodies from the register.

15.—(1) Where a body has been registered in the register of housing associations, that body shall not be removed from the register except by the Corporation in accordance with the provisions of this section.

(2) If it appears to the Corporation that any body which is registered—

(a) is no longer a housing association falling within paragraph (a) or paragraph (b) of section 13(1) above, or

(b) has ceased to exist or does not operate,

the Corporation shall, on giving not less than 14 days' notice to that body, remove it from the register; and in a case where paragraph (b) above applies, any such notice shall be deemed to be given to a body if it is served at the address last known to the Corporation to be the principal place of business of that body.

(3) A body which is aggrieved by a decision of the Corporation to remove it from the register of housing associations may appeal against the decision to the High Court or, as the case may be, the Court of Session.

(4) If an appeal is brought under subsection (3) above and is not withdrawn the Corporation shall not remove the body concerned from the register of housing associations until the appeal has been finally determined.

(5) No sum shall be paid in respect of a grant under section 29, section 32 or section 33 of this Act to a body which has been removed under this section from the register of housing associations.

(6) Where, at the time of its removal under this section from the register of housing associations, a body owns any land,

section 2 of this Act shall continue to apply to that land after the removal as if the body concerned continued to be a registered housing association.

16.—(1) As soon as may be after registering a housing association or removing a body from the register the Corporation shall give notice of the registration or removal—

(*a*) if the association or body is a registered charity and not an exempt charity, to the Charity Commissioners ; and

(*b*) if the association or body is a society registered under the 1965 Act, to the appropriate registrar.

(2) Where notice is given to the Charity Commissioners or to the appropriate registrar as mentioned in subsection (1) above, the Commissioners or the registrar, as the case may be, shall record the registration or removal from the register by the Corporation.

(3) As soon as may be after an appeal is brought under section 15(3) above, the Corporation shall give notice of the appeal,—

(*a*) if the body appealing is a registered charity and not an exempt charity, to the Charity Commissioners ; and

(*b*) if the body appealing is a society registered under the 1965 Act, to the appropriate registrar.

17.—(1) Subject to subsections (3) and (4) below, on and after 1st April 1975 or such later date as the Secretary of State may by order specify for the purposes of this subsection—

(*a*) no such loan as is specified in sub-paragraphs (*b*) and (*c*) of paragraph 3 of Schedule 2 to this Act shall be made to a housing association unless, at the time the loan is made, the association is a registered housing association ; and

(*b*) the powers of a local authority, including a county council, under paragraphs (*a*) and (*c*) of subsection (3) of section 119 of the Housing Act 1957 or under paragraphs (*a*) and (*c*) of subsection (2) of section 152 of the Housing (Scotland) Act 1966 (to make grants and loans to, and to guarantee payments in respect of money borrowed by, housing associations) shall not be exercisable unless, at the time the grant or loan is made or, as the case may be, the guarantee is given, the housing association is a registered housing association.

(2) Subject to subsection (3) below, the power of the Secretary of State to make grants under section 93 of the Finance Act 1965 (grants to housing associations for affording relief from tax) shall not be exercisable on a claim made by a housing association under that section in respect of a period beginning on or after 6th April 1975 or such later date as the Secretary of State may by order specify for the purposes of this subsection unless, throughout that period, the housing association is a registered housing association.

(3) Subsections (1) and (2) above shall not apply in relation to a housing association if—

    (a) it is for the time being specified in an order made by the Secretary of State under section 80 of the Housing Finance Act 1972 (power to apply to certain housing associations provisions of that Act relating to local authorities) ; or

    (b) before the operative date, the association has made an application for registration to the Corporation and the application has not yet been disposed of by the Corporation.

(4) Nothing in subsection (1)(b) above shall prevent a local authority, including a county council, from making loans under section 119(3)(a) of the Housing Act 1957 or section 152(2)(a) of the Housing (Scotland) Act 1966 to an unregistered housing association for the assistance of the association—

    (a) in connection with any works required to be carried out in pursuance of, or the acquisition of any estate or interest in a dwelling or other building for the purposes of, any arrangements under section 121 of the said Act of 1957 or under section 155 of the said Act of 1966 which, before the operative date, have been approved by the Secretary of State ; or

    (b) in connection with the provision of dwellings which are relevant dwellings, within the meaning of section 73 of the Housing Finance Act 1972 (dwellings taken into account for the purposes of special residual subsidy) ; or

    (c) in connection with the provision of works which are relevant works, approved for subsidy, within the meaning of section 53 of the Housing (Financial Provisions) (Scotland) Act 1972 (works taken into account for the purposes of special residual subsidy) ; or

    (d) in connection with a building scheme, within the meaning of section 75 of the Housing Finance Act 1972, which, before the operative date, has been approved by the Secretary of State for the purposes of that section ; or

(e) in connection with a building scheme or improvement scheme, within the meaning of sections 55 and 57 of the Housing (Financial Provisions) (Scotland) Act 1972, which before the operative date has been approved by the Secretary of State for the purposes of those sections.

18.—(1) On and after the operative date, the reference in sub- section (5) of section 5 of the Rent Act 1968 or in subsection (4) of section 5 of the Rent (Scotland) Act 1971 to a housing association shall be construed as not extending to an unregistered housing association unless—

(a) the association is for the time being specified in an order made by the Secretary of State under section 80 of the Housing Finance Act 1972 ; or

(b) the association is a society registered under the 1965 Act and its rules restrict membership to persons who are tenants or prospective tenants of the association and preclude the granting or assignment of tenancies to persons other than members ; or

(c) the association has made an application for registration to the Corporation before the operative date and the application has not been disposed of by the Corporation.

(2) If at any time, by virtue of subsection (1) above, a tenancy ceases to be one to which Part VIII of the Housing Finance Act 1972 applies, or sections 60 to 66 of the Housing (Financial Provisions) (Scotland) Act 1972 apply, and becomes a protected tenancy for the purposes of the Rent Act 1968, or of the Rent (Scotland) Act 1971, that tenancy shall be a regulated tenancy and the housing association which is the landlord under that tenancy shall give notice in writing to the tenant, in such form as may be prescribed, informing him that his tenancy is no longer excluded from protection under the Rent Act 1968 or the Rent (Scotland) Act 1971.

(3) If, without reasonable excuse, a housing association fails to give notice to a tenant under subsection (2) above within the period of 21 days beginning on the day on which his tenancy becomes a protected tenancy, the association shall be liable on summary conviction to a fine not exceeding £100.

(4) Where an offence under subsection (3) above committed by a body corporate is proved to have been committed with the consent or connivance of, or to be attributable to any neglect on the part of, any director, manager or secretary or other similar officer of the body corporate or any person who was purporting to act in any such capacity, he as well as the body corporate shall be guilty of that offence and shall be liable to be proceeded against and punished accordingly.

PART II

(5) In this section "prescribed" means prescribed by order made by the Secretary of State.

(6) The provisions of Schedule 3 to this Act shall have effect for supplementing this section, and Part I of that Schedule shall come into force on the passing of this Act.

Inquiries into affairs of registered 1965 Act associations.

19.—(1) The Corporation may appoint a person (who may or may not be a member of the Corporation's staff) to conduct an inquiry into the affairs of any registered 1965 Act association.

(2) For the purposes of an inquiry under subsection (1) above, the person appointed to conduct the inquiry may, by notice in writing served on the association concerned or on any person who is or has been an officer or member of the association, require the association or that person to produce to the person appointed to conduct the inquiry such books, accounts and other documents relating to the association's business, and to furnish to him such other information relating to that business, as he considers necessary for the purposes of the inquiry.

(3) Any association or other person who without reasonable excuse fails to comply with the requirements of a notice under subsection (2) above shall be liable on summary conviction to a fine not exceeding £400.

(4) For the purposes of an inquiry under subsection (1) above the Corporation may require the accounts and balance sheet of the association concerned, or such of them as the Corporation may specify, to be audited by an auditor appointed by the Corporation being a person who,—

1968 c. 55.

(a) under section 7(1) of the Friendly and Industrial and Provident Societies Act 1968, is a qualified auditor for the purposes of that Act, or

(b) under section 7(2) of that Act, is a qualified auditor in relation to the particular association whose accounts are required to be audited under this subsection.

(5) Any person appointed to conduct an inquiry under subsection (1) above and any person appointed to make an audit under subsection (4) above shall, on completion of the inquiry or, as the case may be, the audit, make a report to the Corporation on such matters and in such form as the Corporation may specify.

(6) The expenses of an audit under subsection (4) above, including the remuneration of the auditor, shall be paid by the Corporation.

(7) An audit under subsection (4) above shall be additional to, and shall not affect, any audit made or to be made under any other enactment.

20.—(1) Where the Corporation are satisfied, as the result of an inquiry or an audit under section 19 above, that there has been in the administration of a registered 1965 Act association any misconduct or mismanagement, the Corporation may do all or any of the following, namely,— PART II
Corporation's
power to
act for
protection of
registered
1965 Act
associations.

> (a) by order remove any member of the committee of the association, or any officer, agent or servant of the association, who has been responsible for or privy to the misconduct or mismanagement or has by his conduct contributed to it or facilitated it;
>
> (b) order any bank or other person who holds money or securities on behalf of the association not to part with the money or securities without the approval of the Corporation;
>
> (c) by order restrict the transactions which may be entered into, or the nature or amount of the payments which may be made, in the administration of the association without the approval of the Corporation.

(2) The Corporation may also by order remove a member of the committee of a registered 1965 Act association where that member—

> (a) is a bankrupt or, in Scotland, is insolvent within the meaning of paragraph 9(2) of Schedule 3 to the Conveyancing and Feudal Reform (Scotland) Act 1970 or is incapable of acting by reason of mental disorder within the meaning of the Mental Health Act 1959 or the Mental Health (Scotland) Act 1960; 1970 c. 35. 1959 c. 72. 1960 c. 61.
>
> (b) has not acted; or
>
> (c) cannot be found or does not act and his absence or failure to act impedes the committee's proper management of the association's affairs.

(3) The Corporation may by order appoint a person to be a member of the committee of a registered 1965 Act association (whether or not he is a member of the association and, if he is not, notwithstanding that the rules of the association restrict membership of the committee to members of the association)—

> (a) in place of a member of the committee removed by them under this section or otherwise;
>
> (b) where there are no members of the committee; or
>
> (c) where the Corporation are of opinion that it is necessary for the proper management of the association's affairs to have an additional member of its committee.

(4) A person appointed to be a member of the committee of a registered 1965 Act association under subsection (3) above shall hold office for such period and on such terms as the

Corporation may specify and, on the expiry of any such period, the Corporation may renew the appointment for such period as they may specify; but nothing in this subsection shall prevent any such person from retiring from the appointment in accordance with the rules of the association.

(5) Any member of the committee of a registered 1965 Act association or any officer, agent or servant of the association who is ordered by the Corporation to be removed under subsection (1)(*a*) or subsection (2) above may appeal against the order to the High Court or, as the case may be, the Court of Session.

(6) Before making an order under subsection (1)(*a*) or subsection (2) above the Corporation shall give not less than 14 days' notice of their intention to do so—

(*a*) to the person whom they intend to remove, and

(*b*) to the registered 1965 Act association concerned,

and any such notice may be given by post and, if so given to the person whom the Corporation intend to remove, may be addressed to the recipient's last known address in the United Kingdom.

(7) If any person contravenes an order under subsection (1)(*b*) above, he shall be liable on summary conviction to a fine not exceeding £400, or to imprisonment for a term not exceeding 3 months, or to both; but no proceedings for an offence punishable under this subsection shall be instituted in England and Wales except by or with the consent of the Corporation.

Corporation's power to require transfer of land of registered 1965 Act associations. **21.**—(1) Where the Corporation are satisfied, as the result of an inquiry or an audit under section 19 above, that—

(*a*) there has been in the administration of a registered 1965 Act association any misconduct or mismanagement, or

(*b*) the management of the land belonging to any such association would be improved if the land were to be transferred in accordance with the provisions of this section,

the Corporation may, with the consent of the Secretary of State, direct the association to transfer the land belonging to it to another body in accordance with subsection (2) below.

(2) A direction under subsection (1) above may require the association concerned to transfer the land belonging to it,—

(*a*) in a case where that association is a charity, to another registered housing association which is a charity and the objects of which appear to the Corporation to be, as nearly as practicable, akin to those of the association directed to make the transfer; and (*b*) in any other case, to the Corporation or to another registered housing association.

(3) A transfer in pursuance of a direction under subsection (1) above shall be made on the terms that the Corporation or, as the case may be, the association to which the land is transferred will pay or undertake to pay to the association making the transfer such sum, if any, as will be necessary to defray all its proper debts and liabilities (including any debts and liabilities secured on the land to be transferred) after taking into account any money or other assets belonging to the association.

(4) If it appears to the Corporation to be likely that, as a result of a transfer in pursuance of a direction under subsection (1) above, the association making the transfer will be dissolved as mentioned in paragraph (*a*) or paragraph (*b*) of section 55 of the 1965 Act, the Corporation shall secure that the costs of such a dissolution are taken into account in determining the sum payable to the association under subsection (3) above.

22.—(1) Without prejudice to the power of any person under any other enactment to petition for the winding up of a registered housing association which is a company incorporated under the Companies Act 1948, the Corporation may present a petition for the winding up under that Act of any such registered housing association on the ground that the association is failing properly to carry out its purposes or objects.

(2) Subject to section 55(*a*) of the 1965 Act, subsection (1) above shall also apply in relation to a registered housing association which is not such a company as is mentioned in that subsection but which is a registered 1965 Act association.

Corporation's power to petition for winding up of certain registered housing associations. 1948 c. 38.

23.—(1) If a registered 1965 Act association is dissolved as mentioned in paragraph (*a*) or paragraph (*b*) of section 55 of the 1965 Act then, notwithstanding anything in that Act or in the rules of the association, there shall be transferred to the Corporation, or, if the Corporation so directs, to such registered housing association as may be specified in the direction, so much of the property of the association as remains after meeting the claims of its creditors and any other liabilities arising on or before the dissolution.

(2) If it appears to the Corporation to be appropriate to do so in order to avoid the necessity for the sale of any land belonging to a registered 1965 Act association which is being dissolved as mentioned in subsection (1) above and thereby secure the transfer of the land under that subsection, the Corporation may make payments to discharge any such claims or liabilities as are referred to in that subsection.

(3) The Corporation may not dispose of any property transferred to them by virtue of subsection (1) above otherwise

Transfer of net assets on dissolution of registered 1965 Act associations.

than to a registered housing association or a subsidiary of the Corporation, and in any case where the property so transferred to the Corporation includes land subject to an existing mortgage or charge, whether in favour of the Corporation or otherwise, the Corporation may, in exercise of their powers under Part I of this Act, dispose of the land subject to that mortgage or charge or subject to a new mortgage or charge in favour of the Corporation, and the amount secured by any such new mortgage or charge shall be such as appears to the Corporation to be appropriate in the circumstances.

(4) Notwithstanding anything in subsection (3) above, where property is transferred to the Corporation by virtue of subsection (1) above on the dissolution of a registered 1965 Act association which is a charity, the Corporation may not dispose of that property except to another registered housing association which is a charity and the objects of which appear to the Corporation to be, as nearly as practicable, akin to those of the association which was dissolved.

Restrictions on exercise of certain powers by registered 1965 Act associations.

24.—(1) The provisions of this section apply in relation to a registered 1965 Act association, the registration of which by the Corporation has been recorded by the appropriate registrar under section 16(2) above, and references in the following provisions of this section to a registered 1965 Act association shall be construed accordingly.

(2) The appropriate registrar shall not register a special resolution, as defined in section 50(2) of the 1965 Act, which is passed by a registered 1965 Act association for the purposes of section 50 or section 51 of that Act (amalgamation of societies and transfer of engagements between societies) unless, together with the copy of the special resolution sent to him as mentioned in section 50(4) of that Act, there is sent a copy of the Corporation's consent to the amalgamation or transfer concerned.

(3) Section 52 of the 1965 Act (power of registered society to convert itself into, to amalgamate with, or to transfer its engagements to, a company registered under the Companies Acts) shall not apply to a registered 1965 Act association.

1948 c. 38.

(4) If, in pursuance of section 55(*a*) of the 1965 Act, a registered 1965 Act association resolves by special resolution, as defined in section 141 of the Companies Act 1948, that it be wound up voluntarily, the resolution shall not have effect for the purposes of that Act as a resolution for voluntary winding up unless—

(*a*) before the passing of the resolution the Corporation have given their consent to the passing of the resolution, and

(b) together with the copy of the resolution required to be forwarded to the appropriate registrar under section 143 of the Companies Act 1948 (as that section has effect by virtue of the said section 55(a)) there is forwarded a copy of the Corporation's consent.

(5) If, in pursuance of section 55(b) of the 1965 Act, a registered 1965 Act association is to be dissolved by an instrument of dissolution, the appropriate registrar shall neither register that instrument, as required by subsection (5) of section 58 of that Act, nor cause notice of the dissolution to be advertised as mentioned in subsection (6) of that section unless, together with the instrument of dissolution required to be sent to him under subsection (4) of that section, there is sent a copy of the Corporation's consent to the making of that instrument.

(6) Any reference in the preceding provisions of this section to the Corporation's consent is a reference to an order under the seal of the Corporation giving their consent.

25.—(1) If, in the case of a registered charity which is a registered housing association,—

    (a) the charity is neither a company incorporated under the Companies Act 1948 nor an exempt charity, and

    (b) its registration by the Corporation has been recorded by the Charity Commissioners under section 16(2) above,

no power contained in the trusts of the charity and permitting any variation of or addition to the objects of the charity may be exercised without the consent of the Charity Commissioners.

(2) Before giving any consent under subsection (1) above, the Charity Commissioners shall consult the Corporation.

(3) In subsection (1) above " trusts " has the same meaning as in the Charities Act 1960.

26.—(1) Subject to subsection (2) below, a registered housing association shall not make a gift or pay any sum by way of dividend or bonus—

    (a) to any person who is or has been a member of the association ; or

    (b) to any person who is a member of the family of any such person as is referred to in paragraph (a) above ; or

    (c) to any company of which a person falling within paragraph (a) or paragraph (b) above is a director or any Scottish firm of which such a person is a member.

(2) Subsection (1) above does not apply to—

(*a*) any sum paid, in accordance with the rules of the assocation concerned, as interest on capital lent to the association or subscribed by way of shares in the association ; or

(*b*) any sum which—

    (i) is paid by an association whose rules restrict membership to persons who are tenants or prospective tenants of the association and preclude the granting or assignment of tenancies to persons other than members ; and

    (ii) is paid to a person who has ceased to be a member of the association ; and

    (iii) is due to that person under the terms of the agreement under which he became a member of the association.

(3) The Corporation may from time to time specify the maximum amounts which may be paid by a registered housing association, other than a registered charity which is not an exempt charity, by way of fees or other remuneration or by way of expenses to a person who is a member of the association, and different amounts may be so specified for different purposes.

(4) Where a sum which exceeds any maximum amount for the time being specified under subsection (3) above is paid to a person who is a member of the association by a registered housing association to which that subsection applies, the amount by which that sum exceeds that maximum amount shall be recoverable by the association.

(5) The Corporation may from time to time specify the conditions subject to which a member of the committee of a registered 1965 Act association may enter into a contract with the association for the provision by that member, directly or indirectly, of goods or services to the association in return for payment ; and any such conditions may be so specified as to apply to particular associations, contracts or sums payable thereunder, or as to apply generally.

(6) Any sum paid to a person under a contract in contravention of any condition specified under subsection (5) above shall be recoverable by the association making the payment.

Disclosure of interest by members of committees of registered 1965 Act associations.

27.—(1) Subject to the provisions of this section, it shall be the duty of a member of the committee of a registered 1965 Act association who is in any way, whether directly or indirectly, interested in a contract or proposed contract with the association to declare the nature of his interest to the committee in accordance with this section.

(2) In the case of a proposed contract, the declaration required by this section to be made by a member of a committee shall be made at the meeting of the committee at which the question of entering into the contract is first taken into consideration, or, if the member was not at the date of that meeting interested in the proposed contract, at the next meeting of the committee held after he becomes interested in the proposed contract.

(3) Where a member of a committee becomes interested in a contract with the association after it is made, the declaration required by this section shall be made at the first meeting of the committee held after he becomes interested in the contract.

(4) For the purposes of this section, a general notice given at a meeting of the committee of an association by a member of the committee to the effect that he is a member of a specified company or firm, and is to be regarded as interested in any contract which may, after the date of the notice, be made with that company or firm, is a sufficient declaration of interest in relation to any contract made after that date with that company or firm.

(5) A member of a committee need not make a declaration or give a notice under this section by attending in person at a meeting of the committee if he takes reasonable steps to secure that the declaration or notice is brought up and read at the meeting.

(6) A member of a committee who fails to comply with the provisions of this section shall be liable on summary conviction to a fine not exceeding £200.

(7) Nothing in this section shall be taken to prejudice the operation of any rule of law restricting members of the committee of a registered 1965 Act association from having any interest in contracts with the association.

28. Except in so far as the context otherwise requires, in this Part of this Act—

Interpretation of Part II.

" appropriate registrar " has the same meaning as in the 1965 Act ;

" charity " and " exempt charity " have the same meanings as in the Charities Act 1960 ;

1960 c. 58.

" committee ", in relation to a society registered under the 1965 Act, has the same meaning as in that Act ;

" house " has the same meaning as in Part I of the Housing Act 1964 ;

1964 c. 56.

" registered 1965 Act association " means a registered housing association which is a society registered under the 1965 Act ; and

B

"the 1965 Act" has the meaning assigned to it by section 13(1)(*b*) above.

PART III

FINANCIAL ASSISTANCE FOR HOUSING ASSOCIATIONS

Housing association grants.

29.—(1) The Secretary of State may, in accordance with the provisions of section 30 below, make grants (in this Part of this Act referred to as "housing association grants") to registered housing associations, other than associations falling within section 18(1)(*b*) of this Act, in respect of their expenditure in connection with housing projects approved by him.

(2) For the purposes of this Part of this Act a project is a housing project if it is undertaken for all or any of the following purposes, namely,—

(*a*) providing housing or residential accommodation,

(*b*) improving such accommodation,

(*c*) repairing such accommodation,

(*d*) providing land or buildings for purposes which, in the opinion of the Secretary of State, will be for the benefit of persons for whom any housing or residential accommodation is or is to be provided, and

(*e*) improving or repairing any such buildings as are referred to in paragraph (*d*) above,

and in this subsection "housing or residential accommodation" means dwellings which are or are to be let or available for letting or a building or part of a building used or for use as a hostel or part of a hostel and for this purpose the grant of a licence to occupy shall be treated as a letting.

(3) No housing association grant shall be paid in respect of any project unless an application therefor is submitted to the appropriate body, that is to say,—

(*a*) in England and Wales, if the registered housing association concerned makes an application to a council for a 1957 c. 56.   loan under section 119 of the Housing Act 1957 in connection with the project, to that council, and in any other case to the Corporation, and

(*b*) in Scotland, to a local authority, the Corporation or the Secretary of State,

and where a council in England and Wales, a local authority in Scotland or the Corporation receive an application under this subsection, they shall forward it to the Secretary of State together with their own assessment of the project.

(4) Subject to subsection (5) below, the housing association grant payable to a registered housing association in respect of a housing project approved by the Secretary of State shall be equal to the net cost of the project to the association.

(5) The Secretary of State may, with the consent of the Treasury, determine maximum levels of cost or of grant applicable to housing projects generally, to any particular housing project or to any description of housing project, and the amount of the housing association grant payable in respect of a project to which any such determination applies shall be limited in accordance with the determination.

(6) Subject to subsection (7) below, for the purposes of this section the net cost of a housing project to a registered housing association means the difference between—

(a) the estimated expenditure of the association which, in the opinion of the Secretary of State, is attributable to the project and reasonable and appropriate, having regard to all the circumstances, and

(b) the estimated income which, in the opinion of the Secretary of State, the association might reasonably be expected to receive in respect of the project, including any sums received or to be received by way of grant or subsidy under any enactment, other than this section,

and for this purpose estimated expenditure and estimated income shall be calculated in such manner as the Secretary of State may, with the consent of the Treasury, from time to time determine, and any such calculation may take account of expenditure likely to be incurred and income likely to be received after the completion of the project in connection with the premises to which the project relates.

(7) If, in the case of an application for a housing association grant in respect of a particular project, it appears to the Secretary of State that it would be appropriate to do so, he may for the purposes of this section determine the net cost of the project to the association in such manner as he considers appropriate instead of in accordance with subsection (6) above.

(8) Before making any general determination for the purposes of subsection (5) or subsection (6) above, the Secretary of State shall consult such bodies appearing to him to be representative of housing associations as he considers appropriate.

30.—(1) According as the Secretary of State may determine, a housing association grant in respect of a housing project shall be payable—

(a) in a single sum at such time as, in the opinion of the Secretary of State, the project is completed, or (*b*) in annual instalments beginning in the financial year in which, in his opinion, the project is completed and continuing over such number of years as he may determine, either generally or in relation to the particular project,

but, in either case, the Secretary of State may, if he considers it appropriate to do so, make payments on account of the grant before the project is completed.

(2) In giving his approval to a housing project for the purposes of a housing association grant, the Secretary of State may provide that payment of the grant is conditional upon compliance by the housing association concerned with such conditions as he may specify, including (in a case where the project has not yet been completed) conditions as to the period within which it is to be completed.

(3) The Secretary of State may reduce the amount of, or of any payment in respect of, a housing association grant or suspend or discontinue any instalments of such a grant—

    (*a*) if he imposed any conditions under subsection (2) above and any of those conditions have not been complied with ; or

    (*b*) if he is satisfied that the whole or any part of a building to which the project relates and which comprises or is intended to comprise housing or residential accommodation as defined in section 29(2) above—

        (i) has been converted, demolished or destroyed ; or

        (ii) is not fit to be used or is not being used for the purpose for which it was intended ; or

        (iii) has been sold or leased ; or

        (iv) has ceased for any reason whatsoever to be vested in the housing association concerned or in trustees for that association.

(4) If at any time any dwelling or hostel or part thereof to which a housing project relates is leased to or becomes vested in a registered housing association or trustees for a registered housing association, other than the association by whom the application for the housing association grant relating to that project was made, the Secretary of State may pay to that other association the whole or any part of the grant or any instalment thereof which would otherwise have been paid after that time to the association by whom the application for the grant was made.

(5) If, at any time after a housing association grant or any payment in respect of such a grant has been made to a registered housing association, it appears to the Secretary of State

that any building to which the housing project concerned relates PART III
has ceased to be available for use for the purpose for which, at
the time the project was approved, it was intended that it should
be used, he may direct the association to pay to him an amount
equal to the whole or such proportion as he may determine
of that grant or, as the case may be, of any payment made in
respect of it ; and any amount which a registered housing association is directed to repay to the Secretary of State under this
subsection shall be recoverable as a simple contract debt, or in
Scotland as a debt due under a contract, in any court of com-
petent jurisdiction.

(6) For the purposes of this section, the whole or any part
of any building is leased if and only if it is leased for a term
exceeding 7 years, or for a term not exceeding 7 years granted
by a lease which confers on the lessee an option for renewal
for a term which, together with the original term, exceeds 7
years.

(7) No housing association grant (or payment in respect of
such a grant) may be made before the operative date, but applications for such grants may be submitted in accordance with
section 29(3) above before that date and may be so submitted
by a housing association notwithstanding that it is not then
registered.

(8) On such terms as he may with the approval of the
Treasury specify, the Secretary of State may appoint the Corporation, the Greater London Council, a district council, a
London borough council, the Common Council of the City of
London or a local authority within the meaning of section 1
of the Housing (Scotland) Act 1966 to act as his agent in con- 1966 c. 49.
nection with the making, in such cases as he may specify, of payments in respect of housing association grant ; and where such an
appointment is made the Corporation, council or local authority,
as the case may be, shall act as such an agent in accordance with
the terms of their appointment.

31.—(1) If it appears to the Secretary of State that— Management
  (a) before 1st January 1973 a housing association provided grants for
      any dwellings without the assistance of any grant, sub- housing
      sidy or contribution from the Secretary of State or a associations.
      local authority under any enactment, other than section
      93 of the Finance Act 1965 (grants for affording relief 1965 c. 25.
      from tax), and
  (b) during the whole or any part of an accounting year of
      the association beginning on or after that date the
      dwellings were subject to tenancies to which Part
      VIII of the Housing Finance Act 1972 or sections 60 1972 c. 47.
      to 66 of the Housing (Financial Provisions) (Scotland) 1972 c. 46.

Act 1972 applied, being tenancies under which the interest of the landlord belonged to the association, and

(c) by reason of the operation of the said Part VIII, or of the said sections 60 to 66, and the association's lack of any other funds, the association has incurred a deficit in that accounting year as a result of its expenditure in connection with those dwellings,

the Secretary of State may, in accordance with the provisions of this section, pay to the association a grant towards the difference between the income arising to the association from those dwellings in that year and so much of the expenditure incurred by the association in that year as, in the opinion of the Secretary of State, was necessary for the proper management of those dwellings.

(2) No grant shall be payable under this section in respect of an accounting year of a housing association unless—

(a) an application in respect of that year is made by the association to the Secretary of State not later than the expiry of the period of 15 months beginning immediately after the end of that year and that application is approved by him; and

(b) the application is made with the consent of the Corporation; and

(c) both at the time the application is made and at the time the grant is paid the association is a registered housing association.

(3) An application under subsection (2) above shall be in such form and contain such information as the Secretary of State may from time to time determine.

(4) A grant to a housing association under this section shall be paid in a single sum in respect of the year to which it relates; and the amount of any such grant shall be calculated in such manner as the Secretary of State may, with the agreement of the Treasury, determine.

(5) No grant shall be paid under this section before the operative date, but an application for such a grant may be made before that date.

Revenue
deficit grants
for registered
housing
associations.

32.—(1) The Secretary of State may, in accordance with the provisions of this section, pay a grant (in this section referred to as a " revenue deficit grant ") to a registered housing association, other than an association falling within paragraph (a) or paragraph (b) of section 18(1) above, if the association incurs a deficit on its annual revenue account for an accounting year of the association ending on or after 1st January 1974.

(2) No revenue deficit grant shall be payable in respect of an accounting year of a registered housing association unless—

　　(*a*) an application in respect of that year is made by the association to the Secretary of State not later than the expiry of the period of 15 months beginning immediately after the end of that year and that application is approved by him ; and

　　(*b*) the application is in such form and contains such information as the Secretary of State may from time to time determine ; and

　　(*c*) the application is accompanied by the audited accounts of the association for the accounting year to which the application relates.

(3) Subject to subsection (4) below, for the purposes of this section, a registered housing association shall be treated as incurring a deficit on its annual revenue account for an accounting year of the association if—

　　(*a*) the expenditure of the association for that year which, in the opinion of the Secretary of State, is attributable to dwellings provided by the association and any related property and is reasonable and appropriate, having regard to all the circumstances,

exceeds

　　(*b*) the income which, in the opinion of the Secretary of State, the association might reasonably be expected to receive in respect of those dwellings and any related property in that year, including any sums received or to be received in respect of that year by way of grant or subsidy under any enactment, other than this section,

and for this purpose expenditure and income shall be calculated in such manner as the Secretary of State may, with the consent of the Treasury, from time to time determine.

(4) Notwithstanding anything in subsection (3) above, no account shall be taken for the purposes of this section of so much of any deficit as, in the opinion of the Secretary of State, arises by virtue of any such difference between income and expenditure as is specified in section 31(1) above.

(5) The revenue deficit grant payable to a registered housing association in respect of any accounting year shall be of such amount as the Secretary of State may determine in relation to that association but shall not be greater than the amount of the excess determined for that year under subsection (3) above.

(6) If he considers it appropriate to do so the Secretary of State may make payments on account of any revenue deficit

grant which he considers is likely to become payable to a registered housing association in respect of any accounting year but, subject thereto, any such grant shall be paid in a single sum in respect of the accounting year to which it relates.

(7) No revenue deficit grant shall be paid before the operative date but applications for such a grant may be made before that date and such an application may be so made by a housing association notwithstanding that it is not then registered.

(8) In subsection (3) above " related property ", in relation to dwellings provided by a housing association, means property of the association which is provided for the benefit of the persons occupying those dwellings.

Hostel deficit grants.

33.—(1) The Secretary of State may, in accordance with the provisions of this section, make a grant (in this section referred to as a " hostel deficit grant ") to any registered housing association which, in relation to a hostel managed by the association, incurs a revenue deficit in respect of an accounting year of the association ending on or after the operative date.

(2) No hostel deficit grant shall be payable to a registered housing association in respect of any accounting year of the association unless an application in respect of that year is made by the association to the Secretary of State not later than the expiry of the period of 15 months beginning immediately after the end of that year and that application is approved by him.

(3) For the purposes of this section, a registered housing association shall be treated as incurring, in relation to any hostel managed by them, a revenue deficit in respect of an accounting year of the association if—

(a) the expenditure of the association for that year which, in the opinion of the Secretary of State, is attributable to the hostel and reasonable and appropriate having regard to all the circumstances

exceeds

(b) the income which, in the opinion of the Secretary of State, the association might reasonably be expected to receive in respect of the hostel in that year, including any sums received or to be received in respect of that year by way of grant or subsidy under any enactment, other than this section, and so much as is reasonably attributable to the hostel of any sums received or to be received by the association in respect of that year otherwise than by reference to a specific hostel or purpose,

and for this purpose expenditure and income shall be calculated
in such manner as the Secretary of State may, with the consent
of the Treasury, from time to time determine.

(4) In any case where more than one hostel is managed by
the same registered housing association and that association
makes an application for a hostel deficit grant in respect of
any accounting year of the association, the Secretary of State
may, if he considers it appropriate to do so, treat all the hostels
managed by the association, or any two or more of them, as a
single hostel for the purpose of determining whether the association incurs a revenue deficit in respect of that year in relation
to those hostels.

(5) The hostel deficit grant payable to a registered housing
association in respect of any accounting year shall be of such
amount as the Secretary of State may determine in relation to
that association but shall not be greater than the amount of the
excess determined for that year under subsection (3) above.

(6) According as the Secretary of State may determine, a
hostel deficit grant payable to a registered housing association
in respect of any accounting year shall be payable—

    (a) in a single sum, or

    (b) in instalments payable at such times and in such
        manner as the Treasury may direct,

but, in either case, if the Secretary of State considers that a
registered housing association is likely to be entitled to a hostel
deficit grant in respect of any accounting year, he may make
payments on account of such a grant before the expiry of that
year.

(7) An application under subsection (2) above shall be in
such form and contain such information as the Secretary of
State may from time to time determine.

34.—(1) On and after the appointed day, any rights or obligations of the Secretary of State under an agreement in force
immediately before that day under section 7 of the Housing Act
1961 or section 23 of the Housing (Financial Provisions) (Scotland) Act 1968 (in this section referred to respectively as " the
principal section " and " the principal Scottish section ") shall,
by virtue of this section, become rights or obligations of the
Corporation.

(2) In accordance with subsection (1) above, on and after the
appointed day—

    (a) any reference in any such agreement as is referred to
        in subsection (1) above to the Secretary of State and

Transfer to Corporation of rights and obligations of Secretary of State in relation to certain advances.
1961 c. 65.
1968 c. 31.

PART III

any reference in any such agreement which immediately before the appointed day falls to be construed as a reference to the Secretary of State shall be construed as a reference to the Corporation ;

(b) in subsections (4), (6) and (7) of the principal section for the word " Minister " there shall be substituted the words " Housing Corporation " and in subsections (3), (6) and (7) of the principal Scottish section for the words " Secretary of State " there shall be substituted the words " Housing Corporation " ; and

(c) any rights and obligations of the Secretary of State in relation to advances made under those sections (whether or not arising by virtue of any such agreement as is referred to in subsection (1) above) shall become rights and obligations of the Corporation.

(3) In any case where an advance under the principal section is, immediately before the appointed day, secured by a mortgage of any property in favour of the Secretary of State, the interest of the Secretary of State as mortgagee shall, by virtue of this section (and without any transfer or conveyance), on that day vest in the Corporation.

(4) In this section " the appointed day " means the day appointed for the coming into operation of this section.

Existing subsidies and grants for housing associations: transition to housing association grants.

1972 c. 47.

1972 c. 46.

1968 c. 31.

35.—(1) After the operative date, no approval may be given by the Secretary of State—

(a) for the purposes of section 75 of the Housing Finance Act 1972 (the new building subsidy) in respect of any building scheme ; or

(b) for the purposes of sections 55 and 57 of the Housing (Financial Provisions) (Scotland) Act 1972 (new building subsidy and improvement subsidy) in respect of any building scheme or improvement scheme ; or

(c) for the purposes of section 92 of the Housing Finance Act 1972 (hostel subsidy) in respect of a hostel scheme ; or

(d) for the purposes of section 21 of the Housing (Financial Provisions) (Scotland) Act 1968 (exchequer contributions for hostels) in respect of the provision of hostels.

(2) If, before the expiry of the period of one year beginning on the operative date, a registered housing association makes an application for housing association grant in respect of a housing project which is or includes a building scheme or improvement scheme which has been previously approved for the purposes of the said section 75 or, as the case may be, the said sections 55

and 57 and the Secretary of State gives his approval to that   PART III
project for the purposes of housing association grant,—

  (a) no further payments of new building subsidy or improve-
      ment subsidy shall be made in respect of that approved
      scheme ;

  (b) the Secretary of State may, under section 30(2) above,
      impose a condition requiring the repayment by the
      association of all or any payments of new building
      subsidy or improvement subsidy already made in
      respect of that approved scheme ; and

  (c) where any such condition as is referred to in paragraph
      (b) above is so imposed, no account shall be taken
      under section 29(6)(b) above of any payments received
      by way of new building subsidy or improvement sub-
      sidy which are required to be so repaid.

(3) If, before the operative date, a registered housing association has applied for the approval of the Secretary of State under
the said section 75 or the said sections 55 and 57 in respect of
a building scheme or improvement scheme or under section 92
of the Housing Finance Act 1972 in respect of a hostel scheme 1972 c. 47.
or under section 21 of the Housing (Financial Provisions) 1968 c. 31.
(Scotland) Act 1968 in respect of the provision of hostels, and
no such approval has been given before that date, then, for the
purposes of section 29 above, the application shall be treated—

  (a) as an application for housing association grant in respect
      of a housing project consisting of that building scheme,
      improvement scheme or hostel scheme (in England
      and Wales) or, as the case may be, the provision of
      hostels (in Scotland), and

  (b) as having been submitted to the appropriate body re-
      ferred to in section 29(3) above and forwarded by that
      body to the Secretary of State,

and for the purpose of his consideration of the application for
housing association grant, the Secretary of State may require the
registered housing association to furnish to him such additional
information as he may determine.

(4) A registered housing association may not make an application for housing association grant in respect of a housing
project which consists of or includes—

  (a) the carrying out of works comprised in a hostel scheme
      which, before the operative date, has been approved
      by the Secretary of State for the purposes of section 92
      of the Housing Finance Act 1972, or

  (b) the carrying out of works for the provision of hostels
      which, before the operative date, have been approved

by the Secretary of State for the purposes of section 21 of the Housing (Financial Provisions) (Scotland) Act 1968, or

(c) the provision or conversion of a building for use as a hostel or part of a hostel in accordance with any such arrangements as are referred to in subsection (2)
of section 15 of the Housing (Financial Provisions) Act 1958 or of section 9 of the Housing Act 1961 (grants for hostels),

if, before the operative date, any payment of subsidy under the said section 92 has been made in respect of that hostel scheme or any contribution has been made in respect of the provision of hostels under the said section 21 or, as the case may be, any contribution has been paid in respect of that building under the said section 15.

(5) If, in a case where subsection (4) above does not prevent the making of such an application, a registered housing association makes an application for housing association grant in respect of a housing project falling within that subsection and the Secretary of State gives his approval to that project for the purposes of housing association grant, then, according to the nature of the housing project,—

(a) section 92 of the Housing Finance Act 1972 shall cease to have effect with respect to the hostel scheme referred to in paragraph (a) of that subsection ; or

(b) section 21 of the Housing (Financial Provisions) (Scotland) Act 1968 shall cease to have effect with respect to the provision of hostels referred to in paragraph (b) of that subsection ; or

(c) section 15 of the Housing (Financial Provisions) Act 1958 shall cease to apply to the building referred to in paragraph (c) of that subsection.

(6) In any case where—

(a) a registered housing association is a party to any such arrangements as are referred to in subsection (1) of
section 21 of the Housing Act 1969 or, in Scotland, subsection (1) of section 16 or section 17 of the Housing (Financial Provisions) (Scotland) Act 1968 (contributions for dwellings provided or improved by housing associations under arrangements with local authorities and, in Scotland, the Secretary of State), and

(b) before the operative date approval has been given in accordance with subsection (2) of the said section 21 or in accordance with section 14 of the said Act of 1968, as applied by section 17(1)(ii) of that Act, to the making and terms of those arrangements, and

(c) before the operative date particulars and estimates in respect of works to which those arrangements relate (in this section referred to as a " related project ") have been submitted in an application made under subsection (3) of the said section 21 or, as the case may require, have been furnished under section 18 of the said Act of 1968,

the registered housing association may not make an application for housing association grant in respect of a housing project which consists of or includes the carrying out of any of the works comprised in the related project if any contribution under the said section 21 or the said sections 16 and 17 has been paid in relation to the related project before the operative date.

(7) If, in a case falling within paragraphs (a) to (c) of subsection (6) above,—

(a) the registered housing association concerned makes an application (permitted by that subsection) for housing association grant in respect of a related project, and

(b) the Secretary of State gives his approval to the related project for the purposes of housing association grant,

section 21 of the Housing Act 1969 or, as the case may be, 1969 c. 33. sections 16 and 17 of the Housing (Financial Provisions) (Scot- 1968 c. 31. land) Act 1968 shall cease to have effect with respect to so much of the arrangements concerned as relates to the carrying out of the related project.

(8) In this section—

" building scheme " has the same meaning as in section 75 of the Housing Finance Act 1972 or, in Scotland, 1972 c. 47. section 55 of the Housing (Financial Provisions) (Scot- 1972 c. 46. land) Act 1972 ; and

" hostel scheme " has the same meaning as in section 92 of the Housing Finance Act 1972 ; and

" improvement scheme " has the same meaning as in section 57 of the Housing (Financial Provisions) (Scotland) Act 1972.

PART IV

HOUSING ACTION AREAS

36.—(1) Where a report with respect to an area consisting Declaration primarily of housing accommodation is submitted to the local of housing authority within whose district the area lies by a person or action areas. persons appearing to the authority to be suitably qualified (whether or not that person is or those persons include an officer

PART IV   of the authority) and, upon consideration of the report and of any other information in their possession, the authority are satisfied that, having regard to—

> (a) the physical state of the housing accommodation in the area as a whole, and
>
> (b) social conditions in the area,

the requirement in subsection (2) below is fulfilled with respect to the area, the authority may cause the area to be defined on a map and by resolution declare it to be a housing action area.

(2) The requirement referred to in subsection (1) above is that the living conditions in the area are unsatisfactory and can most effectively be dealt with within a period of 5 years so as to secure—

> (a) the improvement of the housing accommodation in the area as a whole, and
>
> (b) the well-being of the persons for the time being residing in the area, and
>
> (c) the proper and effective management and use of that accommodation,

by declaring the area to be a housing action area.

(3) In considering whether to take action under subsection (1) above with respect to any area, a local authority shall have regard to such guidance as may from time to time be given by the Secretary of State, either generally or with respect to a particular authority or description of authority or in any particular case, with regard to the identification of areas suitable to be declared as housing action areas.

(4) As soon as may be after passing a resolution declaring an area to be a housing action area, a local authority shall—

> (a) publish in two or more newspapers circulating in the locality (of which at least one shall, if practicable, be a local newspaper) a notice of the resolution identifying the area and naming a place or places where a copy of the resolution, a map on which the area is defined and of the report referred to in subsection (1) above may be inspected at all reasonable times ;
>
> (b) take such further steps as may appear to them best designed to secure that the resolution and the obligations imposed by section 47 below are brought to the attention of persons residing or owning property in the area and that those persons are informed of the name and address of the person to whom should be addressed any inquiries and representations concerning any action to be taken with respect to the area or, as the case may

be, any inquiries concerning the obligations so imposed ;

(c) send to the Secretary of State a copy of the resolution, the map and a copy of the report mentioned in paragraph (a) above, a statement of the numbers of dwellings, houses in multiple occupation and hostels in the area and a statement containing such information as the Secretary of State may for the time being require, either generally or with respect to a particular authority or description of authority or in any particular case, to show the basis on which the local authority satisfied themselves that the area was suitable to be declared a housing action area, having regard to the matters specified in paragraphs (a) and (b) of subsection (1) above and any relevant guidance given under subsection (3) above ; and

(d) send to the Secretary of State a statement of their proposals, whether general or specific, for the participation of registered housing associations in dealing with the living conditions in the area.

(5) As soon as may be after a resolution has been passed declaring an area to be a housing action area, the resolution shall be registered in the register of local land charges—

(a) by the proper officer, for the purposes of section 15 of the Land Charges Act 1925, of the local authority in whose area the housing action area is situated ; and

1925 c. 22.

(b) in such manner as may be prescribed by rules under section 19 of that Act.

(6) In this Part of this Act " housing accommodation " means dwellings, houses in multiple occupation and hostels.

37.—(1) When a local authority have declared an area to be a housing action area and have sent to the Secretary of State the documents referred to in section 36(4)(c) above, he shall send to the authority a written acknowledgment of the receipt of those documents.

Functions of Secretary of State.

(2) If it appears to the Secretary of State to be appropriate to do so, he may, at any time within the period of 28 days beginning with the day on which he sent an acknowledgment under subsection (1) above, send a notification to the local authority concerned—

(a) that the area declared by the authority to be a housing action area is no longer to be such an area ; or

(b) that land which is within the area declared by the authority to be a housing action area and which is defined on a map accompanying the notification is to be excluded from that area ; or

(c) that the Secretary of State requires more time to consider the authority's declaration of the area as a housing action area.

(3) In any case where—

(a) the Secretary of State notifies a local authority as mentioned in paragraph (c) of subsection (2) above, and

(b) by a direction given with respect to the particular area declared by the authority to be a housing action area, he so requires,

the authority shall send to him such information and documents, in addition to the information and documents mentioned in section 36(4)(c) above, as may be specified in the direction.

(4) Where the Secretary of State notifies a local authority as mentioned in paragraph (c) of subsection (2) above, he shall, on completion of his consideration of the matter, send a further notification to the authority—

(a) as mentioned in paragraph (a) or paragraph (b) of that subsection ; or

(b) that he does not propose to take any further action with respect to the local authority's declaration.

(5) With effect from the date on which a local authority is notified as mentioned in paragraph (a) or paragraph (b) of subsection (2) above (whether the notification is sent under that subsection or subsection (4) above) the area concerned shall cease to be a housing action area or, according to the nature of the notification, the land defined on the map accompanying the notification shall be excluded from the housing action area.

(6) Where subsection (5) above applies, the local authority concerned shall, as soon as may be after receipt of the notification,—

(a) publish in two or more newspapers circulating in the locality (of which at least one shall, if practicable, be a local newspaper) a notice of the effect of the Secretary of State's notification and naming a place or places where a copy of the notification and, in the case of such a notification as is mentioned in subsection (2)(b) above, a copy of the amended map of the housing action area may be inspected at all reasonable times ; and

(b) take such further steps as may appear to them best designed to secure that the effect of the notification is brought to the attention of persons residing or owning property in the area declared by the local authority to be a housing action area.

38.—(1) If a local authority propose, by a resolution under Incorporation section 36 above, to declare as a housing action area an area of general which consists of or includes land which, immediately prior to improvement the declaration, areas, priority neighbour-

(*a*) is comprised in a general improvement area declared hoods, or under Part II of the Housing Act 1969, or parts thereof into housing

(*b*) is comprised in a priority neighbourhood declared under action areas. section 52 below 1969 c. 33.

they shall indicate on the map referred to in section 36(1) above the land which is so comprised (in this section referred to as " the relevant land ").

(2) Subject to the following provisions of this section, with effect from the date on which such a resolution as is referred to in subsection (1) above is passed, the relevant land shall be deemed (according to its status) either—

(*a*) to have been excluded from the general improvement area or, as the case may be, to have ceased to be a general improvement area by virtue of a resolution under section 30(1) of the Housing Act 1969 passed on that date and approved by the Secretary of State ; or

(*b*) to have been excluded from the priority neighbourhood by virtue of a resolution passed on that date under section 40(1) below, as that section applies in relation to priority neighbourhoods by virtue of section 54 below or, as the case may be, to have ceased to be a priority neighbourhood by virtue of a resolution passed on that date under section 39(3) below (as that section so applies).

(3) If the Secretary of State notifies the local authority concerned under section 37 above that the area declared by them to be a housing action area is no longer to be such an area, subsection (2) above shall be treated as never having applied in relation to the relevant land.

(4) If the Secretary of State notifies the local authority concerned under section 37 above that any land which—

(*a*) is within the area declared by the authority to be a housing action area, and

(*b*) consists of or includes any of the relevant land,

is to be excluded from the housing action area, subsection (2) above shall be treated as never having applied in relation to so

PART IV

'much of the relevant land as is comprised in the land so
excluded.

Duration of
housing
action areas.

39.—(1) Where a local authority have passed a resolution
with respect to any area under section 36(1) above, then, subject
to section 37(5) above and the following provisions of this
section, the area shall be a housing action area throughout the
period of 5 years beginning on the date on which the resolution
was passed.

(2) If, not less than 3 months before the date on which, apart
from any extension, or further extension, under this subsection,
a housing action area would cease to exist, the local authority
concerned notify the Secretary of State in writing that they have
passed a resolution under this subsection, the duration of the
housing action area shall be extended, subject to subsections (3)
and (6) below, by the addition of a further period of 2 years.

(3) Notwithstanding anything in subsections (1) and (2)
above if a local authority by resolution under this subsection so
declare, an area which they had previously declared to be a
housing action area shall cease to be such an area on the date
on which the resolution under this subsection is passed; and as
soon as may be after passing such a resolution the local
authority shall send a copy of it to the Secretary of State.

(4) On receipt of any notification sent to him under subsection (2) above the Secretary of State shall send a written
acknowledgment to the local authority by whom the notification
was sent and, if it appears to him to be appropriate to do so, he
may, at any time within the period of 28 days beginning with
the day on which he sent an acknowledgment under this
subsection, send a notification to the local authority concerned—

   (*a*) that the duration of the housing action area is not to
      be extended in accordance with the authority's
      resolution ; or

   (*b*) that the Secretary of State requires more time to con-
      sider the authority's extension of the duration of the
      housing action area.

(5) Where the Secretary of State notifies a local authority as
mentioned in paragraph (*b*) of subsection (4) above, he shall,
on completion of his consideration of the matter, send a further
notification to the authority—

   (*a*) as mentioned in paragraph (*a*) of that subsection ; or

   (*b*) if, at the time of the notification, the 2 years' extension
      of the duration of the housing action area by virtue
      of the authority's resolution under subsection (2)
      above has begun to run, that the area concerned is to

cease to be a housing action area on such date as may
be specified in the notification ; or

(c) that he does not propose to take any further action with
respect to the authority's resolution.

(6) Where the Secretary of State notifies a local authority as
mentioned in subsection (4)(*a*) above or subsection (5)(*b*) above
(whether, in the former case, the notification is given under
subsection (4) or subsection (5) above) the duration of the
housing action area shall not be extended by virtue of the
authority's resolution under subsection (2) above or, in the case
of a notification under subsection (5)(*b*) above, the extension by
virtue of that resolution shall be for a period expiring on the
date specified in the notification.

(7) As soon as may be after passing a resolution under subsection (2) or subsection (3) above or, if subsection (6) above
applies, as soon as may be after receipt of the notification from
the Secretary of State, a local authority shall—

(a) publish in two or more newspapers circulating in the
locality (of which at least one shall, if practicable, be
a local newspaper) a notice of the resolution or, as the
case may be, of the effect of the Secretary of State's
notification and naming a place or places where a
copy of the resolution or notification, as the case may
be, may be inspected at all reasonable times ; and

(b) take such further steps as may appear to the authority
best designed to secure that the resolution, or as the
case may be, the effect of the notification, is brought to
the attention of persons residing or owning property in
the housing action area concerned.

40.—(1) A local authority may at any time by resolution   Reduction of
exclude from a housing action area any land for the time being   housing
included therein.   action area.

(2) As soon as may be after passing a resolution under this
section, the local authority shall—

(a) publish in two or more newspapers circulating in the
locality (of which one at least shall, if practicable, be
a local newspaper) a notice of the resolution, identifying the housing action area concerned and the land
excluded from it ;

(b) take such further steps as may appear to the authority
best designed to secure that the resolution is brought
to the attention of persons residing or owning property
in the housing action area ; and

(c) send to the Secretary of State a copy of the resolution.

PART IV
Duty to
publish
information.

41. Where a local authority have declared an area to be a housing action area, it shall be their duty to bring to the attention of persons residing or owning property in the area—

(a) the action which they propose to take in relation to the housing action area, and

(b) the assistance available for the improvement of the housing accommodation in the area,

by publishing from time to time, in such manner as appears to them appropriate, such information as is in their opinion best designed to further the purpose for which the area was declared a housing action area.

Duty to
inform
Secretary of
State of action
taken.

42.—(1) If at any time they are directed by the Secretary of State to do so, a local authority who have declared an area to be a housing action area shall furnish the Secretary of State with such information as may be specified in the direction with respect to the action taken by the authority for the purpose of securing all or any of the objectives specified in paragraphs (a) to (c) of subsection (2) of section 36 above.

(2) A direction for the purposes of subsection (1) above—

(a) may require the information concerned to be furnished within a time specified in the direction or within such further time as the Secretary of State may allow ; and

(b) may be given to local authorities generally or to a particular authority or description of authority or in any particular case.

Acquisition
of land in
housing action
areas.

43.—(1) Where a local authority have declared an area to be a housing action area then, for the purpose of securing or assisting in securing all or any of the objectives specified in paragraphs (a) to (c) of subsection (2) of section 36 above,—

(a) they may be authorised by the Secretary of State to acquire compulsorily any land in the area on which are situated premises which consist of or include housing accommodation ; and

(b) to the extent that they could not do so apart from this subsection, they may acquire any such land by agreement.

1946 c. 49.

(2) The Acquisition of Land (Authorisation Procedure) Act 1946 shall apply in relation to a compulsory acquisition of land under subsection (1) above as if that subsection were contained in an Act in force immediately before the commencement of that Act.

(3) If at any time after—

   (a) a local authority have entered into a contract for the acquisition of land falling within subsection (1) above, or

   (b) a compulsory purchase order authorising the acquisition of any such land has been confirmed,

the housing action area concerned ceases to be such an area or the land concerned is excluded from the area, the provisions of this section shall continue to apply as if the land continued to be in a housing action area.

(4) If, at any time after a compulsory purchase order authorising the acquisition of land falling within subsection (1) above has been made but before it is confirmed, the housing action area concerned ceases to be such an area by virtue of paragraph (a) of subsection (2) of section 53 below or the land concerned is excluded from the area by virtue of that paragraph, the provisions of this section shall continue to apply as if the land continued to be in a housing action area.

(5) Section 72 of the Housing Act 1964 (restriction on recovery 1964 c. 56. of possession after making of compulsory purchase order) shall apply in relation to the compulsory acquisition of land under this section as if—

   (a) the reference in that section to the Housing Act 1957 1957 c. 56. were a reference to this section ; and

   (b) the reference in that section to a house which is occupied by persons who do not form a single household were a reference to the land proposed to be acquired under this section.

(6) In subsection (2) of section 131 of the Local Government 1972 c. 70. Act 1972 (enactments which relate to dealings in land by local authorities and which override the provisions of Part VII of that Act relating to land transactions) after paragraph (j) there shall be inserted the following paragraph : —

   " (jj) section 43 of the Housing Act 1974 ".

(7) In this section " land " includes any estate or interest in land and " local authority " includes the Greater London Council and a county council.

44.—(1) The provisions of this section apply to land in a Provision, housing action area— improvement etc. of
   (a) on which are situated premises which consist of or housing include housing accommodation ; and accommoda-
   (b) which was acquired (by agreement or compulsorily) by tion by local the local authority and for the purpose specified in authorities. section 43(1) above ; and

(c) which was so acquired after the date on which the housing action area was declared.

(2) Subject to section 105 of this Act, the local authority referred to in subsection (1) above may, for the purpose specified in section 43(1) above, undertake on land to which this section applies all or any of the following activities—

(a) the provision of housing accommodation, by the construction, conversion or improvement of buildings or otherwise ;

(b) the carrying out of works required for the improvement or repair of housing accommodation, including works to the exterior, or on land within the curtilage, of buildings containing housing accommodation ;

(c) the management of housing accommodation ; and

(d) the provision of furniture, fittings or services in or in relation to housing accommodation.

Assistance for carrying out environmental works.
45.—(1) For the purpose of effecting or assisting the improvement of living conditions in a housing action area, the local authority may, in accordance with the following provisions of this section, give assistance towards the carrying out of works (in this section referred to as " environmental works ")—

(a) to the exterior, or on land within the curtilage, of buildings containing housing accommodation, not being works in respect of which an application for a grant under Part VII of this Act has been approved ; or

(b) on land not falling within paragraph (a) above for the purpose of improving the amenities of the area.

(2) Subject to subsection (3) below, assistance under subsection (1) above may be given to any person having an interest in the building or land concerned and shall consist of all or any of the following, namely—

(a) a grant in respect of expenditure which appears to the local authority to have been properly incurred in the carrying out of environmental works ;

(b) the provision of materials for the carrying out of environmental works ; and

(c) by agreement with the person concerned, the execution of environmental works at his expense, at the expense of the local authority, or partly, at his expense and partly at the expense of the local authority.

(3) No assistance may be given under subsection (1) above in respect of a building or land in which the local authority have

such a freehold or leasehold interest as would enable the
authority themselves to carry out environmental works in
relation thereto.

(4) A grant under subsection (2)(*a*) above may be paid after
the completion of the works towards the cost of which it is
payable or part of it may be paid in instalments as the works
progress and the balance after the completion of the works;
and where part of any such grant is paid in instalments the
aggregate of the instalments paid shall not at any time before
the completion of the works exceed one-half of the aggregate
cost of the works executed up to that time.

46.—(1) Subject to the following provisions of this section, Contributions
the Secretary of State may pay contributions to local authorities towards
in respect of expenditure incurred or to be incurred by them in expenditure
giving assistance under section 45(1) above.   under
section 45.

(2) No contribution shall be paid to a local authority under
subsection (1) above unless an application therefor is made by
the authority and approved by the Secretary of State; and any
such application—

(*a*) shall be in such form and contain such information as
the Secretary of State may from time to time
determine; and

(*b*) may be made before the expenditure concerned is
incurred by the local authority.

(3) Subject to subsection (4) below, the amount of any
contribution under subsection (1) above shall be 50 per cent. of
the expenditure incurred or to be incurred by the local authority
concerned in giving assistance under section 45(1) above.

(4) The aggregate amount of the expenditure in respect of
which applications for contributions may be approved under
this section shall not exceed the sum arrived at by multiplying
£50 by the aggregate of the number of dwellings, houses in
multiple occupation and hostels stated by the local authority,
in accordance with section 36(4)(*c*) above, to be in the area.

(5) A contribution under subsection (1) above shall be payable
in a single sum in the financial year in which are completed
the external works to which the local authority's expenditure
relates.

(6) The Secretary of State may by order made with the
consent of the Treasury vary the sum of £50 specified in subsection (4) above and any such variation—

(*a*) may be made generally or by reference to housing
action areas declared by any particular authority or

description of authority or by reference to any particular housing action area or description of housing action area ; and

(b) shall have effect with respect to applications for contributions under subsection (1) above approved after such date as may be specified in the order.

(7) A statutory instrument containing an order under subsection (6) above shall be subject to annulment in pursuance of a resolution of the Commons House of Parliament.

Notification of notices to quit and disposals of housing accommodation etc.

47.—(1) Within the period of 7 days beginning with the day on which a notice to quit is served—

(a) in respect of land consisting of or including housing accommodation in a housing action area, and

(b) on a tenant who occupies as a dwelling the whole or any part of that land,

the landlord by or on whose behalf the notice is served shall notify the local authority in accordance with Schedule 4 to this Act, that the notice has been served.

(2) Not less than 4 weeks before the expiry by effluxion of time of any tenancy—

(a) which is a tenancy of land consisting of or including housing accommodation in a housing action area, and

(b) which expires without the service of any notice to quit,

the person who is the landlord under that tenancy shall notify the local authority, in accordance with Schedule 4 to this Act, that the tenancy is about to expire.

(3) Not less than 4 weeks and not more than 6 months before the date on which a person carries out a disposal of land to which this section applies, he shall notify the local authority, in accordance with Schedule 4 to this Act, that the disposal is to take place ; and for the purposes of this section a person carries out a disposal of land if he conveys or enters into a contract to convey a legal estate or interest in the land, whether or not that estate or interest is in existence immediately before the date of the conveyance or contract.

(4) Nothing in the preceding provisions of this section shall impose an obligation on any person to notify a local authority of any matter if, apart from this subsection, the obligation would require him to notify the authority at some time before the expiry of the period of 4 weeks beginning with the date on which the housing action area concerned is declared.

(5) A local authority who receive a notification given in
compliance with any provision of subsections (1) to (3) above
shall,—

  (a) as soon as practicable after the notification is received,
    send to the person by whom it was furnished a written
    acknowledgment of its receipt, stating the day on which
    it was received ; and

  (b) within the period of 4 weeks beginning with the day
    on which the notification was received, inform the per-
    son by whom it was furnished what action, if any,
    they propose to take as a result of the notification with
    respect to the land to which the notification relates.

(6) This section applies to a disposal of land consisting of or
including housing accommodation in a housing action area,
other than a disposal—

  (a) by a person who, throughout the period of 6 months
    ending on the date of the disposal, has been continu-
    ously in exclusive occupation (with or without mem-
    bers of his household) of the land to which the disposal
    relates ; or

  (b) to which the local authority are a party ; or

  (c) consisting of the grant of a protected tenancy, within the
    meaning of the Rent Act 1968, or of a contract to 1968 c. 23.
    which Part VI of that Act applies ; or

  (d) consisting of the grant or assignment of a lease (of
    land or of an interest in land) for a term which expires
    within the period of 5 years and 3 months beginning on
    the date of the grant of the lease, where neither the
    lease nor any other instrument or contract confers
    on the lessor or the lessee an option (however ex-
    pressed) to renew or extend the term so that the new
    term or the extended term would continune beyond
    the end of that period of 5 years and 3 months ; or

  (e) consisting of the grant of an estate or interest by way
    of security for a loan ; or

  (f) consisting of the conveyance of an estate or interest
    where the conveyance gives effect to a contract to
    convey that estate or interest and the proposal to enter
    into that contract was notified to the local authority
    in accordance with subsection (3) above.

(7) Any person who—

  (a) without reasonable excuse fails to comply with an
    obligation imposed on him by subsection (1) or
    subsection (2) above, or

  (b) without reasonable excuse carries out a disposal of
    land to which this section applies without having

complied with the obligation imposed on him by subsection (3) above, or

(c) knowingly or recklessly furnishes a notification which is false in a material particular in purported compliance with any provision of this section, or

(d) knowingly or recklessly omits from any such notification any information which is required to be contained therein by virtue of any provision of Schedule 4 to this Act,

shall be guilty of an offence and liable on summary conviction to a fine not exceeding £400.

(8) Where an offence under subsection (7) above which has been committed by a body corporate is proved to have been committed with the consent or connivance of, or to be attributable to any neglect on the part of, a director, manager, secretary or other similar officer of the body corporate, or any person who was purporting to act in any such capacity, he as well as the body corporate shall be guilty of that offence and be liable to be proceeded against and punished accordingly.

(9) Where the affairs of a body corporate are managed by its members, subsection (8) above shall apply in relation to the acts and defaults of a member in connection with his functions of management as if he were a director of the body corporate.

(10) The conviction of any person for an offence under subsection (7) above shall not affect the date on which any tenancy expires (whether by virtue of a notice to quit or otherwise) or the validity of any disposal of land.

Application of certain provisions of Housing Acts.
1957 c. 56.
48.—(1) The following provisions of the Housing Act 1957,—

(a) section 159 (power of entry for inspection, etc.),

(b) section 160 (penalty for obstructing execution of Act),

(c) section 169 (service of notices, etc., on persons other than local authorities), and

(d) section 170 (power of local authority to require information as to ownership of premises),

shall apply, subject to subsection (2) below, as if references therein to the Housing Act 1957 included references to this Part of this Act.

(2) In its application, by virtue of subsection (1) above, in relation to this Part of this Act, section 170 of the Housing Act 1957 shall have effect with the insertion after the words " in respect of any premises " of the words " within such period of not less than fourteen days from the date on which the requirement is made as may be specified by the authority " and after

the words " that information " of the words " within the period so PART IV specified ".

(3) In section 70 of the Housing Act 1969 (review of housing 1969 c. 33. conditions by local authorities with a view to exercising certain statutory functions) for the words " or Part II of this Act " there shall be substituted the words " Part II of this Act or Part IV of the Housing Act 1974 ".

49.—(1) Subject to subsection (2) below, the local authorities Local for the purposes of this Part of this Act are the councils of authorities districts and London boroughs and the Common Council of the for the purposes of City of London. Part IV.

(2) The Greater London Council may exercise the powers of a local authority under subsections (1) to (3) of section 36 above with respect to any area in Greater London, but only with the agreement of any local authority in whose district the area or any part of the area is situated ; and in relation to, and to any premises in, an area which, in acordance with this subsection, has been declared a housing action area by the Greater London Council, any reference to a local authority in—

(*a*) section 36(4) and sections 37 to 42 and 45 to 47 above, or

(*b*) the provisions of the Housing Act 1957 applied in 1957 c. 56. relation to this Part of this Act by section 48(1) above, or

(*c*) Part III of the Housing Finance Act 1972 (rent of dwell- 1972 c. 47. ings in good repair and provided with standard amenities),

shall be construed, except in so far as the context otherwise requires, as a reference to the Greater London Council, to the exclusion of any other council.

(3) Without prejudice to subsection (2) above, in relation to any premises in a housing action area which, in accordance with that subsection, has been declared by the Greater London Council—

(*a*) the Greater London Council may exercise the functions of a local authority under Part II or Part IV of the Housing Act 1957, Part II of the Housing Act 1961, 1961 c. 65. Part IV of the Housing Act 1964 or Part IV of the 1964 c. 56. Housing Act 1969, and

(*b*) any functions exercisable under the enactments referred to in paragraph (*a*) above by the council of a London borough or the Common Council of the City of London shall be so exercisable only after consultation with the Greater London Council.

PART V

GENERAL IMPROVEMENT AREAS

Consideration
by Secretary
of State of
suitability
of general
improvement
areas.

50.—(1) With a view to affording to the Secretary of State an opportunity to consider in advance the suitability of an area as a general improvement area and, where appropriate, to prevent an area which appears to him to be inappropriate to be declared a general improvement area, for section 28 of the Housing Act 1969 there shall be substituted the sections set out in Part I of Schedule 5 to this Act.

(2) In any case where, on or after 12th June 1973 and before the coming into operation of this section, a local authority have,

(a) by resolution under section 28(1) of the Housing Act 1969, declared an area to be a general improvement area, or

(b) by resolution under section 30(2) of that Act, included any land in an existing general improvement area,

the Secretary of State may, if it appears to him appropriate to do so, at any time within the relevant period serve notice on the authority terminating the status of the area as a general improvement area or, as the case may be, excluding the land from the general improvement area in question, with effect from the date on which the notice is served.

(3) In subsection (2) above " the relevant period ", in relation to a general improvement area or land included in such an area as mentioned in paragraph (b) of that subsection, means the period of 42 days beginning on the day appointed for the coming into operation of this section or, if it is later, the day on which the Secretary of State receives, by virtue of any provision of the Housing Act 1969, a copy of the resolution declaring the area referred to in subsection (2)(a) above to be a general improvement area or, as the case may be, including the land referred to in subsection (2)(b) above in a general improvement area.

1969 c. 33.

(4) As soon as may be after notice has been served on a local authority under subsection (2) above, they shall—

(a) publish in two or more newspapers circulating in the locality (of which one at least shall, if practicable, be a local newspaper) a notice identifying the general improvement area concerned and either stating that its status as such an area has been terminated by the Secretary of State and the date on which it was so terminated or, as the case may be, identifying the land excluded from the general improvement area and stating the date on which it was so excluded ; and

(b) that it is not, at the date of the resolution, p[...]
for the local authority to declare the area
of it to be a housing action area or a gen[...]
ment area or to declare as a housing [...]
general improvement area an area [...]
part of the proposed priority nei[...]

(c) that it is necessary to secure i[...]
the objectives specified in [...]
section 36(2) above and t[...]
by declaring the area t[...]

(4) In considering whethe[...]
above with respect to a[...]
regard to such guidanc[...]
the Secretary of Stat[...]
ticular authority o[...]
case, with regar[...]
declared as pr[...]

(5) As [...]
an area [...]

the requirements in subsection (3) below are fulfilled with respect to the area, the authority may cause the area to be defined on a map and by resolution declare it to be a priority neighbourhood.

(2) For the purposes of this section, an area is appropriate to be declared a priority neighbourhood if, immediately before the declaration, it surrounds, or has a common boundary with,—

(a) a housing action area other than an area in respect of which the Secretary of State has notified the local authority as mentioned in subsection (2)(c) of section 37 above and has not yet sent a further notification under subsection (4) of that section ; or

(b) a general improvement area in respect of which a confirmatory resolution, within the meaning of section 28 of the Housing Act 1969, has been passed. 1969 c. 33.

(3) The requirements referred to in subsection (1) above are—

(a) that the living conditions in the area are unsatisfactory ;

acticable
or any part
eral improve-
action area or a
which includes any
ghbourhood ; and

the area all or any of
paragraphs (a) to (c) of
at that need can best be met
o be a priority neighbourhood.

to take action under subsection (1)
y area, a local authority shall have
as may from time to time be given by
, either generally or with respect to a par-
description of authority or in any particular
d to the identification of areas suitable to be
ority neighbourhoods.

soon as may be after passing a resolution declaring
to be a priority neighbourhood, a local authority shall—

(a) publish in two or more newspapers circulating in the locality (of which at least one shall, if practicable, be a local newspaper) a notice of the resolution identifying the priority neighbourhood and naming a place or places where a copy of the resolution, of the map on which the neighbourhood is defined and of the report referred to in subsection (1) above may be inspected at all reasonable times ;

(b) take such further steps as may appear to them best designed to secure that the resolution is brought to the attention of persons residing or owning property in the priority neighbourhood and that those persons are informed of the name and address of the person to whom any inquiries and representations concerning any action to be taken with respect to the neighbourhood should be addressed ; and

(c) send to the Secretary of State a copy of the resolution, the map and a copy of the report mentioned in paragraph (a) above and a statement containing such information as the Secretary of State may for the time being require, either generally or with respect to a particular authority or description of authority or in any particular case, to show the basis on which the local authority satisfied themselves that the area concerned was suitable to be declared a priority neighbourhood, having regard to the matters specified in

paragraphs (*a*) and (*b*) of subsection (1) above and any   PART VI
relevant guidance given under subsection (4) above.

(6) As soon as may be after a resolution has been passed
declaring an area to be a priority neighbourhood, the resolution
shall be registered in the register of local land charges—

    (*a*) by the proper officer, for the purposes of section 15
of the Land Charges Act 1925, of the local authority in   1925 c. 22.
whose area the priority neighbourhood is situated ; and

    (*b*) in such manner as may be prescribed by rules under
section 19 of that Act.

(7) Section 37 above shall apply in relation to the declaration of a priority neighbourhood with the substitution—

    (*a*) for any reference to a housing action area of a
reference to a priority neighbourhood ; and

    (*b*) for any reference to section 36(4)(*c*) above of a reference
to subsection (5)(*c*) of this section.

(8) In this section "housing accommodation" means
dwellings, houses in multiple occupation and hostels.

53.—(1) If a local authority propose, by a resolution under Incorporation
section 52 above, to declare as a priority neighbourhood an into priority
area which consists of or includes land which, immediately neighbour-
prior to the declaration, is comprised— general

    (*a*) in a housing action area declared under section 36 improvement
above, or areas,

    (*b*) in a general improvement area declared under Part II action areas,
of the Housing Act 1969, or parts
thereof.
they shall indicate on the map referred to in section 52 above 1969 c. 33.
the land which is so comprised (in this section referred to as
" the relevant land ").

(2) Subject to the following provisions of this section, with
effect from the date on which such a resolution as is referred
to in subsection (1) above is passed, the relevant land shall be
deemed (according to its status) either—

    (*a*) to have ceased to be a housing action area by virtue of
a resolution passed on that date under section 39(3)
above or, as the case may be, to have been excluded
from the housing action area by virtue of a resolution
passed on that date under section 40(1) above ; or

    (*b*) to have ceased to be a general improvement area or,
as the case may be, to have been excluded from the
general improvement area by virtue of a resolution
under section 30(1) of the Housing Act 1969 passed
on that date and approved by the Secretary of State.

(3) If the Secretary of State notifies the local authority concerned under section 37 above, as that section applies in relation to priority neighbourhoods by virtue of section 52(7) above, that the area declared by them to be a priority neighbourhood is no longer to be such an area, subsection (2) above shall be treated as never having applied in relation to the relevant land.

(4) If the Secretary of State notifies the local authority concerned under section 37 above, as that section applies in relation to priority neighbourhoods by virtue of section 52(7) above, that any land which—

(a) is within the area declared by the authority to be a priority neighbourhood, and

(b) consists of or includes any of the relevant land,

is to be excluded from the priority neighbourhood, subsection (2) above shall be treated as never having applied in relation to so much of the relevant land as is comprised in the land so excluded.

Application
to priority
neighbour-
hoods of
certain
provisions
of Part IV.   **54.**—(1) Subject to the provisions of this section, the following provisions of Part IV of this Act shall apply in relation to a priority neighbourhood as they apply in relation to a housing action area, namely—

(a) section 39 (duration of housing action areas) ;

(b) section 40 (reduction of housing action areas) ;

(c) section 42 (duty to inform Secretary of State of action taken) ;

(d) section 43 (acquisition of land in housing action areas) ;

(e) section 44 (provision, improvement etc. of housing accommodation by local authorities) ;

(f) section 47 (notification of notices to quit and disposals of housing accommodation etc.) ; and

(g) section 48 (application of certain provisions of Housing Acts).

(2) In the application, by virtue of subsection (1) above, of the provisions of Part IV of this Act specified in that subsection—

(a) for any reference in those provisions to a housing action area there shall be substituted a reference to a priority neighbourhood ; and

(b) any reference in any of those provisions to any other provision of Part IV of this Act shall be construed as a reference to that other provision as it applies in relation to priority neighbourhoods.

(3) Without prejudice to subsection (2) above, in the application, by virtue of subsection (1) above, of section 39 above—

> (*a*) for the reference in subsection (1) of that section to
> section 36(1) above there shall be substituted a
> reference to section 52(1) above ; and

> (*b*) for any reference in subsection (2) or subsection (5) of
> that section to 2 years there shall be substituted a
> reference to 5 years.

(4) A local authority may not exercise the power conferred
by section 40 above, as applied by virtue of subsection (1) above,
in relation to a priority neighbourhood unless the land which
would be left in the priority neighbourhood after the exclusion
of the land in question—

> (*a*) would then constitute an area which, having regard to
> subsection (2) of section 52 above, would be appro-
> priate to be declared a priority neighbourhood ; or

> (*b*) would then surround or have a common boundary with
> an area which, immediately before the priority neigh-
> bourhood was declared, constituted or formed part of a
> housing action area or a general improvement area ; or

> (*c*) would then consist of or include land which, immediately
> before the priority neighbourhood was declared, formed
> part of a housing action area or a general improvement
> area.

(5) In the application, by virtue of subsection (1) above, of
section 43 above, in subsection (4) of that section for the words
" paragraph (*a*) of subsection (2) of section 53 below " there
shall be substituted the words " paragraph (*b*) of subsection (2)
of section 38 above ".

55.—(1) Subject to subsection (2) below, the local authorities Local
for the purposes of this Part of this Act are the councils of authorities
districts and London boroughs and the Common Council of for the
the City of London.   purposes of
Part VI.

(2) The Greater London Council may exercise the powers
of a local authority under subsections (1) to (4) of section 52
above with respect to any area in Greater London, but only
with the agreement of any local authority in whose district the
area or any part of the area is situated.

(3) In relation to, and to any premises in, an area which, in
accordance with subsection (2) above, has been declared a
priority neighbourhood by the Greater London Council, any
reference to a local authority in—

> (*a*) sections 52(5), 53 and 54 above, or

C

PART VI

1957 c. 56.

(b) any provision of Part IV of this Act specified in section 52(7) or section 54 above, as that provision has effect by virtue of either of those sections, or

(c) the provisions of the Housing Act 1957 applied in relation to priority neighbourhoods by section 48(1) above, as that section has effect by virtue of section 54(1)(g) above,

shall be construed, except in so far as the context otherwise requires, as a reference to the Greater London Council, to the exclusion of any other council.

PART VII

FINANCIAL ASSISTANCE TOWARDS WORKS OF IMPROVEMENT, REPAIR AND CONVERSION

Grants by local authorities

Grants for provision, improvement and repair of dwellings.

56.—(1) Grants of the descriptions specified in subsection (2) below shall be payable by local authorities in accordance with the following provisions of this Part of this Act towards the cost of works required for—

(a) the provision of dwellings by the conversion of houses or other buildings,

(b) the improvement of dwellings,

(c) the repair of dwellings, and

(d) the improvement of houses in multiple occupation by the provision of standard amenities,

where the provision, improvement or repair is by a person other than a housing authority.

(2) The grants referred to in subsection (1) above are—

(a) an " improvement grant " in respect of works required for the provision of a dwelling (as mentioned in paragraph (a) of that subsection) or for the improvement of a dwelling or, in the case of a registered disabled person, works required for his welfare, accommodation or employment where the existing dwelling is inadequate or unsuitable for those purposes, not being works falling entirely within paragraph (b) below;

(b) an " intermediate grant " in respect of works required for the improvement of a dwelling by the provision of standard amenities which it lacks or which in the case of a registered disabled person are inaccessible to that person by virtue of his disability;

(*c*) a " special grant " in respect of works required for the
improvement of a house in multiple occupation by the
provision of standard amenities ; and

(*d*) a " repairs grant " in respect of works of repair or
replacement relating to a dwelling in a housing action
area or a general improvement area, not being works
associated with other works required for the provision
(as mentioned in subsection (1)(*a*) above) or improvement of the dwelling.

(3) Except in a case where a local authority exercise their
power under subsection (4) below, they shall not entertain—

(*a*) an application for an improvement grant in respect of
works required for the provision of a dwelling by the
conversion of a house or other building which was
erected after 2nd October 1961 ; or

(*b*) an application for any grant for the improvement or
repair of a dwelling which was provided after that
date.

(4) Notwithstanding the prohibition in subsection (3) above,
but subject to such general or special directions as may from
time to time be given by the Secretary of State, where an application is made which falls within paragraph (*a*) or paragraph (*b*)
of that subsection, the local authority to whom it is made may
entertain the application if they consider it appropriate to do so.

57.—(1) No grant shall be paid by a local authority unless   General
an application therefor is made to the Authority in accordance   provisions
with the provisions of this Part of this Act.   relating to
                                                                   applications
(2) An application for a grant shall—   for grants.

(*a*) specify the premises to which the application relates ;

(*b*) contain particulars of the works in respect of which the
grant is sought (in this Part of this Act referred to as
" the relevant works ") and an estimate of their cost ;
and

(*c*) contain such other particulars as may for the time being
be specified by the Secretary of State.

(3) Subject to section 83 below, a local authority shall not
entertain an application for a grant unless they are satisfied
that the applicant has, in every parcel of land on which the
relevant works are to be or have been carried out, an interest
which is either an estate in fee simple absolute in possession or
a term of years absolute of which not less than 5 years remain
unexpired at the date of the application.

(4) If the Secretary of State has given directions for the
purposes of this subsection, either to local authorities generally

or to a particular local authority, applying to any application for an improvement grant or an intermediate grant which is of a description specified in the directions, a local authority affected by the directions shall not approve an application to which they apply except with the consent of the Secretary of State ; and any such consent may be given generally or with respect to a particular authority or with respect to a particular description of application.

(5) A local authority may not approve an application for a grant if the relevant works have been begun unless they are satisfied that there were good reasons for beginning those works before the application was approved.

(6) Except in so far as this Act otherwise provides, a local authority may not entertain an application for a grant if the relevant works are or include—

    (*a*) works which were the relevant works in relation to an application which has previously been approved under this Part of this Act ; or

    (*b*) works which were specified in an application for a grant under Part I of the Housing Act 1969 which was approved,

and the applicant for the grant is, or is the personal representative of, the person who made the earlier application.

(7) If, after an application for a grant has been approved by a local authority, the authority are satisfied that owing to circumstances beyond the control of the applicant the relevant works will not be carried out on the basis of the estimate contained in the application, they may, on receiving a further estimate, redetermine the estimated expense in relation to the grant and make such other adjustments relating to the amount of the grant as appear to them to be appropriate, but the amount of a grant shall not be increased by virtue of this subsection beyond the amount which could have been notified as the amount of the grant when the application was approved if the estimate contained in the application had been for the same amount as the further estimate.

Standard amenities.   **58.**—(1) Subject to subsection (2) below, the " standard amenities " for the purposes of this Part of this Act are the amenities which are described in the first column of Part I of Schedule 6 to this Act and which conform to such of the provisions of Part II of that Schedule as are applicable.

(2) The Secretary of State may by order vary the provisions of Schedule 6 to this Act and any such order may contain such transitional or other supplemental provisions as appear to the Secretary of State to be expedient.

59.—(1) In this Part of this Act " the appropriate percentage " PART VII (which is relevant for determining the amount, or the maximum Appropriate amount, of any grant) shall be determined according to whether, percentage. on the date on which the application for the grant concerned is approved, the premises to which the application relates are in a housing action area, a general improvement area or neither and, subject to the following provisions of this section, the appropriate percentage is—

(a) in a case where those premises are on that date in a housing action area, 75 per cent. ;

(b) in a case where those premises are on that date in a general improvement area, 60 per cent. ; and

(c) in any other case, 50 per cent.

(2) If, in the case of premises which are in a housing action area on the date on which the application for the grant concerned is approved, it appears to the local authority by whom the application is approved that the applicant will not without undue hardship be able to finance the cost of so much of the relevant works as is not met by the grant, they may treat the appropriate percentage as increased to such percentage not exceeding 90 per cent. as they think fit.

(3) If, at any time after an application for a grant has been approved but before the relevant works have been begun, an area which includes the land on which the premises concerned are situated is declared to be a housing action area or a general improvement area, the local authority by whom the application was approved shall allow the application to be withdrawn with a view to enabling the applicant to make a further application for a grant.

(4) The Secretary of State may by order made with the consent of the Treasury vary all or any of the percentages specified in subsections (1) and (2) above, and any such variation shall have effect with respect to applications for grants approved after such date as may be specified in the order.

(5) An order under subsection (4) above—

(a) shall not be made unless a draft thereof has been approved by a resolution of the Commons House of Parliament ; and

(b) shall not specify a date earlier than the date of the laying of the draft.

60.—(1) Subject to section 83 below, a local authority shall Certificates not entertain an application for a grant other than a special of future grant unless the application is accompanied by a certificate occupation. under this section as to future occupation of the dwelling or,

C 3

as the case may be, each of the dwellings for the provision, improvement or repair of which the grant is sought.

(2) A certificate of future occupation shall be either a certificate of owner-occupation under subsection (3) or subsection (4) below or a certificate of availability for letting under subsection (5) below.

(3) Subject to subsection (4) below, for the purposes of this Part of this Act a " certificate of owner-occupation " is a certificate stating that the applicant for the grant intends that, on or before the first anniversary of the certified date and throughout the period of 4 years beginning on that first anniversary, the dwelling will be his only or main residence and will be occupied exclusively by himself and members of his household (if any).

(4) For the purposes of this Part of this Act, in a case where an application for a grant is made by the personal representatives of a deceased person or by trustees, a " certificate of owner-occupation " is a certificate stating that the applicants are personal representatives or trustees and intend that, on or before the first anniversary of the certified date and throughout the period of 4 years beginning on that first anniversary, the dwelling will be the only or main residence of, and exclusively occupied by, a person who, under the will or intestacy or, as the case may require, under the terms of the trust, is beneficially entitled to an interest in the dwelling or the proceeds of sale thereof and members of his household (if any).

(5) For the purposes of this Part of this Act a " certificate of availability for letting " is a certificate stating that the applicant for the grant intends that, throughout the period of 5 years beginning with the certified date,—

(a) the dwelling will be let or available for letting as a residence, and not for a holiday, to a person other than a member of the applicant's family ; or

(b) the dwelling will be occupied or available for occupation by a member of the agricultural population in pursuance of a contract of service and otherwise than as a tenant.

Improvement grants

Improvement grants.   **61.**—(1) A local authority shall pay an improvement grant if—

(a) an application for such a grant, made in accordance with this Part of this Act, is approved by them, and

(b) the conditions for the payment of the grant are fulfilled,

and, subject to the provisions of this Part of this Act, a local

authority may approve an application for an improvement grant
in such circumstances as they think fit.

(2) A local authority shall not approve an application for an
improvement grant unless they are satisfied that, on completion
of the relevant works, the dwelling or, as the case may be, each
of the dwellings to which the application relates will attain the
required standard.

(3) For the purposes of this section a dwelling shall be taken,
subject to subsections (4) and (5) below, to attain the required
standard if the following conditions are fulfilled with respect to
it, namely—

    (a) that it is provided with all the standard amenities for the
        exclusive use of its occupants; and

    (b) that it is in good repair (disregarding the state of
        internal decorative repair) having regard to its age and
        character and the locality in which it is situated; and

    (c) that it conforms with such requirements with respect
        to construction and physical conditions and the pro-
        vision of services and amenities as may for the time
        being be specified by the Secretary of State for the
        purposes of this section; and

    (d) that it is likely to provide satisfactory housing accom-
        modation for a period of 30 years.

(4) If it appears to a local authority that it is not practicable
at reasonable expense for a dwelling to which an application
for an improvement grant relates—

    (a) to be provided with all the standard amenities, or

    (b) to attain the standard of repair required by the con-
        dition in paragraph (b) of subsection (3) above, or

    (c) to conform in every respect with the requirements re-
        ferred to in paragraph (c) of that subsection,

the authority may, in the case of that dwelling, reduce the
required standard by dispensing with the condition in question
to such extent as will enable them, if they think fit, to approve
the application.

(5) If it appears to a local authority reasonable to do so in
the case of any dwelling to which an application for an improvement grant relates, they may reduce the required standard by
substituting for the period specified in paragraph (d) of subsection (3) above such shorter period of not less than 10 years
as appears to them to be appropriate in the circumstances.

PART VII
Rateable
value limit on
improvement
grants for
dwellings for
owner
occupation.

62.—(1) If an application for an improvement grant in respect of works required for the improvement of a dwelling or dwellings is accompanied by a certificate of owner-occupation relating to that dwelling or, as the case may be, one of those dwellings, the local authority shall not approve the application if, on the date of the application, the rateable value of the dwelling to which that certificate relates is in excess of the relevant limit.

(2) If an application for an improvement grant in respect of works required for the provision of a dwelling or dwellings by the conversion of any premises which consist of or include a house or two or more houses is accompanied by a certificate of owner-occupation in respect of that dwelling or, as the case may be, one of those dwellings, the local authority shall not approve the application if, on the date of the application,—

    (*a*) the rateable value of that house or, as the case may be, any of those houses, or

    (*b*) where the certificate relates to a dwelling to be provided by the conversion of premises consisting of or including two or more houses, the aggregate of the rateable values of those houses,

is in excess of the relevant limit.

(3) In this section " the relevant limit " means such limit of rateable value as the Secretary of State may with the consent of the Treasury by order specify ; and different limits may be so specified in relation to dwellings falling within subsection (1) above and houses converted as mentioned in subsection (2) above and also in relation to property in different areas.

(4) For the purposes of this section the rateable value on any day of a dwelling or house shall be determined as follows : —

    (*a*) if the dwelling or house is a hereditament for which a rateable value is then shown in the valuation list, it shall be that rateable value ;

    (*b*) if the dwelling or house forms part only of such a hereditament or consists of or forms part of more than one such hereditament, its rateable value shall be taken to be such value as the local authority, after consultation with the applicant as to an appropriate apportionment or aggregation, shall determine.

Determination
of estimated
expense in
relation to
improvement
grant.

63.—(1) Where a local authority approve an application for an improvement grant they shall determine the amount of the expenses which, in their opinion, are proper to be incurred for the execution of the relevant works and shall notify the applicant of that amount ; and, in relation to an improvement grant which has been approved, the amount so notified is in this section

and section 64 below referred to as " the estimated expense " of
the relevant works.

(2) Not more than 50 per cent., or such other percentage as
may for the time being be prescribed, of the estimated expense of
any works shall be allowed for works of repair and replacement.

(3) If the applicant satisfies the local authority that the
relevant works cannot be or could not have been carried out
without the carrying out of additional works and that this
could not have been reasonably foreseen at the time the application was made, the local authority may, subject to subsection
(2) above, determine a higher amount as the amount of the
estimated expense.

64.—(1) Subject to the following provisions of this section, Amount of
the amount of an improvement grant shall be such as may be improvement
fixed by the local authority when they approve the application grant.
for the grant but shall not exceed the appropriate percentage
of the eligible expense.

(2) Together with the notification under section 63(1) above,
the local authority shall send to the applicant a notification of
the amount of the grant.

(3) Except in a case or description of case in respect of which
the Secretary of State approves a higher eligible expense, the
eligible expense for the purposes of an improvement grant shall
be so much of the estimated expense as does not exceed the relevant limit ; and, subject to subsections (4) and (7) below, " the
relevant limit ", in relation to an improvement grant, is the
amount for the dwelling, or if the application for the grant
relates to more than one dwelling the total of the amounts
for each of the dwellings, applicable under the following
paragraphs, that is to say—

(a) for a dwelling which is improved by the relevant works
or is provided by them otherwise than as mentioned
in paragraph (b) below, £2,000, or such other amount
as the Secretary of State may by order specify ; and

(b) for a dwelling which is provided by the conversion
of a house or other building consisting of three or
more storeys, £2,400, or such other amount as the
Secretary of State may by order specify.

(4) A statutory instrument containing an order under subsection (3) above shall be subject to annulment in pursuance
of a resolution of the Commons House of Parliament.

(5) If the local authority are satisfied in a particular case
that there are good reasons for increasing the amount which,

apart from this subsection, would constitute the relevant limit, they may substitute for that amount such higher amount as the Secretary of State may approve; and the approval of the Secretary of State may be given either with respect to a particular case or with respect to any description of case.

(6) In any case where, after the amount of an improvement grant has been fixed under subsection (1) above, the local authority, in exercise of their powers under section 63(3) above, substitute a higher amount as the amount of the estimated expense, the eligible expense shall be re-calculated under subsection (3) above and if, on that re-calculation, the amount of the eligible expense is greater than it was at the time when the application was approved,—

(*a*) the amount of the improvement grant shall be increased accordingly ; and

(*b*) the local authority shall notify the applicant of the increased amount of the grant.

(7) In any case where—

(*a*) an intermediate grant, a repairs grant or a standard grant (within the meaning of Part I of the Housing Act 1969) has been made in respect of a dwelling, and

1969 c. 33.

(*b*) within the period of 10 years beginning on the date on which that grant was paid or, if it was paid by instalments, the date on which the last instalment was paid, an improvement grant is made in respect of that dwelling,

the amount which, by virtue of subsection (3) above, would otherwise be the relevant limit in relation to the improvement grant shall be reduced by the amount which was the eligible expense for the purposes of the grant referred to in paragraph (*a*) above or, where that grant was a standard grant (within the meaning of Part I of the Housing Act 1969) by an amount determined by reference to the amount of that grant and the rate at which it was made, namely, twice the amount of the grant where that rate was one-half and one and one-third times the amount of the grant where (by virtue of the Housing Act 1971) that rate was 75 per cent.

1971 c. 76.

(8) For the purposes of this section, where an improvement grant is to be paid towards the cost of works required for the provision of a dwelling all or part of which is in the basement of a building, the basement shall count as a storey.

Intermediate grants

Intermediate grants. **65.**—(1) A local authority shall pay an intermediate grant if—

(*a*) an application for such a grant, made in accordance with this Part of this Act, is approved by them ; and (*b*) the conditions for the payment of the grant are fulfilled.

(2) An application for an intermediate grant shall—

(*a*) specify the standard amenity or amenities which it is intended to provide by the relevant works ; and

(*b*) if some only of the standard amenities are specified as mentioned in paragraph (*a*) above, state whether the dwelling is already provided with the remainder ; and

(*c*) contain a statement, with respect to each of the standard amenities specified as mentioned in paragraph (*a*) above, whether, to the best of the knowledge and belief of the applicant, the dwelling has been without that amenity for a period of not less than 12 months ending with the date on which the application is made.

(3) A local authority shall not approve an application for an intermediate grant unless they are satisfied, with respect to each of the standard amenities specified as mentioned in subsection (2)(*a*) above, either—

(*a*) that the dwelling concerned, except in the case of a registered disabled person when this subsection shall not apply, has been without the amenity in question for a period of not less than 12 months ending with the date on which the application is made ; or

(*b*) that the dwelling is provided with the amenity in question on the date of the application but the relevant works, exclusive of those for the provision of that amenity, involve interference with or replacement of that amenity and it would not be reasonably practicable to avoid the interference or replacement.

66.—(1) A local authority shall not approve an application for an intermediate grant unless they are satisfied that, on completion of the relevant works, the dwelling or, as the case may be, each of the dwellings to which the application relates will attain the full standard or, if any of subsections (3) to (5) below applies, the reduced standard.

(2) For the purposes of this section a dwelling shall be taken to attain the full standard if the following conditions are fulfilled with respect to it, namely,—

(*a*) that it is provided with all the standard amenities for the exclusive use of its occupants ; and

(*b*) that it is in good repair (disregarding the state of internal decorative repair) having regard to its age and character and the locality in which it is situated ; and

PART VII

1957 c. 56.

1961 c. 65.

(c) that it conforms with such requirements with respect to thermal insulation as may for the time being be specified by the Secretary of State for the purposes of this section ; and

(d) that it is in all other respects fit for human habitation, construing that expression in accordance with Part II of the Housing Act 1957 ; and

(e) that it is likely to be available for use as a dwelling for a period of 15 years or such other period as may for the time being be specified by the Secretary of State for the purposes of this subsection.

(3) Where an application for an intermediate grant contains a statement, and the local authority are satisfied, that it is not practicable at reasonable expense for the dwelling to which the application relates to be provided with all the standard amenities, they shall dispense with the condition in paragraph (*a*) of subsection (2) above unless they are satisfied that the dwelling is, or forms part of, a house or building in respect of which they could, by a notice under section 15 of the Housing Act 1961, require the execution of such works as are referred to in subsection (1) of that section.

(4) If it appears to a local authority that it is not practicable at reasonable expense for a dwelling to which an application for an intermediate grant relates—

(a) to attain the standard of repair required by the condition in paragraph (*b*) of subsection (2) above, or

(b) to conform in every respect with the requirements referred to in paragraph (*c*) of that subsection, or

(c) to comply with the condition in paragraph (*d*) of that subsection,

the authority may, in the case of that dwelling, dispense with the condition in question to such extent as will enable them, if they think fit, to approve the application.

(5) If it appears to a local authority reasonable to do so in the case of any dwelling to which an application for an intermediate grant relates, they may in the case of that dwelling vary the condition in paragraph (*e*) of subsection (2) above by substituting for the period of 15 years or such other period as may for the time being be specified as mentioned in that paragraph such shorter period as appears to them to be appropriate in the circumstances.

(6) If, in relation to any dwelling, a local authority by virtue of subsection (3), subsection (4) or subsection (5) above dispense, in whole or in part, with any of the conditions in paragraphs (*a*) to (*d*) of subsection (2) above or vary the condition in para-

graph (e) of that subsection, then for the purposes of this section the dwelling concerned shall be taken to attain the reduced standard if, subject to any such dispensation or variation, the conditions in subsection (2) above are fulfilled with respect to it.

67.—(1) Subject to sections 57, 60, 65(2), 65(3) and 66 above, a local authority shall approve an application for an intermediate grant which is duly made in accordance with this Part of this Act.

(2) If an application for an intermediate grant is duly made in accordance with this Part of this Act and the relevant works consist solely of works which the applicant is required to carry out by an improvement notice served or an undertaking accepted under Part VIII of this Act,—

   (a) subsections (3) to (5) of section 57 and sections 60 and 65(2) above shall not apply, and

   (b) if it appears to the local authority to whom the application is made that, on completion of the relevant works, the dwelling concerned will not attain the full standard, they shall be treated as having exercised their powers under subsections (4) and (5) of section 66 above and, where appropriate, as being satisfied as mentioned in subsection (3) of that section, to such extent as is necessary to secure that on completion of the relevant works the dwelling will attain the reduced standard,

and subsection (1) above shall apply accordingly.

(3) Where the relevant works specified in an application for an intermediate grant include works of repair or replacement which go beyond those needed, in the opinion of the local authority, for the purposes of enabling the dwelling concerned to attain the full standard or the reduced standard, as the case may require, the local authority may, with the consent of the applicant, treat the application as varied so that the relevant works—

   (a) are confined to works other than works of repair or replacement, or

   (b) include only such works of repair or replacement as (taken with the rest of the relevant works) will secure, in the opinion of the local authority, that the dwelling will attain the full standard or the reduced standard as the case may require,

and may approve the application as so varied.

(4) In this section " the full standard " and " the reduced standard " have the same meanings as in section 66 above.

PART VII
Determination
of estimated
expense and
amount of
intermediate
grant.

68.—(1) Where a local authority approve an application for an intermediate grant they shall determine separately—

> (a) the amount of the expenses which in their opinion are proper to be incurred for the execution of those of the relevant works which consist of works of repair or replacement, and

> (b) the amount of the expenses which in their opinion are proper to be incurred for the execution of those of the relevant works which relate solely to the provision of standard amenities,

and shall notify the applicant of the amounts determined by them under this subsection.

(2) If the applicant satisfies the local authority that the relevant works cannot be or could not have been carried out without the carrying out of additional works and that this could not have been reasonably foreseen at the time the application was made, the local authority may determine a higher amount under either or both of paragraphs (a) and (b) of subsection (1) above.

(3) Except in a case or description of case in respect of which the Secretary of State approves a higher eligible expense, the eligible expense for the purposes of an intermediate grant shall be the aggregate of—

> (a) so much of the amount determined under subsection (1)(a) above as does not exceed £800 or such other amount as may be prescribed ; and

> (b) so much of the amount determined under subsection (1)(b) above as does not exceed the total of the amounts specified in the second column of Part I of Schedule 6 to this Act in relation to each of the standard amenities which are to be provided by the relevant works.

(4) In any case where the relevant works make provision for more than one standard amenity of the same description, only one amenity of that description shall be taken into account under subsections (1) to (3) above.

(5) Subject to subsection (6) below, the amount of an intermediate grant shall be the appropriate percentage of the eligible expense and, together with the notification under subsection (1) above, the local authority shall send to the applicant a notification of the amount of the grant.

(6) In any case where, after the amount of an intermediate grant has been notified to the applicant under subsection (5) above, the local authority, in exercise of their powers under subsection (2) above, determine a higher amount under either or both of paragraphs (a) and (b) of subsection (1) above, the

eligible expenses shall be re-calculated under subsection (3) above and if, on that re-calculation, the amount of the eligible expense is greater than it was at the time when the application was approved,—

  (a) the amount of the intermediate grant shall be increased accordingly ; and

  (b) the local authority shall notify the applicant of the increased amount of the grant.

Special grants

69.—(1) A local authority shall pay a special grant if—   Special

  (a) an application for such a grant, made in accordance grants. with this Part of this Act, is approved by them, and

  (b) the conditions for the payment of the grant are ful-filled,

and, subject to the provisions of this Part of this Act, a local authority may approve an application for a special grant in such circumstances as they think fit.

(2) An application for a special grant shall specify by how many households and individuals the house concerned is occupied and with what standard amenities it is already provided.

(3) In its application in relation to special grants, Part II of Schedule 6 to this Act shall have effect as if paragraphs 2 and 3 and, in paragraph 1, the words " Except as provided by paragraph 2 below " were omitted.

70.—(1) Where a local authority approve an application for Amount of a special grant they shall determine the amount of the expenses special which in their opinion are proper to be incurred for the execution grant. of the relevant works and shall notify the applicant of that amount.

(2) If any of the relevant works are not exclusively for the purpose of providing one or more of the standard amenities, only so much of the cost of carrying out those works as is, in the opinion of the local authority, attributable to the provision of the standard amenity or standard amenities shall be taken into account for the purpose of the determination under sub-section (1) above.

(3) If the applicant satisfies the local authority that the relevant works cannot be or could not have been carried out without the carrying out of additional works and that this could not have been reasonably foreseen at the time the

application was made, the local authority may, subject to subsection (2) above, determine a higher amount under subsection (1) above.

(4) Except in a case or description of case in respect of which the Secretary of State approves a higher eligible expense, the eligible expense for the purposes of a special grant shall be so much of the amount determined under subsection (1) above as does not exceed the aggregate of the amounts specified in the second column of Part I of Schedule 6 to this Act in relation to each of the standard amenities which are to be provided by the relevant works (so that, where the relevant works make provision for more than one standard amenity of the same description, a separate amount shall be aggregated for each of those amenities).

(5) The amount of a special grant shall be such as may be fixed by the local authority when they approve the application for the grant but shall not exceed the appropriate percentage of the eligible expense and, together with the notification under subsection (1) above, the local authority shall send to the applicant a notification of the amount of the grant.

Repairs grants

Repairs grants.   **71.**—(1) A local authority shall pay a repairs grant if—

(a) an application for such a grant, made in accordance with this Part of this Act, is approved by them, and

(b) the conditions for the payment of the grant are fulfilled,

and, subject to the provisions of this Part of this Act, a local authority may approve an application for a repairs grant in such circumstances as they think fit.

(2) In considering whether or not to exercise their discretion to approve an application for a repairs grant, a local authority shall have regard to the question whether, in their opinion, the applicant would without undue hardship be able to finance the cost of the relevant works without the assistance of a repairs grant.

(3) A local authority shall not approve an application for a repairs grant unless they are satisfied—

(a) that the dwelling or, as the case may be, each of the dwellings to which the application relates is situated in a general improvement area or a housing action area, and

(b) that on completion of the relevant works the dwelling or, as the case may be, each of the dwellings to which the application relates will attain the relevant standard of repair.

(4) Without prejudice to the discretion of a local authority PART VII
to approve or decline to approve an application for a repairs
grant, if, in the opinion of the authority, the relevant works are
more extensive than is necessary for the purpose of securing
that the dwelling or, as the case may be, any of the dwellings
to which the application relates will attain the relevant standard
of repair, the authority may, with the consent of the applicant,
treat the application as varied so that the relevant works include
only such works as seem to the authority to be necessary for
that purpose, and may approve the application as so varied.

(5) For the purposes of this section a dwelling shall be taken
to attain the relevant standard of repair if it is in good repair
(disregarding the state of internal decorative repair) having
regard to its age and character and the locality in which it is
situated.

72.—(1) Where a local authority approve an application for a Determination
repairs grant they shall determine the amount of the expenses of estimated
which in their opinion are proper to be incurred for the execu- expense and
tion of the relevant works and shall notify the applicant of that amount of
amount. repairs grant.

(2) If the applicant satisfies the local authority that the relevant
works cannot be or could not have been carried out without
the carrying out of additional works and that this could not
have been reasonably foreseen at the time the application was
made, the local authority may determine a higher amount under
subsection (1) above.

(3) Except in a case or description of case in respect of which
the Secretary of State approves a higher eligible expense, the
eligible expense for the purposes of a repairs grant shall be so
much of the amount determined under subsection (1) above as
does not exceed £800 or such other amount as may be prescribed.

(4) The amount of a repairs grant shall be such as may be
fixed by the local authority when they approve the application
for the grant but, subject to subsection (5) below, shall not
exceed the appropriate percentage of the eligible expense and,
together with the notification under subsection (1) above, the
local authority shall send to the applicant a notification of the
amount of the grant.

(5) In any case where, after the amount of a repairs grant has
been notified to the applicant under subsection (4) above, the
local authority, in exercise of their powers under subsection (2)
above, determine a higher amount under subsection (1) above,
the eligible expense shall be re-calculated under subsection (3)
above, and if, on that re-calculation, the amount of the eligible

PART VII expense is greater than it was at the time when the application was approved,—

> (*a*) the amount of the repairs grant shall be increased accordingly ; and
>
> (*b*) the local authority shall notify the applicant of the increased amount of the grant.

Grant conditions

Conditions as to future occupation.
73.—(1) Subject to section 83 below, where an application for an improvement grant, an intermediate grant or a repairs grant has been approved by a local authority the provisions of this section shall apply with respect to the occupation, during the period of 5 years beginning with the certified date (in this section referred to as " the initial period "), of the dwelling or, as the case may be, each of the dwellings to which the grant relates.

(2) In any case where the application for the grant was accompanied by a certificate of owner-occupation with respect to the dwelling, it shall be a condition of the grant—

> (*a*) that throughout the first year of the initial period the dwelling will, as a residence, be occupied exclusively by, or be available for the exclusive occupation of, a qualifying person and members of his household (if any) ; and
>
> (*b*) that if, at any time during the second or any subsequent year of the initial period, the dwelling is not occupied exclusively as his only or main residence by a qualifying person and members of his household (if any), the dwelling will at that time be let or available for letting by a qualifying person as a residence, and not for a holiday, to persons other than members of that person's family.

(3) For the purposes of this section, the following are " qualifying persons " in relation to a dwelling, namely,—

> (*a*) the applicant for the grant and any person who derives title to the dwelling through or under the applicant, otherwise than by a conveyance for value ; and
>
> (*b*) at any time when personal representatives or trustees as such are the qualifying person by virtue of paragraph (*a*) above, any person who, under the will or intestacy or, as the case may require, under the terms of the trusts concerned, is beneficially entitled to an interest in the dwelling or the proceeds of sale thereof.

(4) In any case where the application for the grant was accompanied by a certificate of availability for letting with

respect to the dwelling, it shall be a condition of the grant that, PART VII
throughout the initial period,

(*a*) the dwelling will be let or available for letting as a
residence, and not for a holiday, by a qualifying person
to persons other than members of the family of that
qualifying person or any other person who is for the
time being a qualifying person in relation to the
dwelling; or

(*b*) the dwelling will be occupied or available for occupation
by a member of the agricultural population in
pursuance of a contract of service and otherwise than
as a tenant.

(5) In determining, in a case where subsection (2) above
applies, whether there is a breach of the condition specified in
that subsection, there shall be disregarded any period of not
more than 12 months during which that condition is not fulfilled
if—

(*a*) that period begins on the death of a qualifying person
who, immediately before his death, was occupying the
dwelling concerned as his residence ; and

(*b*) throughout that period an interest in the dwelling or
the proceeds of sale thereof, being either the interest
which belonged to the deceased or an interest which
arose or fell into possession on his death, is vested in
his personal representatives acting in that capacity or in
trustees as such or, by virtue of section 9 of the
Administration of Estates Act 1925, in the Probate 1925 c. 23.
Judge, within the meaning of that Act.

(6) In any case where subsection (1) above applies, it shall
be a condition of the grant that if, at any time within the
initial period, the local authority by whom the grant was paid
serve notice on the owner of the dwelling requiring him to do
so, the owner shall, within the period of 21 days beginning
with the date on which the notice is served, furnish to the
authority a certificate giving such information as the authority may reasonably require with respect to the occupation of
the dwelling, and for this purpose it shall also be a condition
of the grant that, if required to do so by the owner of the
dwelling, any tenant of the dwelling will furnish the owner
with such information as he may reasonably require to enable
him to furnish the certificate to the authority.

74.—(1) Subject to section 83 below, where an application Power
for an improvement grant, an intermediate grant or a repairs of local
grant is approved by a local authority then, subject to sub- authorities to
section (3) below, the authority may and, in the case of a conditions.

dwelling or dwellings situated in an area which, on the date on which the application is approved, is a housing action area, a general improvement area or a priority neighbourhood, they shall impose, with respect to the dwelling or, as the case may be, each of the dwellings to which the grant relates, the conditions specified in subsection (2) below as conditions of the grant, but may impose no other condition in relation to the approval or making of the grant, whether the condition purports to operate by way of a condition of the grant, a personal covenant or otherwise.

(2) The conditions referred to in subsection (1) above are—

 (a) that the dwelling will be let or available for letting on a regulated tenancy or a Part VI contract;

 (b) that, if the local authority by whom the grant in question was paid serve notice on the owner of the dwelling requiring him to do so, the owner will within the period of 21 days beginning with the date on which the notice is served furnish to the authority a certificate that the condition set out in paragraph (a) above is being fulfilled;

 (c) that, if required to do so by the owner of the dwelling, any tenant of the dwelling will furnish the owner with such information as he may reasonably require for the purpose of enabling him to comply with the condition set out in paragraph (b) above;

 (d) that, if on the certified date there is no registered rent for the dwelling and no such application or reference is pending, an application for the registration of a rent for the dwelling will be made to the rent officer before the expiry of the period of 14 days beginning on the relevant day or, as the case may require, the Part VI contract will be referred to the rent tribunal for the district in question before the expiry of that period;

 (e) that any such application or reference as is referred to in paragraph (d) above which is either pending on the certified date or made as mentioned in that paragraph will be diligently proceeded with and not withdrawn; and

 (f) that no premium shall be required as a condition of the grant, renewal or continuance on or after the certified date of any lease, agreement for a lease or Part VI contract of or relating to the dwelling.

(3) To the extent that a grant relates to a dwelling—

 (a) in which a registered housing association or an unregistered housing association falling within section 18(1)(b) of this Act has an estate or interest on the date on which the application for the grant is approved (in this subsection referred to as " the approval date "), or

(b) in respect of which a certificate of owner-occupation has been given and which has not at any time during the period of 12 months immediately preceding the approval date been let in whole or in part for residential purposes, or

(c) which is occupied or available for occupation by a member of the agricultural population in pursuance of a contract of service and otherwise than as a tenant,

no condition may be imposed under this section as a condition of the grant.

(4) In this section—

" Part VI contract " has the same meaning as in Part VI of the Rent Act 1968 ; 1968 c. 23.

" premium " has the same meaning as in Part VII of that Act ;

" registered rent " means,—

(a) in relation to a dwelling which is subject to, or available for letting on, a regulated tenancy, a rent registered under Part IV of that Act ; and

(b) in relation to a dwelling which is let, or available for letting, on a Part VI contract, a rent registered in the register kept under section 74 of that Act ;

" regulated tenancy " has the same meaning as in that Act ; and

" relevant day ", in relation to a dwelling for which there is no registered rent on the certified date, means the first day, not being earlier than the certified date, on which the dwelling is or becomes subject to a regulated tenancy or let on a Part VI contract.

75.—(1) The provisions of this section shall apply in any case Enforceability where, under or by virtue of any provision of this Part of this and registra- Act, a condition (in this section referred to as a " grant condi- tion of grant tion ") is imposed as a condition of a grant. conditions.

(2) If and so long as a grant condition remains in force—

(a) it shall be binding on any person, other than a housing authority or registered housing association, who is for the time being the owner of the dwelling to which the grant relates ; and

PART VII

(*b*) it shall be enforceable against all other persons having any interest in that dwelling as if it were a condition of the terms of every lease, agreement for a lease or statutory tenancy of, or of property including, that dwelling.

(3) Subject to subsection (4) below, a grant condition shall be in force throughout the period of 5 years beginning on the certified date.

(4) If, on the date on which an application for a grant is approved, the dwelling to which the grant relates is in a housing action area, subsection (3) above shall have effect, except in the case of a grant condition imposed under section 73 above, with the substitution for the words " 5 years " of the words " 7 years ".

1925 c. 22.

(5) A grant condition shall be treated as not being registrable by virtue of section 15 of the Land Charges Act 1925 (either as, or as if it were, a local land charge) but, as soon as may be after an application for a grant has been approved, any condition of that grant shall be registered in the register of local land charges—

(*a*) by the proper officer, for the purposes of section 15 of the Land Charges Act 1925, of the council in whose area the dwelling concerned is situated, and

(*b*) in such manner as may be prescribed by rules under section 19 of that Act,

and in this subsection " council " means a district council, a London borough council or the Common Council of the City of London.

(6) In this Part of this Act " the certified date ", in relation to a dwelling in respect of which an application for a grant has been approved, means the date certified by the local authority by whom the application was approved as the date on which the dwelling first becomes fit for occupation after the completion of the relevant works to the satisfaction of the local authority.

Repayment of grant for breach of condition.

76.—(1) The provisions of this section shall have effect in the event of a breach of a condition of a grant (in this section referred to as " the relevant grant ") at a time when the condition is binding on the owner of the dwelling concerned by virtue of section 75(2) above.

(2) Where the relevant grant related to a single dwelling, an amount equal to the amount of the relevant grant, together with compound interest thereon as from the certified date, calculated at the appropriate rate and with yearly rests, shall, on being

demanded by the local authority forthwith become payable to the authority by the owner for the time being of the dwelling.

(3) Where the relevant grant related to two or more dwellings, an amount equal to such part of the relevant grant as appears to the authority to be referable to the dwelling to which the breach relates, together with compound interest on that part as from the certified date, calculated at the appropriate rate and with yearly rests, shall, on being demanded by the local authority, forthwith become payable to the authority by the owner for the time being of that dwelling.

(4) Nothing in subsection (2) or, as the case may be, subsection (3) above shall prevent a local authority from determining not to demand any such amount as is referred to in that subsection or from demanding an amount less than that which they are entitled to demand under that subsection.

(5) Upon satisfaction of the liability of an owner of a dwelling to make a payment under this section to a local authority in respect of a breach of a condition of a grant, the condition shall cease to be in force with respect to that dwelling.

(6) In this section " the appropriate rate " means the rate of interest for the time being fixed by subsection (2) of section 171 of the Local Government Act 1972 for the purposes of the 1972 c. 70. enactments specified in subsection (1) of that section.

77.—(1) If, at any time while a condition of a grant remains Voluntary in force, the owner of the dwelling to which the condition repayment relates or a mortgagee of the interest of the owner in that dwell- of grants. ing, being a mortgagee entitled to exercise a power of sale, pays to the local authority by whom the grant was made the like amount as would (on a demand by the local authority) become payable under section 76 above in the event of a breach of that condition, all conditions of the grant shall cease to be in force with respect to that dwelling.

(2) Any amount paid under subsection (1) above by a mortgagee shall be treated as part of the sum secured by the mortgage and may be discharged accordingly.

(3) The purposes authorised for the application of capital money—

(a) by section 73 of the Settled Land Act 1925 and by that 1925 c. 18. section as applied by section 28 of the Law of Property 1925 c. 20. Act 1925 in relation to trusts for sale, and

(b) by section 26 of the Universities of College Estates 1925 c. 24. Act 1925,

shall include the payment to a local authority under subsection (1) above of the amount mentioned in that subsection in respect of a dwelling.

Contributions

Contributions
by Secretary
of State
towards
grants.

78.—(1) The Secretary of State may make a contribution towards the expense incurred by a local authority in making a grant.

(2) The contributions shall be a sum payable annually for a period of 20 years beginning with the financial year in which the works towards the cost of which the grant was made were completed, equal to the relevant percentage of the annual loan charges referable to the amount of the grant.

(3) In subsection (2) above "the relevant percentage" means—

(a) in a case where, on the date on which the application for the grant concerned is approved, the premises to which the application relates are in a general improvement area or a housing action area, 90 per cent., and

(b) in any other case, 75 per cent.

(4) The Secretary of State may by order made with the consent of the Treasury vary either or both of the percentages specified in subsection (3) above, and any such variation shall have effect with respect to applications for grants approved after such date as may be specified in the order.

(5) An order under subsection (4) above—

(a) shall not be made unless a draft thereof has been approved by a resolution of the Commons House of Parliament ; and

(b) shall not specify a date earlier than the date of the laying of the draft.

(6) For the purposes of this section " the annual loan charges " referable to the amount of a grant means the annual sum which, in the opinion of the Secretary of State, would fall to be provided by a housing authority for the payment of interest on, and the repayment of, a loan of that amount repayable over a period of 20 years.

(7) In any case where, on the date on which the application for a grant is approved, the premises to which the application relates are in an area declared by the local authority concerned to be a housing action area and, after that date, the Secretary of State notifies the local authority that the area is no longer to be such an area, or that land on which the premises are situated is to be excluded from the area, he may, without prejudice to his discretion under subsection (1) above not to make a contribution under this section, make such a contribution on the basis that the relevant percentage is 75 per cent.

79.—(1) The Secretary of State may pay contributions (in this section referred to as "improvement contributions") to housing authorities towards the expenses incurred by them in—

(a) the provision of dwellings by the conversion of houses or other buildings, or

(b) the improvement of dwellings,

in such circumstances as appear to him to be sufficiently similar to those in which an improvement grant might be paid by a local authority had the provision or improvement been by a person other than a housing authority.

(2) The Secretary of State may pay an improvement contribution with respect to any dwellings if an application therefor containing such estimates and particulars as he may require is made by a housing authority and approved by him.

(3) Where the Secretary of State approves an application for an improvement contribution, he shall determine the amount of the expenses which, in his opinion, are proper to be incurred by the housing authority for the execution of any works required for the provision or improvement of the dwellings.

(4) The eligible expense for the purposes of an improvement contribution shall be so much of the amount determined under subsection (3) above as does not exceed the amount arrived at by taking, for each dwelling provided or improved, £2,000.

(5) The improvement contribution shall be a sum payable annually for a period of 20 years, beginning with the financial year in which the works required for the provision or improvement of the dwellings are completed, equal to 37·5 per cent. of the annual loan charges referable to the eligible expense.

(6) Subsection (6) of section 78 above shall apply for the purposes of this section as it applies for the purposes of that.

80. If a local authority—

(a) do not approve an application for a grant, or

(b) fix the amount of an improvement grant, a special grant or a repairs grant at less than the appropriate percentage of the eligible expense within the meaning of section 64, section 70 or, as the case may be, section 72 above,

they shall state to the applicant in writing their reasons for doing so.

PART VII
Grants
restricted to
applicant and
his personal
representa-
tives.

81.—(1) In relation to a grant or an application therefor, any reference in the preceeding provisions of this Part of this Act and in subsection (2) below to the applicant shall be construed, in relation to any time after his death, as a reference to his personal representatives.

(2) If, before the certified date, an applicant for a grant ceases to have such an interest as is referred to in section 57(3) above,—

(a) no grant shall be paid or, if any instalment of the grant was paid before the applicant ceased to have such an interest, no further instalments shall be paid ; and

(b) any instalment of the grant which has been paid to the applicant shall, on being demanded by the local authority who approved the application for the grant, forthwith become repayable to them by the applicant together with interest thereon from the date on which it was paid until repayment at the rate for the time being fixed by subsection (2) of section 171 of the Local Government Act 1972 for the purposes of the enactments specified in subsection (1) of that section.

1972 c. 70.

Payment of grants.

82.—(1) In approving an application for a grant a local authority may require as a condition of paying the grant that the relevant works are carried out within such time, not being less than 12 months, as the authority may specify or such further time as they may allow.

(2) Where a local authority are satisfied under section 63(3), section 68(2), section 70(3) or section 72(2) above that the relevant works cannot be or could not have been carried out without the carrying out of additional works, they may, without prejudice to subsection (1) above, allow further time as the time within which the relevant works and the additional works are to be carried out.

(3) A grant may be paid after the completion of the works towards the cost of which it is payable or part of it may be paid in instalments as the works progress and the balance after the completion of the works.

(4) Where a grant is paid in instalments the aggregate of the instalments paid shall not at any time before the completion of the works exceed one half of the aggregate cost of the works executed up to that time.

(5) The payment of a grant or of any part thereof shall be conditional upon the works or the corresponding part of the works being executed to the satisfaction of the local authority.

(6) If an instalment of a grant is paid before the completion PART VII
of the works and the works are not completed within the time
specified in subsection (7) below, that instalment and any
further sums paid by the local authority as part of the grant
shall, on being demanded by the authority, forthwith become
repayable to them by the person who made the application
for the grant or his personal representatives and shall carry
interest from the date on which it was paid until repayment
at the rate for the time being fixed by subsection (2) of section
171 of the Local Government Act 1972 for the purposes of the 1972 c. 70.
enactments specified in subsection (1) of that section.

(7) Where the local authority have specified no time under
subsection (1) above for the completion of the works, the time
referred to in subsection (6) above is 12 months from the date
on which the instalment is paid or such further time as the
authority may allow ; and where they have specified a time
under subsection (1) above or allowed further time under that
subsection or subsection (2) above the time referred to in subsection (6) above is the time so specified or allowed.

83.—(1) Sections 57(3), 60, 73 and 74 above shall not apply Special
in relation to— provisions as
to parsonages,
    (*a*) an application for a grant in respect of glebe land or etc.
        the residence house of an ecclesiastical benefice made,
        during a period when the benefice is vacant, by a
        sequestrator of the profits thereof ; or

    (*b*) an application for a grant made by a charity or on
        behalf of a charity by the charity trustees thereof.

(2) Section 57(3) above shall not apply in relation to land
which is proposed to be sold or leased under section 105(2) of
the Housing Act 1957 (power to dispose of land for the purpose 1957 c. 56.
of carrying out works in connection with work on an adjoining
house) to the applicant for a grant.

84. In this Part of this Act— Interpretation
    " agricultural population " means— of Part VII.
        (*a*) persons whose employment or latest employ-
        ment is or was employment in agriculture or in an
        industry mainly dependent on agriculture, and
        (*b*) the dependants of such persons,
    and for this purpose " agriculture " includes dairy-
farming and poultry-farming and the use of land as
grazing, meadow or pasture land, or orchard or osier
land or woodland, or for market gardens or nursery
grounds ;
    " appropriate percentage " has the meaning assigned to it
    by section 59 above ;

" certificate of owner-occupation " and " certificate of availability for letting " have the meanings assigned to them by section 60 above ;

" certified date " has the meaning assigned to it by section 75(6) above ;

" charity " and " charity trustees " have the same meanings as in the Charities Act 1960 ;

" grant " means a grant of a description specified in section 56(2) above ;

" housing authority " means a local authority, the council of a county, the Greater London Council, the Commission for the New Towns or a redevelopment corporation within the meaning of the New Towns Act 1965 ;

" improvement " includes alteration and enlargement, and any reference to works required for the provision or improvement of a dwelling (whether generally or in any particular respect) includes a reference to any works of repair or replacement needed (in the opinion of the person paying any grant or contribution) for the purpose of enabling the dwelling to which the improvement relates to attain the relevant standard ;

" let " includes " sub-let " ;

" local authority ",—

(a) in relation to premises in a general improvement area or a housing action area, means the council by whom the area was declared to be such an area ; and

(b) in relation to any other premises, means the council of a district or London borough or the Common Council of the City of London ;

" owner ", in relation to a dwelling, means the person who—

(a) is for the time being entitled to receive from a lessee of the dwelling, or would be so entitled if the dwelling were let, a rent of not less than two-thirds of the net annual value of the dwelling ; and

(b) is himself not liable, as a lessee of, or of any property which includes, the dwelling, to pay to a superior landlord a rent of not less than two-thirds of the net annual value of the property of which he is such a lessee ;

" prescribed " means prescribed by order made by the Secretary of State ;

" the relevant standard " means—

(a) in relation to an improvement grant, the required standard referred to in section 61 above ;

(b) in relation to an intermediate grant, the full standard or, as the case may require, the reduced standard referred to in section 66 above; and

(c) in relation to a repairs grant, the relevant standard of repair referred to in section 71 above;

" the relevant works " has the meaning assigned to it by section 57(2)(b) above;

" standard amenities " has the meaning assigned to it by section 58 above.

PART VIII

COMPULSORY IMPROVEMENT OF DWELLINGS

Dwellings in general improvement areas and housing action areas

85.—(1) If it appears to the local authority by whom a general improvement area or a housing action area has been declared that a dwelling in that area—

Provisional notice of local authority's proposals for improvement of dwelling.

(a) is without one or more of the standard amenities, whether or not it is also in a state of disrepair, and

(b) is capable at reasonable expense of improvement to the full standard or, failing that, to the reduced standard, and

(c) was provided (by erection or by the conversion of a building already in existence) before 3rd October 1961,

then, subject to subsection (3) below, the authority may serve a notice under subsection (2) below on the person having control of the dwelling.

(2) A notice under this subsection (in the following provisions of this Part of this Act referred to as a " provisional notice ") shall—

(a) specify the works which in the opinion of the local authority are required for the dwelling to be improved to the full standard or, as the case may be, to the reduced standard ; and

(b) state the date, being a date not less than 21 days after service of the provisional notice, and time and place at which the authority's proposals for the carrying out of the works, any alternative proposals, any proposed housing arrangements, the views and interests of the occupying tenant (if any) and any other matters may be discussed.

(3) A local authority may not serve a provisional notice in respect of a dwelling which is owner-occupied unless it appears to them that the circumstances are such that it is not reasonably practicable for another dwelling—

(a) which is in the same building as, or is adjacent to, the dwelling which is owner-occupied, and

(b) which is not owner-occupied or in respect of which an application for a grant under Part VII of this Act has been approved,

to be improved to the full standards or, as the case may be, to the reduced standard without effecting the improvement to one of those standards of the dwelling which is owner-occupied.

(4) A local authority shall, not less than 21 days before the date stated in a provisional notice as mentioned in subsection (2)(b) above, in addition to serving the notice on the person having control of the dwelling, serve a copy of the notice on the occupying tenant (if any) of the dwelling and on every other person who, to the knowledge of the local authority, is an owner, lessee or mortgagee of the dwelling; and the person having control of the dwelling, the occupying tenant (if any) and every other person who is an owner, lessee or mortgagee of the dwelling shall be entitled to be heard when the authority's proposals are discussed in accordance with the notice.

(5) After the service of a provisional notice and before taking any other action under this Part of this Act, a local authority shall take into consideration all representations made on or before the occasion when their proposals with respect to the dwelling are discussed in accordance with the notice and, in particular, any representations with respect to the nature of the works proposed by them for improving the dwelling or with respect to any proposed housing arrangements.

Housing arrangements.

86.—(1) In this Part of this Act " housing arrangements ", in relation to a dwelling falling within section 85(1) above, means arrangements falling within subsection (2) below and making provision for the housing of an occupying tenant of the dwelling and his household—

(a) during the period when improvement works are being carried out, or

(b) after the completion of those works, or

(c) during that period and after completion of those works,

and for any matters incidental or ancillary thereto.

(2) The arrangements referred to in subsection (1) above are arrangements contained in a written agreement to which the

occupying tenant and either or both of his landlord and the PART VIII
local authority concerned are parties.

87.—(1) In any case where an improvement notice has not Acceptance of
yet been served in respect of a dwelling falling within subsection undertakings
(1) of section 85 above, the local authority referred to in that to do works.
subsection may, subject to subsection (3) below, accept from the
person having control of the dwelling or from any other person
having an estate or interest in the dwelling an undertaking
in writing to improve the dwelling to the full standard or, if in
the opinion of the local authority it is not practicable at reasonable expense for the dwelling to be improved to the full standard,
to the reduced standard.

(2) The undertaking shall specify the works agreed to be
carried out and the period within which (subject to any variation by the local authority as mentioned in subsection (4)(*a*)
below) the works are to be carried out, being a period ending
not more than 9 months after the date on which the undertaking
is accepted.

(3) Before accepting an undertaking under this section with
respect to any dwelling, the local authority shall satisfy
themselves—

   (*a*) that, if there is an occupying tenant, the housing
       arrangements are satisfactory or no housing arrange-
       ments are required and the undertaking incorporates
       the written consent of the occupying tenant signed by
       him, to the carrying out of the works specified in the
       undertaking ; and

   (*b*) that the person giving the undertaking has a right to
       carry out the works specified in the undertaking as
       against all other persons having an estate or interest
       in the dwelling.

(4) Where a local authority accept an undertaking under this
section with respect to any dwelling, they shall serve a notice
to that effect on the person by whom the undertaking was given
and shall not thereafter serve an improvement notice with
respect to that dwelling—

   (*a*) unless any works specified in the undertaking are not
       carried out within the period so specified, or within
       such longer period as the local authority may by
       permission in writing have allowed ; or

   (*b*) unless the local authority are satisfied that, owing to a
       change of circumstances since the undertaking was
       accepted by them, the undertaking is unlikely to be
       fulfilled.

(5) A local authority who have accepted an undertaking under this section—

(a) shall discharge the undertaking if at any time they consider that the dwelling no longer falls within paragraph (a) or paragraph (b) of subsection (1) of section 85 above, and

(b) may discharge the undertaking in any other case,

and the discharge of an undertaking under this subsection shall be effected by serving a notice of the discharge on the person by whom the undertaking was given.

(6) Where a local authority serve a notice under subsection (4) or subsection (5) above on the person by whom an undertaking was given, they shall at the same time serve a copy of the notice on the person (if any) who is at that time the occupying tenant of the dwelling and on every other person who, to the knowledge of the authority, is at that time an owner, lessee or mortgagee of the dwelling.

Conditions for
service of
improvement
notices.

88.—(1) If a local authority have served a provisional notice in respect of a dwelling and—

(a) no undertaking has yet been accepted in respect of the dwelling under section 87 above, or

(b) such an undertaking has been accepted but paragraph (a) or paragraph (b) of subsection (4) of section 87 above applies,

the local authority may, subject to the following provisions of this section, serve an improvement notice on the person having control of the dwelling.

(2) Before serving an improvement notice in respect of any dwelling by virtue of subsection (1) above, a local authority shall satisfy themselves—

(a) that the dwelling continues to be in a general improvement area or a housing action area; and

(b) that the provisions of paragraphs (a) and (b) of subsection (1) of section 85 above still apply in relation to the dwelling; and

(c) that the dwelling is not for the time being owner-occupied or that the circumstances specified in subsection (3) of that section apply or still apply in relation to it; and

(d) if there is an occupying tenant, that the housing arrangements are satisfactory or that no housing arrangements are required or that the occupying tenant has unreasonably refused to enter into any housing arrangements.

(3) An improvement notice may not be served in respect of   PART VIII
any dwelling by virtue of subsection (1) above,—

    (a) if paragraph (a) of that subsection applies, more than
       9 months after the service of the provisional notice
       referred to in that subsection ; and

    (b) if paragraph (b) of that subsection applies, more than
       6 months after the expiry of the period specified in
       the undertaking mentioned in that paragraph or, as
       the case may be, such longer period as the local
       authority may by permission in writing have allowed
       for the completion of the works specified in the
       undertaking.

(4) Where, by virtue of subsection (1) above, a local authority
serve an improvement notice on the person having control of
a dwelling, they shall at the same time serve a copy of the
notice on the occupying tenant (if any) of the dwelling and on
every other person who, to the knowledge of the authority, is
an owner, lessee or mortgagee of the dwelling.

Dwellings outside general improvement areas and
housing action areas

89.—(1) An occupying tenant of a dwelling which—   Compulsory
    (a) is not in a general improvement area or a housing action   improvement
       area, and   of dwellings
       outside
    (b) is without one or more of the standard amenities,   general
       whether or not it is also in a state of disrepair, and   improvement
       areas and
    (c) was provided (by erection or by the conversion of   housing
       a building already in existence) before 3rd October   action areas.
       1961,

may make representations in writing to the local authority for
the area in which the dwelling is situated with a view to the
exercise by the authority of their powers under this section.

(2) A local authority shall notify the person having control of
the dwelling of any representations made to them under subsection (1) above.

(3) If, on taking the representations into consideration, the
local authority are satisfied—

    (a) that the person making the representations is an occupy-
       ing tenant of the dwelling in question, and

    (b) that the provisions of paragraphs (a) to (c) of subsection
       (1) above apply in relation to the dwelling, and

    (c) that the dwelling is capable at reasonable expense of
       improvement to the full standard or, failing that, to the
       reduced standard, and

D

(*d*) that, having regard to all the circumstances, the dwelling ought to be improved to the full standard or, as the case may be, to the reduced standard, and that it is unlikely that it will be so improved unless the local authority exercise their powers under this section,

the following provisions of this section shall apply.

(4) If the local authority are satisfied as mentioned in subsection (3) above, they shall either—

(*a*) serve a provisional notice on the person having control of the dwelling, or

(*b*) notify the occupying tenant of the dwelling of their decision not to serve a provisional notice and give him a written statement setting out their reasons for making that decision,

and where a provisional notice is served by virtue of paragraph (*a*) above, the provisions of subsections (4) and (5) of section 85 above shall apply accordingly and the dwelling shall be treated for the purposes of section 86 above as being one falling within section 85(1) above.

(5) Subject to subsection (6) below, in any case where—

(*a*) representations have been made to a local authority under subsection (1) above, and

(*b*) as a result of those representations, a provisional notice has been served by virtue of subsection (4)(*a*) above,

the local authority may, at any time before the expiry of the period of 12 months beginning with the date on which the representations were received by them, serve an improvement notice on the person having control of the dwelling; and subsection (4) of section 88 above shall apply as it applies in relation to an improvement notice served by virtue of subsection (1) of that section.

(6) Before serving an improvement notice in respect of a dwelling by virtue of subsection (5) above, a local authority shall satisfy themselves—

(*a*) that the provisions of paragraphs (*b*) to (*d*) of subsection (3) above still apply in relation to the dwelling; and

(*b*) that the housing arrangements are satisfactory or that no housing arrangements are required or that the occupying tenant has unreasonably refused to enter into any housing arrangements.

(7) The power of serving a provisional notice by virtue of subsection (4)(*a*) above and of taking any further steps authorised under this Part of this Act may be exercised by a local authority notwithstanding that the occupying tenant who made

representations under subsection (1) above quits the dwelling and notwithstanding that, after the occupying tenant has made those representations, the authority pass a resolution declaring an area in which the dwelling is situated to be a general improvement area or a housing action area. PART VIII

General provisions as to improvement notices

90.—(1) Subject to the following provisions of this section, a notice under this section (in this Part of this Act referred to as an " improvement notice ") shall— Improvement notices: content and registration.

    (*a*) specify the works which in the opinion of the local authority are required to improve the dwelling to the full standard or, as the case may be, to the reduced standard;

    (*b*) state the authority's estimate of the cost of carrying out those works; and

    (*c*) require the person having control of the dwelling to carry out to the authority's satisfaction the works specified in the notice within the period of 12 months beginning with the date when the improvement notice becomes operative or such longer period as the authority may by permission in writing from time to time allow.

(2) The works specified in an improvement notice may be different from the works specified in the provisional notice but shall not require the improvement of a dwelling to the full standard if the provisional notice specified works for improving the dwelling only to the reduced standard.

(3) In an improvement notice which requires the improvement of a dwelling only to the reduced standard the local authority may, if they think fit, substitute for the period of 12 months specified in paragraph (*c*) of subsection (1) above such shorter period as appears to them to be appropriate.

(4) As soon as may be after an improvement notice has been served it shall be registered in the register of local land charges—

    (*a*) by the proper officer, for the purposes of section 15 of the Land Charges Act 1925, of the council in whose area the dwelling concerned is situated, and 1925 c. 22.

    (*b*) in such manner as may be prescribed by rules under section 19 of that Act,

and in this subsection " council " means a district council, a London borough council or the Common Council of the City of London.

91.—(1) Within 6 weeks from the service on the person having control of the dwelling of an improvement notice, that person, the occupying tenant (if any) of the dwelling or any other person having an estate or interest in the dwelling may appeal to the county court against the improvement notice in accordance with the following provisions of this section.

(2) Subject to subsection (3) below, the grounds on which an appeal may be brought under this section are all or any of the following,—

> (a) that it is not practicable to comply with the requirements of the improvement notice at reasonable expense ;

> (b) that the local authority have refused unreasonably to approve the execution of alternative works, or that the works specified in the notice are otherwise unreasonable in character or extent ;

> (c) that the dwelling is within an area declared to be a clearance area under Part III of the Housing Act 1957 and, having regard to all the circumstances of the case, it would be unreasonable for the local authority to require the works specified in the improvement notice to be carried out ;

> (d) that the dwelling is not, or is no longer, without one or more of the standard amenities ;

> (e) that, in a case where the improvement notice requires the improvement of the dwelling to the full standard, the works specified in the notice are inadequate to secure that the dwelling will attain that standard ;

> (f) that some person other than the appellant will, as the holder of an estate or interest in the dwelling (whether or not that estate or interest entitles him to occupation), derive a benefit from the execution of the works and that that person ought to pay the whole or part of the cost of the execution of the works ;

> (g) that the improvement notice is invalid on the ground that any requirement of this Part of this Act has not been complied with or on the ground of some informality, defect or error in or in connection with the improvement notice.

(3) Without prejudice to the grounds on which he may appeal by virtue of subsection (2) above,—

> (a) an owner-occupier may bring an appeal under this section on the ground that the local authority are in error in considering that the circumstances specified

in section 85(3) above exist in relation to the dwelling;   PART VIII
and

(*b*) the occupying tenant may bring an appeal under this
section on the ground that the condition in section
88(2)(*d*) above or, as the case may be, section 89(6)(*b*)
above for the service of the improvement notice is
not fulfilled.

(4) Subject to the following provisions of this section, on an
appeal under this section the court may make such order either
confirming or quashing or varying the improvement notice as
the court thinks fit.

(5) An improvement notice shall not be varied on an appeal
under this section—

(*a*) so as to extend the period within which the works
specified in the notice are to be carried out; or

(*b*) so as to require the carrying out of works to improve
a dwelling to the full standard if the works specified
in the notice were works to improve the dwelling to
the reduced standard ; or

(*c*) so as to require the carrying out of works to improve
a dwelling to the reduced standard if the work specified in the notice were works to improve the dwelling
to the full standard.

(6) Where an appeal is brought under this section on the
grounds specified in paragraph (*f*) of subsection (2) above (with
or without other grounds), the court may on hearing of the
appeal make such order as it thinks fit with respect to the payment to be made by the other person referred to in that paragraph to the appellant or where, by virtue of section 93 below,
the works are carried out by the local authority to the local
authority.

(7) In so far as an appeal under this section is based on the
ground that the improvement notice is invalid, the court shall
confirm the improvement notice unless satisfied that the interests
of the appellant have been substantially prejudiced by the facts
relied on by him.

92.—(1) If no appeal is brought against an improvement notice Operative
under section 91 above, the notice shall become operative at effect and
the expiry of the period of 6 weeks beginning with the date of withdrawal of
the service of the notice on the person having control of the notices.
dwelling, and any improvement notice against which an appeal
is so brought shall, if and so far as it is confirmed by the county
court, or on appeal from the county court, become operative on
the final determination of the appeal.

D 3

(2) For the purposes of subsection (1) above the withdrawal of an appeal shall be deemed to be the final determination thereof, having the like effect as a decision confirming the improvement notice or decision appealed against.

(3) An improvement notice shall, subject to the right of appeal conferred by section 91 above, be final and conclusive as to any matters which could be raised on any such appeal.

(4) A local authority may, if they think fit, at any time withdraw an improvement notice by serving notice of the withdrawal on the person having control of the dwelling, and the local authority shall serve a copy of any such notice on the occupier of the dwelling (if different from the person having control of it) and on every other person who, to the knowledge of the authority, is an owner, lessee or mortgagee of the dwelling.

Enforcement of improvement notices. **93.**—(1) If the works to be carried out in compliance with an improvement notice have not been carried out in whole or in part within the period specified in the notice, or within such longer period as the local authority by whom the notice was served may by permission in writing have allowed, the authority may themselves carry out so much of the works as has not been completed.

(2) If before the expiry of the period mentioned in subsection (1) above the person who is for the time being the person having control of the dwelling notifies the local authority in writing that he does not intend or is unable to do the works in question, the authority may, if they think fit, do the works before the expiry of that period.

(3) If the local authority by whom an improvement notice was served have reason to believe that the person who is for the time being the person having control of the dwelling does not intend or is unable to do the works in question in compliance with the notice,—

   (a) the authority may, before the expiry of the period mentioned in subsection (1) above, but not earlier than 6 months after the date on which the improvement notice becomes operative, serve on that person a notice requiring him to furnish them, within 21 days of the service of the notice, with evidence of his intentions with respect to the carrying out of the works ; and

   (b) if, from any evidence furnished to them in pursuance of a notice under paragraph (a) above or otherwise, the authority are not satisfied that that person intends to carry out the works in compliance with the notice, they may, if they think fit, do the works before the expiry of the period mentioned in subsection (1) above.

(4) Not less than 21 days before beginning to do the works the local authority shall serve notice of their intention on the occupier of the dwelling, on the person having control of the dwelling and on every other person who, to the knowledge of the authority, is an owner, lessee or mortgagee of the dwelling.

94.—(1) Subject to subsections (2) and (3) below, any expenses reasonably incurred by a local authority under section 93 above in carrying out works may, except so far as they are by any direction of the court on appeal recoverable under an order of the court, be recovered by them by action from the person having control of the dwelling.

(2) A demand for the expenses recoverable by a local authority under subsection (1) above, together with interest thereon in accordance with subsection (3) below, shall be served on the person having control of the dwelling; and on the date on which a demand is so served, the local authority shall serve a copy of the demand on every other person who, to the knowledge of the authority, is an owner, lessee or mortgagee of the dwelling concerned.

(3) Expenses in respect of which a demand is served under subsection (2) above shall carry interest—

(a) from the date on which the demand is so served until payment of all sums due thereunder, and

(b) at the rate fixed by section 171(2) of the Local Government Act 1972 (rates of interest in relation to various sums due to local authorities).

(4) The amount of any expenses and interest thereon due to an authority under this section shall, as from the date when the demand under subsection (2) above becomes operative, be a charge on the premises in respect of which the expenses were incurred, and on all estates and interests in those premises, and the authority shall for the purpose of enforcing that charge have all the same powers and remedies under the Law of Property Act 1925 and otherwise as if they were mortgagees by deed having powers of sale and lease, of accepting surrenders of leases and of appointing a receiver; and the power of appointing a receiver under this subsection shall be exercisable at any time after the expiry of one month from the date when the said demand becomes operative.

(5) Within 21 days from the date of service of a demand under subsection (2) above, any person on whom the demand or a copy thereof was so served may appeal to the county court against the demand, but on such an appeal no question may be raised which might have been raised on an appeal against the improvement notice relating to the dwelling in question.

PART VIII

Recovery of expenses incurred by local authority on default under improvement notice.

1972 c. 70.

1925 c. 20.

D 4

(6) A demand served under subsection (2) above—

(a) against which no appeal is brought under subsection (5) above shall become operative on the expiry of 21 days from the date of service of the demand,

(b) against which an appeal is so brought shall, if and so far as it is confirmed on appeal, become operative on the final determination of the appeal,

and for the purposes of this subsection the withdrawal of an appeal shall be deemed to be the final determination thereof, having the like effect as a decision confirming the demand appealed against.

(7) A demand served under subsection (2) above shall, subject to the right of appeal conferred by subsection (5) above, be final and conclusive as to any matters which can be raised on such an appeal.

Charging orders in favour of persons carrying out works.
1957 c. 56.

95. Sections 14 and 15 of the Housing Act 1957 (charging orders in favour of owner executing works) shall apply as if any reference to works required to be executed by a notice under Part II of that Act included a reference to works required to be carried out by an improvement notice, and in the application of those sections by virtue of this section any reference to a house or the owner of a house shall be construed as a reference to a dwelling, within the meaning of this Part of this Act, or, as the case may require, the person having control of it, within the meaning of this Part.

Supplementary

Provisions as to carrying out of works.

96.—(1) The person having control of any premises—

(a) which consist of or include a dwelling in a general improvement area or a housing action area which is without all or any of the standard amenities, or

(b) which consist of or include a dwelling in respect of which representations have been made by the occupying tenant under section 89 above,

shall, as against the occupying tenant of the dwelling and any other person having an estate or interest in the premises, have the right to enter the premises in order to carry out any survey or examination required with a view to providing the dwelling with any of the standard amenities and, where appropriate, of putting it in good repair (disregarding internal decorative repair) having regard to its age and character and the locality in which it is situated.

(2) On and after the date on which an improvement notice in respect of a dwelling becomes operative, the person having

control of the dwelling shall have the right, as against the occupying tenant (if any) of the dwelling and any other person having an estate or interest in the premises which consist of or include the dwelling, to take any reasonable steps for the purpose of complying with the improvement notice ; and any person bound by an undertaking accepted under this Part of this Act shall have the right as against the occupying tenant (if any) of the dwelling to which the undertaking relates to take any reasonable steps for the purpose of complying with the undertaking.

(3) Section 161 of the Housing Act 1957 (penalty for 1957 c. 56. preventing execution of works) shall apply as if—

(a) any reference in that section to Part II of that Act included a reference to this Part of this Act ;

(b) the reference therein to receiving notice of the intended action included a reference to receiving an improvement notice or a copy thereof ; and

(c) any reference therein to the owner of any premises included a reference to the person having control thereof.

(4) Without prejudice to subsection (2) above, the carrying out of works in pursuance of an improvement notice or an undertaking accepted under this Part of this Act shall not give rise to any liability on the part of a lessee to reinstate any premises at any time in the condition in which they were before the works were carried out, or to any liability for failure so to reinstate the premises.

97.—(1) Section 159 of the Housing Act 1957 (powers of Further entry of local authorities for certain purposes) shall apply to powers and entry for the purpose of survey and examination of any dwelling duties of local with a view to ascertaining whether the requirements of an authorities. improvement notice served, or undertaking accepted, under this Part of this Act have been complied with, and section 160 of that Act (penalty for obstructing execution of Act) shall apply accordingly.

(2) A local authority may by agreement with a person having control of a dwelling or any other person having an estate or interest in a dwelling execute at his expense any works which that person is required to carry out in the dwelling in pursuance of an improvement notice served, or undertaking accepted, under this Part of this Act, and for that purpose the local authority shall have all such rights as that person would have as against the occupying tenant (if any) of the dwelling and any other person having an interest in the dwelling.

PART VIII

(3) Where under this Part of this Act a local authority are required to serve a copy of a notice on any person who, to their knowledge, is an owner, lessee or mortgagee of any dwelling, any person having an estate or interest in the dwelling who is not served with a copy of the notice shall, on application in writing to the local authority, be entitled to obtain a copy of that notice.

Consequential modifications of Agricultural Holdings Act 1948.
1948 c. 63.

98.—(1) Section 9 of the Agricultural Holdings Act 1948 (increases of rent for improvements carried out by landlord) shall apply, subject to subsection (2) below, as if references in subsection (1) of that section to improvements carried out at the request of the tenant included references to improvements carried out in compliance with an improvement notice or an undertaking accepted under this Part of this Act.

(2) Where a tenant has contributed to the cost incurred by his landlord in carrying out such an improvement as is referred to in subsection (1) above, the increase in rent provided for by the said section 9 shall be reduced proportionately.

(3) Any works carried out in compliance with an improvement notice or an undertaking accepted under this Part of this Act shall be included among the improvements specified in paragraph 8 of Schedule 3 to the Agricultural Holdings Act 1948 (tenant's right to compensation for erection, alteration or enlargement of buildings), but subject to the power conferred by section 78 of that Act to amend that Schedule ; and section 49 of that Act (tenant's right to compensation conditional on the landlord consenting to the carrying out of the improvements) shall not apply to any works carried out in compliance with such a notice or undertaking.

(4) Where a person other than the tenant claiming compensation has contributed to the cost of carrying out the works in compliance with an improvement notice or an undertaking accepted under this Part of this Act, compensation in respect of the works, as assessed under section 48 of the Agricultural Holdings Act 1948, shall be reduced proportionately.

Exclusion of dwellings controlled by Crown or a public authority.

99.—(1) No provisional notice or improvement notice may be served in respect of a dwelling in which there is a Crown or Duchy interest except with the consent of the appropriate authority and, where a provisional notice or improvement notice is served with the consent of the appropriate authority, this Part of this Act shall apply in relation to the dwelling as it applies in relation to a dwelling in which there is no such interest.

(2) No provisional notice or improvement notice may be served in respect of a dwelling if the person having control of the dwelling is—

(*a*) a local authority ;

(*b*) the Commission for the New Towns ;

(*c*) the Housing Corporation ;

(*d*) a registered housing association ;

(*e*) a development corporation within the meaning of the New Towns Act 1965 ; or

(*f*) a housing trust as defined in section 5(3) of the Rent Act 1968 which is a charity within the meaning of the Charities Act 1960.

(3) If, after a provisional notice or an improvement notice has been served in respect of any dwelling,—

(*a*) any such body as is mentioned in paragraphs (*a*) to (*f*) of subsection (2) above becomes the person having control of the dwelling, or

(*b*) in the case of a dwelling in which there is a Crown or Duchy interest, the appropriate authority becomes the person having control of the dwelling,

any such notice with respect to the dwelling and any undertaking accepted under this Part of this Act with respect to the dwelling shall cease to have effect.

(4) If, by virtue of subsection (3) above, an improvement notice with respect to any dwelling ceases to have effect, it shall be the duty of the body which or person who has become the person having control of the dwelling as mentioned in that subsection to notify the officer who registered the notice in the register of local land charges and to furnish him with all information required by him for the purpose of cancelling the registration.

(5) In this section " Crown or Duchy interest " means an interest belonging to Her Majesty in right of the Crown or of the Duchy of Lancaster, or belonging to the Duchy of Cornwall or belonging to a government department, or held in trust for Her Majesty for the purposes of a government department, and " the appropriate authority ",—

(*a*) in relation to land belonging to Her Majesty in right of the Crown and forming part of the Crown Estate, means the Crown Estate Commissioners, and, in relation to any other land belonging to Her Majesty in right of the Crown, means the government department having the management of that land ;

(*b*) in relation to land belonging to Her Majesty in right of the Duchy of Lancaster, means the Chancellor of the Duchy ;

(*c*) in relation to land belonging to the Duchy of Cornwall, means such person as the Duke of Cornwall, or the possessor for the time being of the Duchy of Cornwall, appoints ; and

PART VIII   (*d*) in relation to land belonging to a government department or held in trust for Her Majesty for the purposes of a government department, means that department;

and if any question arises as to what authority is the appropriate authority in relation to any land, that question shall be referred to the Treasury, whose decision shall be final.

(6) In this section " local authority " includes, in addition to the bodies which, by virtue of section 104(1) below, are local authorities for the purposes of this Part of this Act,—

(*a*) a county council;

(*b*) the Greater London Council;

(*c*) a parish or community council;

(*d*) the trustees of the Honourable Society of the Inner Temple;

(*e*) the trustees of the Honourable Society of the Middle Temple;

(*f*) the police authority for any police area; and

(*g*) any joint board or joint committee all the constituent members of which are local authorities for the purposes of this section.

Duty of local authority to offer loans to meet expenses of compulsory improvement.   **100.**—(1) Any person who is liable to incur expenditure in complying with an improvement notice served, or undertaking accepted, under this Part of this Act, or who is liable to make a payment as directed by a court under section 91(6) above, may apply to the local authority for a loan.

(2) Subject to the following provisions of this section, if the local authority are satisfied that the applicant for a loan can reasonably be expected to meet obligations assumed by him in pursuance of this section in respect of a loan of the amount of the expenditure or payment to which the application relates, the local authority shall offer to enter into a contract with the applicant for a loan by the local authority to the applicant of that amount, to be secured to the local authority by a mortgage of the applicant's interest in the dwelling concerned.

(3) Subject to the following provisions of this section, if the local authority are not satisfied as mentioned in subsection (2) above but consider that the applicant can reasonably be expected to meet obligations assumed by him in pursuance of this section in respect of a loan of a smaller amount, the local authority may, if they think fit, offer to enter into a contract with the applicant for a loan by the local authority to the applicant of that smaller amount, to be secured as mentioned in subsection (2) above.

(4) Any contract entered into by a local authority under this section shall contain a condition to the effect that, if an improvement grant or intermediate grant becomes payable under Part VII of this Act in respect of the expenditure or payment to which the application under this section relates, the local authority shall not be required to lend a sum greater than the amount of the expenditure or payment to which the application relates after deduction of the amount of the improvement grant, or, as the case may be, the intermediate grant.

(5) A local authority shall not make an offer under the preceding provisions of this section unless they are satisfied—

    (a) that the applicant's interest in the dwelling concerned amounts to an estate in fee simple absolute in possession or an estate for a term of years which will not expire before the date for final repayment of the loan ; and

    (b) that, according to a valuation made on behalf of the local authority, the amount of the principal of the loan does not exceed the value which it is estimated that the mortgaged security will bear after improvement of the dwelling to the full standard or, as the case may be, to the reduced standard.

(6) The rate of interest payable on a loan under this section shall be such as the Secretary of State may direct either generally or in any particular case and the Secretary of State may, if he thinks fit, give directions, either generally or in any particular case, as to the time within which a loan under this section, or any part of such a loan, is to be repaid.

(7) Subject to the preceding provisions of this section, the contract offered by a local authority under this section shall require proof of title and contain such other reasonable terms as the local authority may specify in their offer and, in particular, may provide for the advance being made by instalments from time to time as the works specified in the improvement notice progress.

(8) An application under this section shall be made in writing within the period of 3 months beginning with the date when the improvement notice becomes operative or the undertaking is accepted or the payment is to be made as directed by the court, as the case may be, or such longer period as the local authority by permission given in writing may allow.

(9) Where an improvement grant or intermediate grant is payable under Part VII of this Act partly in respect of expenditure or a payment to which the application under this section relates and partly in respect of other expenditure or another payment, the references in subsection (4) above to an inter-

PART VIII mediate grant or an improvement grant shall be taken as a reference to the part of the intermediate grant or improvement grant which in the opinion of the local authority is attributable to the expenditure or payment to which the application under this section relates.

Right of
person
served with
improvement
notice to serve
purchase
notice.

101.—(1) Where a local authority have served an improvement notice under this Part of this Act on the person having control of a dwelling, that person may, by notice in writing served on the local authority at any time within the period of 6 months beginning with the date on which the improvement notice becomes operative, require the local authority to purchase his interest in the dwelling in accordance with this section.

(2) Where the person having control of a dwelling serves a notice on a local authority under subsection (1) above—

1957 c. 56.

(a) the authority shall be deemed to be authorised under and for the purposes of Part V of the Housing Act 1957 to acquire that person's interest in the dwelling compulsorily and to have served a notice to treat in respect of that interest on the date of the service of the notice under subsection (1) above ; and

1961 c. 33.

(b) the power conferred by section 31 of the Land Compensation Act 1961 to withdraw a notice to treat shall not be exercisable in the case of the notice to treat which is deemed to have been so served.

(3) Within 21 days of the receipt of a notice under subsection (1) above served by the person having control of a dwelling the local authority shall notify every other person who, to their knowledge, is an owner, lessee or mortgagee of the dwelling or who is the occupier thereof.

Effect of an
area ceasing
to be a general
improvement
area or
housing action
area after
improvement
notice is
served.

102. If, after an undertaking has been accepted under this Part of this Act in respect of a dwelling or an improvement notice has been served in respect of a dwelling by virtue of section 88(1) above, the general improvement area or housing action area in which the dwelling is situated ceases to be such an area or the land on which the dwelling is situated is excluded from such an area, the provisions of this Part of this Act shall continue to apply in relation to that undertaking or notice as if the dwelling continued to be in a general improvement area or housing action area declared by the local authority by whom the undertaking was accepted or, as the case may be, the notice was served.

Service of
notices, etc.
1964 c. 56.

103.—(1) In section 102(1) of the Housing Act 1964 (where a local authority are under a duty to serve a notice on a person described in a particular way, the local authority are to take reasonable steps to identify the person coming within that description) for the words "or Part II, Part III" there shall be substituted the words "Part VIII of the Housing Act 1974".   PART VIII

(2) In section 103(1) of the Housing Act 1964 (method of service of notices, etc.) after the words "those Acts" there shall be inserted the words "or under Part VIII of the Housing Act 1974".   1964 c. 56.

(3) In section 103(2) of the Housing Act 1964 (service of notices, etc. where more than one person comes within the description of the person to be served) for the words "Part II", in the last place where they occur, there shall be substituted the words "Part VIII of the Housing Act 1974".

104.—(1) In this Part of this Act, unless the context otherwise requires,—   Interpretation of Part VIII.

"the full standard" has the same meaning as it has for the purposes of section 66 of this Act (intermediate grants);

"housing arrangements" has the meaning assigned to it by section 86 above;

"improvement" includes alteration and enlargement and, so far as also necessary to enable a dwelling to reach the full standard or the reduced standard, repair, and "improved" shall be construed accordingly;

"improvement notice" means a notice under section 90 above;

"lessee" includes any person entitled, at law or in equity, to a tenancy or any other term of years certain, whether in possession or in reversion;

"local authority", subject to section 99(6) above, has the same meaning as in Part VII of this Act;

"occupying tenant", in relation to a dwelling, means the person who is not an owner-occupier, but who—

(a) occupies or is entitled to occupy the dwelling as a lessee; or

(b) is a statutory tenant of the dwelling, within the meaning of the Rent Act 1968; or   1968 c. 23.

(c) occupies the dwelling as a residence under a Part VI contract, within the meaning of Part VI of the Rent Act 1968 (furnished lettings); or

(d) is employed in agriculture (as defined in section 17(1) of the Agricultural Wages Act 1948) and occupies or resides in the dwelling as part of the terms of his employment;   1948 c. 47.

" owner ", in relation to a dwelling, means the person who, otherwise than as a mortgagee in possession, is for the time being entitled to dispose of the fee simple in the dwelling ;

" owner-occupier ", in relation to a dwelling, means the person who, as owner or as lessee under a long tenancy, occupies or is entitled to occupy the dwelling, and " owner-occupied " shall be construed accordingly ;

" the person having control ", in relation to a dwelling shall be determined in accordance with subsection (2) below ;

" provisional notice " means a notice under section 85(2) above ;

" the reduced standard " has the same meaning as it has for the purposes of section 66 of this Act (intermediate grants) ;

" standard amenities " has the same meaning as in Part VII of this Act.

(2) References in this Part of this Act to the person having control of a dwelling shall be construed as follows : —

(*a*) if the dwelling is owner-occupied, the person having control of it is the owner-occupier ;

(*b*) if there is an occupying tenant of the dwelling and he is a person employed in agriculture (as defined in

1948 c. 47.   section 17(1) of the Agricultural Wages Act 1948) who occupies or resides in the dwelling as part of the terms of his employment, the employer or other person by whose authority the occupying tenant occupies or resides in the dwelling is the person having control of it ; and

(*c*) in any other case, the person who has control of a dwelling is the person who is either the owner of it or the lessee of it under a long tenancy and whose interest in the dwelling is not in reversion on that of another person who has a long tenancy.

1967 c. 88.   (3) Section 3 of the Leasehold Reform Act 1967 (meaning of " long tenancy ") shall apply for the purposes of subsections (1) and (2) above as it applies for the purposes of Part I of that Act.

1957 c. 56.   (4) References in the following provisions of the Housing Act 1957 to that Act shall be construed as including a reference to this Part of this Act, that is to say—

(*a*) section 169 (service of notices etc. on persons other than local authorities) ;

(*b*) section 170 (power of local authority to require infor- PART VIII
mation as to ownership of premises) ;

(*c*) section 178 (power of Secretary of State to prescribe
information, etc.) ; and

(*d*) section 179 (dispensation with advertisements and
notices).

PART IX

MISCELLANEOUS

105.—(1) A housing authority may not incur any expenses Secretary
in— of State's
control over
(*a*) providing dwellings by the conversion of houses or certain
other buildings, or expenditure by
housing
(*b*) carrying out works required for the improvement of authorities
dwellings, with or without associated works of repair, in England
except in accordance with proposals submitted by the authority and Wales.
to the Secretary of State and for the time being approved by
him.

(2) Any approval given by the Secretary of State under subsection (1) above may be given subject to such conditions, and
may be varied in such circumstances, as appear to him to be
appropriate, but before varying the terms of any such approval
the Secretary of State shall consult the housing authority
concerned.

(3) In this section " housing authority " and " dwelling " have
the same meanings as in Part VII of this Act.

106.—(1) For the year 1975-76 and subsequent years, Lodging-
buildings, or parts of buildings, provided or converted for use houses and
as lodging-houses (that is to say, houses not occupied as separate hostels
provided
dwellings) or as hostels shall be included among the buildings by local
to which the requirements in subsection (1) of section 12 of the authorities
Housing Finance Act 1972 relate and, accordingly, subsection and new town
(2) of that section shall cease to have effect except with respect corporations
in England
to years prior to the year 1975-76. and Wales.
1972 c. 47.

(2) No payment shall be made for the year 1975-76 or any
subsequent year to a local authority or a new town corporation—

(*a*) under section 40 of the Housing Act 1949 (Exchequer 1949 c. 60.
contributions for hostels),

(*b*) under section 15 or section 22 of the Housing (Finan- 1958 c. 42.
cial Provisions) Act 1958 (grants for hostels),

PART IX
1972 c. 47.

1959 c. 62.
1965 c. 59.
1967 c. 29.

1957 c. 56.

(c) under section 92 of the Housing Finance Act 1972 (hostel subsidy), or

(d) so far as it relates to hostels, under any provision of the New Towns Act 1959 or the New Towns Act 1965,

nor shall any such payment be made by virtue of section 14(6) of the Housing Subsidies Act 1967; and in this section "local authority" has, in relation to any of the enactments specified in paragraphs (a) to (c) above, the same meaning as in that enactment and "new town corporation" has the meaning assigned to it by section 106 of the Housing Finance Act 1972.

(3) For the purposes of Part V of the Housing Act 1957 "housing accommodation" shall include, and be deemed always to have included, hostels (within the meaning of this Act), and any reference in that Part to a house shall be, and shall be deemed always to have been, construed accordingly.

(4) In accordance with the preceding provisions of this section, Schedule 1 to the Housing Finance Act 1972 (the Housing Revenue Account) shall be amended in accordance with Schedule 7 to this Act.

(5) In this section "year" means a financial year, and "the year 1975-76" means the financial year beginning in 1975.

107. For the purpose of enabling the Secretary of State to make grants to housing authorities within the meaning of section 5(3)(c) of this Act in respect of their expenditure on housing projects relating to hostels, such an authority shall be treated as a registered housing association, and sections 29(1) to (7), 30(1) to (7), 33 and 35 of this Act shall apply accordingly, but otherwise for the said purpose Parts I to III of this Act shall not apply.

108.—(1) The power of a local authority for the purposes of the Housing Act 1957 to make a clearance order under Part III of that Act (clearance and re-development) for the demolition of any building in a clearance area—

(a) shall not be available with respect to any clearance area declared on or after the commencement date; and

(b) shall cease to be available with respect to any other clearance area after the expiry of the period of 12 months beginning on the commencement date.

(2) In the application of section 60 of the Housing Act 1957 (payments in respect of well-maintained houses in clearance areas) in relation to a house which is the subject of a compulsory purchase order or a clearance order made on or after the commencement date, for subsection (1) of that section there

shall be substituted the subsections set out in Schedule 9 to   PART IX
this Act.

(3) This section shall come into operation at the expiry of the period of one month beginning with the date on which this Act is passed, and any reference in subsections (1) and (2) above to the commencement date is a reference to the day on which this section comes into operation.

109.—(1) In sections 110 to 115 the reference to an English General enactment includes a reference to the corresponding Scottish interpretation enactment, and the corresponding Scottish enactments, except of sections where the context otherwise implies or provides, are as follows— Scotland.

110 to 115 for

(a) the corresponding Scottish enactments to Part III of the Housing Act 1957 are Part III of the Housing (Scot- 1957 c. 56. land) Act 1966 and Part I of the Housing (Scotland) 1966 c. 49. Act 1969 ; 1969 c. 34.

(b) the corresponding Scottish enactments to sections 54 and 55 of the Town and Country Planning Act 1971 1971 c. 78. are respectively sections 52 and 53 of the Town and 1972 c. 52. Country Planning (Scotland) Act 1972 ;

(c) the corresponding Scottish enactment to section 5 of the Compulsory Purchase Act 1965 is section 17 of the 1965 c. 56. Lands Clauses Consolidation (Scotland) Act 1845 ; 1845 c. 19.

(d) the corresponding Scottish enactments to section 9 of the Housing Act 1957 are section 11 of the Housing (Scotland) Act 1966 and section 24 of the Housing (Scotland) Act 1969 ;

(e) the corresponding Scottish enactment to Part V of the Housing Act 1957 is Part VII of the Housing (Scotland) Act 1966 ;

(f) the corresponding Scottish enactment to Part VI of the Town and Country Planning Act 1971 is Part VI of the Town and Country Planning (Scotland) Act 1972 ;

(g) the corresponding Scottish enactments to section 60 of, and Schedule 2 to, the Housing Act 1957 are section 49 of the Housing (Scotland) Act 1966 and section 11 of the Housing (Scotland) Act 1969 ;

(h) the corresponding Scottish enactment to section 8 of the Town and Country Planning (Amendment) Act 1972 c. 42. 1972 is section 9 of that Act ;

(i) the corresponding Scottish enactment to Schedule 2 to the Town and Country Planning (Amendment) Act 1972 is Schedule 3 to that Act ;

(j) the corresponding Scottish enactment to Schedule 3 to the Housing Act 1957 is Schedule 3 to the Housing 1957 c. 56. (Scotland) Act 1966 by virtue of section 7(3) of the 1966 c. 49. Housing (Scotland) Act 1969 ; 1969 c. 34.

PART IX
1957 c. 56.
1966 c. 49.
1969 c. 34.

1947 c. 42.

1965 c. 56.

1845 c. 19.

1961 c. 33.
1963 c. 51.

1969 c. 33.

1973 c. 26.
1973 c. 56.

1961 c. 33.

(*k*) the corresponding Scottish enactments to section 43(2) of the Housing Act 1957 are section 37 of the Housing (Scotland) Act 1966 and section 6 of the Housing (Scotland) Act 1969 ;

(*l*) the corresponding Scottish enactments to section 49 of the Housing Act 1957 are section 41 of the Housing (Scotland) Act 1966 and section 9 of the Housing (Scotland) Act 1969,

(*m*) the corresponding Scottish enactments to section 169 of the Housing Act 1957 are section 5(3) of, and paragraph 19 of Schedule 1 to, the Acquisition of Land (Authorisation Procedure) (Scotland) Act 1947 ;

(*n*) the corresponding Scottish enactments to Schedule 4 to the Housing Act 1957 are paragraphs 6, 15 and 16 of Schedule 1 to the said Act of 1947, and the corresponding Scottish enactment to paragraph 1 of the said paragraph 6 ;

(*o*) the corresponding Scottish enactment to section 30 of the Compulsory Purchase Act 1965 is paragraph 19 of Schedule 1 to the Acquisition of Land (Authorisation Procedure) (Scotland) Act 1947 ;

(*p*) the corresponding Scottish enactments to section 22 of the Compulsory Purchase Act 1965 are sections 117 and 118 of the Lands Clauses Consolidation (Scotland) Act 1845 ;

(*q*) the corresponding Scottish enactment to section 32 of the Land Compensation Act 1961 is section 40 of the Land Compensation (Scotland) Act 1963 ;

(*r*) the corresponding Scottish enactments to the reference to section 68 of and Schedule 5 to the Housing Act 1969 are sections 18 to 20 of the Housing (Scotland) Act 1969.

(*s*) the corresponding Scottish enactment to section 37 of the Land Compensation Act 1973 is section 34 of the Land Compensation (Scotland) Act 1973 ;

(*t*) the corresponding Scottish enactment to section 30 of the Land Compensation Act 1961 is section 38 of the Land Compensation (Scotland) Act 1963.

(2) (*a*) The expression " clearance area " includes a housing treatment area which is to be dealt with by securing the demolition of all or some of the buildings in that area under section 4(2)(*a*) or 4(2)(*c*) of the Housing (Scotland) Act 1969 ;

(*b*) " mortgagee " means the creditor in a heritable security.

110.—(1) In this section references to a compulsory purchase order are to a compulsory purchase order made (at any time before or after the coming into operation of this section) under Part III of the Housing Act 1957.

(2) Where a building to which a compulsory purchase order applies is (at any time after the making of the order) included in a list of buildings of special architectural or historic interest under section 54 of the Town and Country Planning Act 1971, the authority making the order may, subject to subsection (3) below, apply to the Secretary of State (and only to him) under section 55 of the Act of 1971 for his consent to the demolition of the building.

(3) No such application may be made by virtue of subsection (2) above after the expiry of the period of three months beginning with the date—

    (*a*) on which the building is included in the said list, or

    (*b*) on which this section comes into force,
whichever is the later.

(4) The following provisions of this section shall have effect where—

    (*a*) an application for consent has been made under the said section 55, by virtue of subsection (2) above, and has been refused, or

    (*b*) in a case falling within subsection (3) above, the period of three months has expired without the authority having made such an application,

and in this section " relevant date " means the date of the refusal or, as the case may be, of the expiry of the period of three months.

(5) If, at the relevant date—

    (*a*) the building has not vested in the authority, and

    (*b*) no notice to treat has been served by the authority under section 5 of the Compulsory Purchase Act 1965, in respect of any interest in the building,

the compulsory purchase order shall cease to have effect in relation to the building and, where applicable, the building shall cease to be comprised in a clearance area.

(6) Where a building, which was included in a clearance area solely by reason of its being unfit for human habitation, ceases to be comprised in the clearance area by virtue of subsection (5) above, the authority concerned shall, in respect of the building, forthwith—

    (*a*) serve a notice under section 9 of the Act of 1957 (power of local authority to require repair of unfit houses), or

PART IX

Listed buildings subject to compulsory purchase orders under Part III of the Housing Act 1957.

1957 c. 56.

1971 c. 78.

1965 c. 56.

(*b*) make a closing order under Part II of that Act,

whichever is appropriate ; and in the application of this subsection to Scotland the words from " solely " to " habitation " shall be omitted.

(7) Where subsection (5) above does not apply, the authority shall cease to be subject to the duty imposed by Part III of the Act of 1957 to demolish the building, and in relation to any interest in the building which at the relevant date has not vested in the authority the compulsory purchase order shall have effect as if—

> (*a*) in the case of a house, it had been made and confirmed under Part V of the Act of 1957, and

> (*b*) in any other case, it had been made and confirmed under Part VI of the Act of 1971.

(8) If the building, or any interest in the building, was vested in the authority at the relevant date it shall be treated—

> (*a*) in the case of a house, as appropriated to the purposes of Part V of the Act of 1957, and

> (*b*) in any other case, as appropriated to the purposes of Part VI of the Act of 1971.

(9) As respects a building falling within subsection (2) above, the authority shall not serve notice to treat under section 5 of the Compulsory Purchase Act 1965 in respect of the building until after the relevant date.

1965 c. 56.

Listed
buildings in
clearance
areas,
acquired by
agreement.
1957 c. 56.
1971 c. 78.

111.—(1) Where Part III of the Housing Act 1957 applies to a building purchased by a local authority by agreement, and at any time (before or after the coming into operation of this section) the building is included in a list of buildings of special architectural or historic interest under section 54 of the Town and Country Planning Act 1971, the authority may, subject to subsection (2) below, apply to the Secretary of State (and only to him) under section 55 of the Act of 1971 for his consent to the demolition of the building.

(2) No such application may be made by virtue of subsection (1) above after the expiry of the period of three months beginning with the date—

> (*a*) on which the building is included in the said list, or

> (*b*) on which this section comes into force,

whichever is the later.

(3) where—

> (*a*) an application for consent has been made under the said section 55, by virtue of subsection (1) above ; and has been refused, or

(*b*) the period of three months mentioned in subsection (2) PART IX
above has expired without the authority having made
such an application,

the authority shall cease to be subject to the duty, imposed by
Part III of the Act of 1957, to demolish the building, which
shall be treated—

(i) in the case of a house, as appropriated to the purposes
of Part V of the Act of 1957, and

(ii) in any other case, as appropriated to the purposes of
Part VI of the Act of 1971.

112.—(1) In this section references to a " clearance order " Temporary
are to a clearance order made (at any time before or after the provision for
coming into operation of this section) under Part III of the buildings
Housing Act 1957. subject to

clearance
(2) Where a building to which a clearance order applies is, orders.
at any time after the confirmation of the order, included in a 1957 c. 56.
list of buildings of special architectural or historic interest under
section 54 of the Town and Country Planning Act 1971, the 1971 c. 78.
authority making the order may, subject to subsection (3) below,
apply to the Secretary of State (and only to him) under section
55 of the Act of 1971 for his consent to the demolition of the
building.

(3) No such application may be made by virtue of subsection (2) above after the expiry of the period of three months
beginning with the date—

(*a*) on which the building is included in the said list, or

(*b*) on which this section comes into force,

whichever is the later.

(4) Where—

(*a*) an application for consent has been made under the
said section 55, by virtue of subsection (2) above, and
has been refused, or

(*b*) the period of three months mentioned in subsection (3)
above has expired without the authority having made
such an application,

the building shall cease to be comprised in a clearance area or
to be subject to the clearance order.

(5) Where a building, which was included in a clearance area
solely by reason of its being unfit for human habitation, ceases
to be comprised in the clearance area by virtue of subsection (4)

PART IX   above, the authority concerned shall, in respect of the building, forthwith—

> (a) serve a notice under section 9 of the Act of 1957 (power of local authority to require repair of unfit house) or
>
> (b) make a closing order under Part II of that Act,

whichever is appropriate; and in the application of this subsection to Scotland the words from "solely" to "habitation" shall be omitted.

1969 c. 33.

(6) Where a payment in respect of a house has been made by a local authority under section 60 of, or Schedule 2 to, the Act of 1957, or Schedule 5 to the Housing Act 1969, in connection with a clearance order, and by virtue of this section the house is excluded from the clearance area, then, if the person to whom the payment was made is entitled to an interest in the house he shall, subject to subsection (7) below, repay the payment to the authority on demand.

(7) No repayment shall be required by virtue of subsection (6) above in a case where the authority have made a closing order in respect of the house and—

> (a) no appeal has, within the time allowed, been made against the making of the order, or
>
> (b) such an appeal has been made and has failed.

Application of provisions about listed buildings to buildings in conservation areas.
1972 c. 42.

113.—(1) Sections 110, 111 and 112 above shall, with the modifications mentioned in subsection (2) below, have effect in relation to buildings subject to directions made and confirmed under section 8 of the Town and Country Planning (Amendment) Act 1972 (control of demolition in conservation areas in England and Wales) as they have effect in relation to listed buildings.

(2) The modifications subject to which those sections are to have effect by virtue of subsection (1) above are—

1971 c. 78.

> (a) for references to section 55 of the Town and Country Planning Act 1971 there shall be substituted references to that section as applied by Schedule 2 to the Act of 1972; and
>
> (b) for references to a building being included in a list under section 54 of the Act of 1971 there shall be substituted references to a building being subject to a direction made and confirmed under section 8 of the Act of 1972.

114.—(1) This section applies to any building comprised in a clearance area under Part III of the Housing Act 1957 which—

(a) at any time before the date on which this section comes into operation, has been purchased by agreement by the local authority in whose area the clearance area falls, or

(b) is subject to a compulsory purchase order—

(i) made at any time before that date under the said Part III, and

(ii) which, at any time before the expiry of the period of three months beginning with that date, has been confirmed in accordance with Schedule 3 to the Act of 1957.

(2) Where any building to which this section applies—

(a) was included in the clearance area solely by reason of its being unfit for human habitation, and

(b) in the opinion of the authority concerned is capable of being, and ought to be, improved to the full standard,

the authority may, subject to the provisions of this section and of Schedule 10 to this Act, make and submit to the Secretary of State an order under this section (a " rehabilitation order ") in relation to that building.

(3) In subsection (2) above " full standard " in England and Wales means the standard attained by a dwelling in respect of which the conditions mentioned in section 66(2) of this Act are fulfilled and in Scotland means the standard specified by virtue of section 16(3) of the Housing (Scotland) Act 1974 ; and in the application to Scotland of subsection (2)(a) above the words from " solely " to " habitation " shall be omitted.

(4) Schedule 10 to this Act shall have effect for the purpose of supplementing the provisions of this section.

115.—(1) It is hereby declared that where, under section 110 above, or Schedule 10 to this Act, a compulsory purchase order is to be treated as made under Part V of the Housing Act 1957 or Part VI of the Town and Country Planning Act 1971 compensation for the compulsory acquisition of the land comprised in the compulsory purchase order is to be assessed in accordance with the provisions applying to a compulsory acquisition under the said Part V (or, as the case may be, the said Part VI).

(2) Where under section 110 above, or Schedule 10 to this Act, land or any interest in land within a clearance area is to be treated as appropriated by a local authority to the purposes of

PART IX
Temporary provision for rehabilitation of unfit houses.
1957 c. 56.

1974 c. 45.

Compensation.
1971 c. 78.

the said Part V, compensation for its compulsory acquisition shall (where it increases the amount) be assessed or reassessed in accordance with the provisions applying to a compulsory acquisition under the said Part V.

(3) Where under section 111 above or Schedule 10 to this Act, any interest in land acquired by a local authority by agreement (after the declaration of the clearance area) is to be treated as appropriated for the purposes of the said Part V—

    (*a*) compensation shall (where subsection (2) above would have increased the amount) be assessed and paid as if the acquisition were a compulsory acquisition, under the said Part III, to which subsection (2) applied, but

    (*b*) there shall be deducted from the amount of compensation so payable any amount previously paid in respect of the acquisition of that interest by the authority.

(4) Where subsection (2) or subsection (3) above applies, the local authority shall serve on the person entitled to the compensation a notice in the prescribed form giving particulars of the amount of compensation payable in accordance with the provisions applying to a compulsory acquisition under the said Part V, and if the person served does not within twenty-one days from service of the notice accept the particulars, or if he disputes the amount stated, the question of disputed compensation shall be referred to the Lands Tribunal.

(5) The notice shall be served not later than six months after (as the case may be)—

    (*a*) the relevant date as defined in section 110 above, or

    (*b*) confirmation of the rehabilitation order,

1965 c. 56. and section 30 of the Compulsory Purchase Act 1965 (service of notices) shall apply to the notice.

(6) Subsection (2) above shall be left out of account in considering whether under section 22 of the Compulsory Purchase Act 1965 compensation has been properly paid for the land; and accordingly subsection (2) above shall not prevent an acquiring authority from remaining in undisputed possession of the land.

(7) Where subsection (2) above makes an increase in compensation to be assessed in accordance with Schedule 2 to the Compulsory Purchase Act 1965 (absent and untraced owners)—

    (*a*) a deed poll executed under paragraph 2(2) of that Schedule before the latest date for service of a notice under subsection (5) above shall not be invalid because the increase in compensation had not been paid, and (*b*) it shall be the duty of the local authority not later than six months after the said date to proceed under the said Schedule 2 and pay the proper additional amount into court.

(8) In Scotland where subsection (2) makes an increase in compensation to be assessed in accordance with sections 56 to 60 and 63 of the Lands Clauses (Consolidation) (Scotland) Act 1845 c. 19. 1845 (provisions dealing with absent and untraced owners)—

(*a*) a notarial instrument executed under section 76 of that Act before the latest date for service of a notice under subsection (4) above shall not be invalid because the increase in compensation had not been paid and

(*b*) it shall be the duty of the local authority not later than six months after the said date to proceed under the said sections and pay the proper additional amount into the Bank.

(9) Any sum payable by virtue of this section shall carry interest at the rate prescribed under section 32 of the Land 1961 c. 33. Compensation Act 1961 from the time of entry by the local authority on the land, or from vesting of the land or interest, whichever is the earlier, until payment.

(10) In this section references to an increase in compensation shall be read as if payments under—

(*a*) sections 60 and 61 of and Schedule 2 to the Act of 1957 (payments in respect of well-maintained houses and payments to owner-occupiers),

(*b*) section 63(1) of the Act of 1957 or section 30 of the Land Compensation Act 1961 (allowances to persons displaced),

(*c*) section 68 of and Schedule 5 to the Housing Act 1969 1969 c. 33. (payments to owner-occupiers and others in respect of unfit houses purchased or demolished), and

(*d*) section 37 of the Land Compensation Act 1973 1973 c. 26. (disturbance payments for persons without compensatable interests),

and any extra-statutory payments made by way of additional compensation were, to the extent that they were made to the person holding the interest in question, compensation in respect of the compulsory purchase.

(11) In this section " prescribed " means prescribed by order made by the Secretary of State for the purposes of this section ; and any order under this subsection shall be contained in a statutory instrument which shall be subject to annulment in pursuance of a resolution of either House of Parliament.

PART IX
Amendment of
section 4 of
the
Compulsory
Purchase Act
1965.
1965 c. 56.

116. In section 4 of the Compulsory Purchase Act 1965 (time limits for exercising powers under compulsory purchase orders) there shall be added at the end, the following paragraph:—

"For the purposes of this section no account shall be taken of any period during which an authority are, by virtue of section 110, 113, or 114 of the Housing Act 1974 (which relate among other things to unfit buildings in clearance or conservation areas) prevented from serving notice to treat under section 5 of this Act.",

1845 c. 19.

and the same amendment shall be made to section 116 of the Lands Clauses Consolidation (Scotland) Act 1845 with the substitution for the reference to section 5 of the Compulsory Purchase Act 1965 of a reference to section 17 of the said Act of 1845.

Removal of
time limit for
completing
certain works
eligible for
higher rates
of grants or
contributions.
1971 c. 76.

117.—(1) In section 1 of the Housing Act 1971 (certain works carried out in local government areas wholly or partly in development areas or intermediate areas to be eligible for increased rates of grants or contributions) paragraph (b) of each of subsections (1) and (2) (which requires the works concerned to be completed before the expiration of a period of 3 years beginning with 23rd June 1971) shall not have effect in the case of works falling within subsection (2), subsection (3) or subsection (4) below.

(2) Subsection (1) above applies to works which were the subject of an application to a local authority for an improvement grant, a standard grant or a special grant if the application was approved by the local authority on or before 30th September 1973 and—

1969 c. 33.

(a) in the case of an application to a local authority in England and Wales for an improvement grant, if the local authority have, before 23rd June 1974, fixed as the amount of the grant (either originally or by way of variation under subsection (2) of section 2 of the Housing Act 1971) an amount which took account of the amendments of Part I of the Housing Act 1969 effected by subsection (1) of that section (increase of grant or maximum grant from one-half to 75 per cent. of the cost of the works); and

(b) in the case of an application to a local authority in Scotland for an improvement grant or a standard grant, if the local authority have, before 23rd June 1974, fixed as the amount of the grant (either originally or by way of variation under subsection (2) of section 3 of the Housing Act 1971) an amount which took account of the amendments of Parts I and II of the Housing (Financial Provisions) (Scotland) Act 1968

1968 c. 31.

effected by subsection (1) of that section (increase of grant or maximum grant from one-half to 75 per cent. of the cost of the works).

(3) Subsection (1) above also applies to works comprised in arrangements to which subsection (1) of section 21 of the Housing Act 1969 applies (contributions for dwellings pro- 1969 c. 33. vided or improved by housing associations under arrangements with local authorities) if an application for a contribution under that section containing particulars and estimates of those works was received by the Secretary of State on or before 30th September 1973.

(4) Subsection (1) above also applies to works comprised in arrangements to which subsection (1) of section 16 or section 17 (in so far as the latter section applies to housing associations) of the Housing (Financial Provisions) (Scotland) Act 1968 applies 1968 c. 31. (contributions for dwellings provided or improved by housing associations under arrangements with the Secretary of State or local authorities) if the Secretary of State had made arrangements under the said section 16 or had approved improvement pro-posals made under the said section 17 on or before 30th September 1973.

(5) In this section " local authority ", " improvement grant ", " standard grant " and " special grant " have, in England and Wales, the same meanings as in Part I of the Housing Act 1969, and in Scotland " local authority " has the same meaning as in section 1 of the Housing (Scotland) Act 1966 and " improve- 1966 c. 49. ment grant " and " standard grant " have the same meanings as in Part II of the Housing (Financial Provisions) (Scotland) Act 1968.

118.—(1) In section 1 of the Leasehold Reform Act 1967, Rateable in subsection (1)(*a*) (certain tenants entitled to enfranchisement value or extension of their leaseholds where rateable value is within limits for certain limits on a particular day) after the words " rent and " ment or there shall be inserted the words " subject to subsections (5) extension and (6) below " and after subsection (4) there shall be added under the following subsections:— Leasehold Reform Act 1967.

" (5) If, in relation to any house and premises, the appro- 1967 c. 88. priate day for the purposes of subsection (1)(*a*) above falls on or after 1st April 1973 that subsection shall have effect in relation to the house and premises,—

(*a*) in a case where the tenancy was created on or before 18th February 1966, as if for the sums of £200 and £400 specified in that subsection there were substituted respectively the sums of £750 and £1,500 ; and

(b) in a case where the tenancy was created after 18th February 1966, as if for those sums of £200 and £400 there were substituted respectively the sums of £500 and £1,000.

(6) If, in relation to any house and premises,—

(a) the appropriate day for the purposes of subsection (1)(a) above falls before 1st April 1973, and

(b) the rateable value of the house and premises on the appropriate day was more than £200 or, if it was then in Greater London, £400, and

(c) the tenancy was created on or before 18th February 1966,

subsection (1)(a) above shall have effect in relation to the house and premises as if for the reference to the appropriate day there were substituted a reference to 1st April 1973 and as if for the sums of £200 and £400 specified in that subsection there were substituted respectively the sums of £750 and £1,500."

1967 c. 88.

(2) In any case where, by virtue only of the amendments of section 1 of the Leasehold Reform Act 1967 effected by subsection (1) above, the right specified in subsection (1) of that section is conferred on a tenant, section 19 of that Act (retention of management powers for general benefit of neighbourhood) shall have effect in relation to the house and premises to which the tenant's right applies as if for the reference in subsection (1) of that section to an application made within two years beginning with the commencement of Part I of that Act there were substituted a reference to an application made within two years beginning with the date on which this Act is passed.

(3) After subsection (4) of section 1 of the Leasehold Reform Act 1967 there shall be inserted—

" (4A) At any time the tenant may take the action provided in Schedule 8 to the Housing Act 1974 for his rateable value to be adjusted and in all such cases the agreed rateable value or that determined by the Court or District Valuer shall be the rateable value for the purposes of that Act."

(4) In section 9 of the Leasehold Reform Act 1967 (purchase price of enfranchisement) there shall be inserted after subsection (1):—

" (1A) Notwithstanding, the foregoing subsection, the price payable for a house and premises, the rateable value of which is above £1,000 in Greater London and £500 elsewhere, on a conveyance under section 8 above, shall be

the amount which at the relevant time the house and
premises, if sold in the open market by a willing seller,
might be expected to realise on the following
assumptions: —

(a) on the assumption that the vendor was selling for
an estate in fee simple, subject to the tenancy, but
on the assumption that this Part of this Act conferred no right to acquire the freehold;

(b) on the assumption that at the end of the tenancy
the tenant has the right to remain in possession
of the house and premises under the provisions
of Part I of the Landlord and Tenant Act 1954; 1954 c. 56.

(c) on the assumption that the tenant has no liability
to carry out any repairs, maintenance or redecora-
tions under the terms of the tenancy or Part I
of the Landlord and Tenant Act 1954;

(d) on the assumption that the price be diminished by
the extent to which the value of the house and
premises has been increased by any improvement
carried out by the tenant or his predecessors in
title at their own expense;

(e) on the assumption that (subject to paragraph (a)
above) the vendor was selling subject, in respect
of rentcharges and other rents to which section
11(2) below applies, to the same annual charge as
the conveyance to the tenant is to be subject to,
but the purchaser would otherwise be effectively
exonerated until the termination of the tenancy
from any liability or charge in respect of tenant's
incumbrances; and

(f) on the assumption that (subject to paragraphs (a)
and (b) above) the vendor was selling with and
subject to the rights and burdens with and subject to which the conveyance to the tenant is to
be made, and in particular with and subject to
such permanent or extended rights and burdens
as are to be created in order to give effect to
section 10 below.

(1B) For the purpose of determining whether the rateable value of the house and premises is above £1,000 in
Greater London, or £500 elsewhere, the rateable value shall
be adjusted to take into account any tenant's improvements
in accordance with Schedule 8 to the Housing Act 1974."

(5) This section shall come into force on the passing of this
Act.

119.—(1) Subject to the following provisions of this section, Part II of the Housing Subsidies Act 1967 (assistance for house purchase and improvement) shall be amended in accordance with Schedule 11 to this Act and the amendments of section 28 of that Act contained in paragraph 5 of that Schedule shall be deemed to have taken effect on 18th April 1974.

(2) Until 6th April 1980, nothing in paragraphs 1(2) and 2 of Schedule 11 to this Act or in paragraphs (ix) to (xi) of section 24(3) of the said Act of 1967 shall have effect in relation to a loan if—

(a) the option notice in respect of the loan was signed on or before 26th June 1974, or

(b) the loan was made in pursuance of an offer in writing made by the lender to the borrower on or before 26th June 1974 and the option notice was signed as mentioned in section 24(3)(b) of the said Act of 1967.

(3) Until the expiry of the period of 3 months beginning on the appointed day, nothing in paragraphs 1(2) and 2 of Schedule 11 to this Act or in paragraphs (ix) to (xi) of section 24(3) of the said Act of 1967 shall have effect in relation to a loan (being a loan to which subsection (2) above does not apply) if the option notice in respect of the loan was signed after 26th June 1974 and before the day appointed for the coming into operation of this section.

(4) The Secretary of State may by regulations made by statutory instrument make such transitional provisions as he considers appropriate for the purpose of securing the proper application of Part II of the said Act of 1967—

(a) on and after 6th April 1980 in relation to a loan to which subsection (2) above applies ; and

(b) after the expiry of the period specified in subsection (3) above in relation to a loan to which that subsection applies.

(5) Without prejudice to the generality of the power conferred by subsection (4) above, in relation to a loan to which the power applies, regulations under that subsection—

(a) may require things to be done before the date on which the said Part II is to apply to the loan ; and

(b) may make such modifications of the said Part II as the Secretary of State considers appropriate.

(6) A statutory instrument containing regulations under subsection (4) above shall be subject to annulment in pursuance of a resolution of either House of Parliament.

120. After section 341 of the Income and Corporation Taxes
Act 1970 there shall be inserted the following section:—

"Self-build
societies.

341A.—(1) Where a self-build society makes a
claim in that behalf for any year or part of a year
of assessment during which the society was approved
for the purposes of this section, rent to which the
society was entitled from its members for the year
or part shall be disregarded for tax purposes.

PART XI
Tax
exemptions
for self-build
societies.
1970 c. 10.

(2) Where a claim under subsection (1) of this
section has effect, any adjustment of the society's
liability to tax which is required in consequence of
the claim may be made by an assessment or by
repayment or otherwise, as the case may require.

(3) Where a self-build society makes a claim in
that behalf for an accounting period or part of an
accounting period during which it was approved for
the purposes of this section, the society shall be
exempt from corporation tax on chargeable gains
accruing to it in the accounting period or part thereof
on the disposal of any land to a member of the
society.

(4) References in this section to the approval of a
self-build society are references to its approval by
the Secretary of State, and the Secretary of State
shall not approve a self-build society for the purposes
of this section unless he is satisfied—

(*a*) that the society is, or is deemed to be, duly
registered under the Industrial and
Provident Societies Act 1965; and

1965 c. 12.

(*b*) that the society satisfies such other requirements as may be prescribed by or under
regulations under subsection (6) below and
will comply with such conditions as may
for the time being be so prescribed.

(5) An approval given for the purposes of this
section shall have effect as from such date (whether
before or after the giving of the approval) as may be
specified by the Secretary of State and shall cease
to have effect if revoked by him.

(6) The Secretary of State may by statutory instrument make regulations for the purpose of carrying
out the provisions of this section; and a statutory
instrument containing any such regulations shall be
subject to annulment in pursuance of a resolution
of the Commons House of Parliament.

E

(7) Section 42 of the Taxes Management Act 1970 (procedure for making claims) shall not apply to a claim under this section, but such a claim shall be made to the inspector and shall be made not later than two years after the end of the year of assessment or accounting period to which, or to a part of which, it relates.

(8) Subject to subsection (9) below, no claim under this section shall have effect unless it is proved that during the year or accounting period, or part thereof, to which the claim relates—

   (a) no land owned by the society was occupied, in whole or in part and whether solely or as joint occupier, by a person who was not, at the time of his occupation, a member of the society ; and

   (b) the society making the claim satisfies the condition specified in paragraph (a) of subsection (4) above and has complied with the conditions prescribed under paragraph (b) of that subsection and for the time being in force ;

and for the purposes of paragraph (a) above, occupation by any other person in accordance with the will, or the provisions applicable on the intestacy, of a deceased member, shall be treated during the first six months after the death as if it were occupation by a member.

(9) Notwithstanding the provisions of subsection (8) above, where, on a claim under this section, the Board are satisfied that the requirements of paragraphs (a) and (b) of that subsection are substantially complied with, they may direct that the claim shall have effect ; but if, subsequently, information comes to the knowledge of the Board which satisfies them that the direction was not justified, they may revoke the direction and thereupon the liability of the society to tax for all relevant years or accounting periods shall be adjusted by the making of assessments or otherwise.

(10) A claim under this section shall be in such form and contain such particulars as may be prescribed by the Board.

(11) In this section—

   " self-build society " has the same meaning as in Part I of the Housing Act 1974 ; and

" rent " includes any sums to which a self-
build society is entitled in respect of the
occupation of any of its land under a
licence or otherwise."

121.—(1) If after the coming into operation of this section Disclosure of landlord's
the tenant of premises occupied as a dwelling makes a written identity.
request for the landlord's name and address to any person who
demands or to the last person who received rent payable under
the tenancy or to any other person for the time being acting
as agent for the landlord in relation to the tenancy, and that
person fails without reasonable excuse to supply a written statement of the name and address within the period of 21 days
beginning with the day on which he receives the tenant's
request, that person shall be guilty of an offence and liable on
summary conviction to a fine not exceeding £200.

(2) In any case where—

(a) in response to a request under subsection (1) above, a
tenant is supplied with the name and address of the
landlord of the premises concerned ; and

(b) the landlord is a body corporate ; and

(c) the tenant makes a further written request to the landlord for information under this subsection,

the landlord shall, within the period of 21 days beginning with
the day on which he receives the request under this subsection,
supply to the tenant a written statement of the name and
address of every director and the secretary of the landlord.

(3) Any reference in subsection (1) or subsection (2) above
to a person's address is a reference to his place of abode or his
place of business or, in the case of a company, its registered
office.

(4) A request under subsection (2) above shall be deemed to
be duly made to the landlord if it is made to an agent of the
landlord or to a person who demands the rent of the premises
concerned, and any such agent or person to whom such a
request is made shall as soon as may be forward it to the
landlord.

(5) A landlord who fails without reasonable excuse to comply
with a request under subsection (2) above within the period
mentioned in that subsection and a person who fails without
reasonable excuse to comply with any requirement imposed on
him by subsection (4) above shall be guilty of an offence and
liable on summary conviction to a fine not exceeding £200.

E 2

(6) Where an offence under subsection (1) or subsection (5) above which has been committed by a body corporate is proved to have been committed with the consent or connivance of, or to be attributable to any neglect on the part of, a director, manager, secretary or other similar officer of the body corporate, or any person who was purporting to act in any such capacity, he, as well as the body corporate, shall be guilty of that offence and be liable to be proceeded against and punished accordingly.

(7) Where the affairs of a body corporate are managed by its members, subsection (6) above shall apply in relation to the acts and defaults of a member in connection with his functions of management as if he were a director of the body corporate.

(8) In England and Wales proceedings for an offence under this section may be instituted by any of the following local authorities,—

(a) the council of a district or London borough ;

(b) the Greater London Council ; and

(c) the Common Council of the City of London.

(9) In this section—

" landlord " means the immediate landlord and, in relation to premises occupied under a right conferred by an enactment, includes the person who, apart from that right, would be entitled to possession of the premises ;

" tenant " includes a sub-tenant and a tenant under a right conferred by an enactment, except that it does not include a tenant under a tenancy to which Part II of the Landlord and Tenant Act 1954 (business tenancies) applies.

(10) This section shall come into operation at the expiry of the period of one month beginning with the date on which this Act is passed.

Duty to inform tenant of a dwelling of assignment of landlord's interest.

122.—(1) If the interest of the landlord under a tenancy of premises which consist of or include a dwelling is assigned, the person to whom that interest is assigned (in this section referred to as " the new landlord ") shall, within the appropriate period, give notice in writing to the tenant of the assignment and of the name and address of the new landlord.

(2) In subsection (1) above " the appropriate period " means the period beginning on the date of the assignment in question and ending either two months after that date or, if it is later, on the first day after that date on which rent is payable under the tenancy.

(3) Subject to subsection (4) below, the reference in subsection (1) above to the new landlord's address is a reference to his place of abode or his place of business or, if the new landlord is a company, its registered office.

(4) If trustees as such constitute the new landlord, it shall be a sufficient compliance with the obligation in subsection (1) above to give the name of the new landlord to give a collective description of the trustees as the trustees of the trust in question, and where such a collective description is given—

  (a) the address of the new landlord for the purpose of that subsection may be given as the address from which the affairs of the trust are conducted ; and

  (b) a change in the persons who are for the time being the trustees of the trust shall not be treated as an assignment of the interest of the landlord.

(5) If any person who is the new landlord under a tenancy falling within subsection (1) above fails, without reasonable excuse, to give the notice required by that subsection, he shall be guilty of an offence and liable on summary conviction to a fine not exceeding £200.

(6) Where an offence under subsection (5) above which has been committed by a body corporate is proved to have been committed with the consent or connivance of, or be attributable to any neglect on the part of, a director, manager, secretary or other similar officer of the body corporate, he, as well as the body corporate, shall be guilty of that offence and be liable to be proceeded against and punished accordingly.

(7) Where the affairs of a body corporate are managed by its members, subsection (6) above shall apply in relation to the acts and defaults of a member in connection with his functions of management as if here were a director of the body corporate.

(8) In this section " tenancy " includes a subtenancy and a statutory tenancy, within the meaning of the Rent Act 1968 or of the Rent (Scotland) Act 1971, but does not include a tenancy to which Part II of the Landlord and Tenant Act 1954 (business tenancies) applies, and " tenant " shall be construed accordingly. 1968 c. 23.
1971 c. 28.
1954 c. 56.

(9) In this section—

  (a) in relation to England and Wales " assignment " includes any conveyance other than a mortgage or charge ; and

  (b) in relation to Scotland " assignment " means a conveyance or other transfer (other than in security), and any reference to the date of the assignment means the date on which the conveyance or other transfer was granted, delivered or otherwise made effective.

E 3

(10) This section shall come into operation at the expiry of the period of one month beginning with the date on which this Act is passed.

Form and content of certain notices to quit.
1957 c. 25.
1971 c. 28.

123.—(1) In section 16 of the Rent Act 1957 or, in Scotland, section 131 of the Rent (Scotland) Act 1971 (minimum length of notice to quit) after the words " shall be valid unless it " there shall be inserted the words " is in writing and contains such information as may be prescribed and " and at the end of that section there shall be added the following subsections:—

" (2) In this section " prescribed " means prescribed by regulations made by the Secretary of State by statutory instrument, and a statutory instrument containing any such regulations shall be subject to annulment in pursuance of a resolution of either House of Parliament.

(3) Regulations under this section may make different provision in relation to different descriptions of lettings and different circumstances."

(2) This section does not apply in relation to a notice to quit given before the day appointed for the coming into operation of this section.

Service charges.
1972 c. 47.

124.—(1) After section 91 of the Housing Finance Act 1972 there shall be inserted the following section:—

" Right to challenge service charges.

91A.—(1) A service charge shall only be recoverable from the tenant of a flat—

    (a) in respect of the provision of chargeable items to a reasonable standard ; and

    (b) to the extent that the liability incurred or amount defrayed by the landlord in respect of the provision of such items is reasonable ; and if any works in respect of which a service charge is claimed are estimated to cost more than £250, at least two estimates of the cost of such works shall be obtained by the landlord or agent and one of the said estimates shall be from a firm wholly unconnected with them, in the manner described in Schedule 12 to this Act;

and if any work in respect of which a service charge is claimed is estimated to cost more than £2,000, there shall be a duty upon the landlord or agent first to discuss it with the tenants' association or if no such body exists or is not wholly independent, then with individual tenants before it is proceeded with (except in cases of emergency) and only after such

consultation shall estimates be obtained in accordance with the provisions of this section; and the
consultation and expressed views of tenants or their
association or both shall be produced to the Court
in case of any dispute arising out of the operation
of this section.

(2) Any agreement made by a tenant of a flat
other than an arbitration agreement within the meaning of section 32 of the Arbitration Act 1950 1950 c. 23.
(whether the agreement is contained in an instrument
letting the flat or not and whether it is made before
the flat is let or not) shall be void in so far as it
purports to provide for determination in a particular
manner or on particular evidence (including, without prejudice to the generality of this subsection,
determination on the basis of a certificate given by
any person) of any question—

> (*a*) whether chargeable items have been pro-
> vided to a reasonable standard; or
>
> (*b*) whether the liability incurred or amount
> defrayed by the landlord in respect of them
> was reasonable.

(3) The High Court or the county court, on the
application of the landlord or tenant of a flat, may
by order, in relation to any chargeable items specified in the order, declare—

> (*a*) that they have or have not been provided
> to a reasonable standard; and
>
> (*b*) that the amount alleged to be payable in
> respect of them is or is not reasonable,

and may direct the amount to be paid by the tenant
in consequence of the declaration.

(4) Where in proceedings brought under the foregoing subsection (3) it is proved to the satisfaction
of the Court that an association has been formed
to represent the tenants one or more of whom are
parties to the application and that the membership
of such association comprises not less than 60 per
cent. of the tenants eligible to belong thereto the
Court may in making any order on the application
further declare that the said association shall until
further order of the Court be recognised for the
purposes of this Act as the tenants' association
entitled to exercise the rights conferred by this Act
and the term " tenants' association " shall refer to
such association so long as it is so recognised.

PART XI

(5) Regulations relating to the formation of such tenants' association may be made by the Secretary of State.

(6) The county court may make a declaration under this section notwithstanding that the declaration is the only relief sought.

(7) In this section " chargeable items " means any items for which a service charge may be payable, and other expressions used in this section have the meanings assigned to them by section 90(12) above.

(8) This section does not apply—

(a) where the landlord is—

(i) a local authority or a county council, or

(ii) a new town corporation, or

(iii) the Housing Corporation, or

(iv) a housing association falling within paragraph (d) of subsection (1) of section 91 above, or

(v) an association or company the membership of which is wholly or mainly restricted to persons who are tenants in the same block or blocks of flats, or

1968 c. 23.

(b) where the tenant is a protected tenant or a statutory tenant within the meaning of the Rent Act 1968 or a lessee within the meaning of Part VI of that Act (furnished lettings).

(9) This section does not apply in relation to an accounting year ending before 1st August 1974."

1972 c. 47.

(2) The amendments of the Housing Finance Act 1972 specified in Schedule 12 to this Act shall have effect, subject to paragraph 5 of that Schedule.

(3) This section shall come into operation at the expiry of the period of one month beginning with the date on which this Act is passed.

Specific performance of landlord's repairing covenants, etc.

125.—(1) In any proceedings in which a tenant of a dwelling alleges a breach on the part of his landlord of a repairing covenant relating to any part of the premises in which the dwelling is comprised, the court may, in its discretion, order specific performance of that covenant, whether or not the breach relates to a part of the premises let to the tenant and notwithstanding any equitable rule restricting the scope of that remedy, whether on the basis of a lack of mutuality or otherwise.

(2) In this section—

" landlord ", in relation to a tenant, includes any person against whom the tenant has a right to enforce a repairing covenant;

" repairing covenant " means a covenant to repair, maintain, renew, construct or replace any property;

" statutory tenant " has the same meaning as in the Rent Act 1968; and

" tenant " includes a sub-tenant and a statutory tenant but does not include a tenant under a tenancy to which Part II of the Landlord and Tenant Act 1954 (business tenancies) applies, and any reference to the premises let to a tenant means, in relation to a statutory tenant, the premises of which he is the statutory tenant.

(3) This section shall come into operation on the passing of this Act.

126.—(1) The provisions of this section shall apply if a principal council (in the exercise of their powers under section 111 of the Local Government Act 1972 or otherwise) and a person having an interest in land in their area become parties to an instrument under seal executed for the purpose of securing the carrying out of works on that land or of facilitating the development of that land or of other land in which that person has an interest and the instrument is registered in the register of local land charges—

(a) by the proper officer, for the purposes of section 15 of the Land Charges Act 1925, of the local authority in whose area the land is situated, and

(b) in such manner as may be prescribed by rules under section 19 of that Act,

and in this subsection " local authority " means a district council, a London borough council or the Common Council of the City of London.

(2) If, in a case where this section applies,—

(a) the instrument contains a covenant on the part of any person having an interest in land, being a covenant to carry out any works or do any other thing on or in relation to that land, and

(b) the instrument defines the land to which the covenant relates, being land in which that person has an interest at the time the instrument is executed, and

(c) the covenant is expressed to be one to which this section applies,

the covenant shall be enforceable (without any limit of time) against any person deriving title from the original covenantor

PART IX

1968 c. 23.

1954 c. 56.

Enforceability of certain covenants in agreements relating to development of land.
1972 c. 70.

1925 c. 22.

in respect of his interest in any of the land defined as mentioned in paragraph (*b*) above and any person deriving title under him in respect of any lesser interest in that land as if that person had also been an original covenanting party in respect of the interest for the time being held by him.

(3) Without prejudice to any other method of enforcement of a covenant falling within subsection (2) above, if there is a breach of the covenant as a result of a failure to carry out any works or to do any other thing on or in relation to any of the land to which the covenant relates, then, subject to subsection (4) below, the principal council who are a party to the instrument in which the covenant is contained may—

> (*a*) enter on the land concerned and carry out the works or do any other thing which the covenant requires to be carried out or done ; and

> (*b*) recover from any person against whom the covenant is enforceable (whether by virtue of subsection (2) above or otherwise) any expenses incurred by the council in exercise of their powers under this subsection.

(4) Before a principal council exercise their powers under subsection (3)(*a*) above they shall give not less than 21 days notice of their intention to do so to any person—

> (*a*) who has for the time being an interest in the land on or in relation to which the works are to be carried out or other thing is to be done ; and

> (*b*) against whom the covenant is enforceable (whether by virtue of subsection (2) above or otherwise).

1936 c. 49. (5) The Public Health Act 1936 shall have effect as if any reference to that Act in—

> (*a*) section 277 thereof (power of councils to require information as to ownership of premises),

> (*b*) section 283 thereof (notices to be in writing ; forms of notices, etc.),

> (*c*) section 288 thereof (penalty for obstructing execution of Act), and

> (*d*) section 291 thereof (certain expenses recoverable from owners to be a charge on the premises ; power to order payment by instalments),

included a reference to subsections (1) to (4) above and as if any reference in those sections of that Act—

> (i) to a local authority were a reference to a principal council ; and

(ii) to the owner of premises were a reference to the holder of an interest in land.

(6) In its application to a notice or other document authorised to be given or served under subsection (4) above or by virtue of any provision of the Public Health Act 1936 specified in 1936 c. 49. subsection (5) above, section 233 of the Local Government Act 1972 c. 70. 1972 (service of notices by local authorities) shall have effect as if any reference in that section to a local authority included a reference to the Common Council of the City of London.

(7) In this section " principal council " means the council of a county, district or London borough, the Common Council of the City of London or the Greater London Council, and, subject to subsection (8) below, in relation to the Isles of Scilly, the Council of those Isles.

(8) The Secretary of State may, after consultation with the Council of the Isles of Scilly, by order direct that the provisions of subsections (1) to (6) of this section shall apply to the Isles of Scilly subject to such exceptions, adaptations and modifications, if any, as may be specified in the order.

127.—(1) Except as provided by section 7 of this Act, there Expenses and shall be defrayed out of money provided by Parliament— terms of payment of

(*a*) any sums required for the payment by the Secretary of grants, etc. State of grants, subsidies or contributions under this Act and any other expenses or outgoings of the Secretary of State under this Act ;

(*b*) any increase attributable to the provisions of this Act in the sums payable out of such money under any other Act ;

and any sums received by the Secretary of State under this Act shall be paid into the Consolidated Fund.

(2) Any grant, subsidy or contribution payable by the Secretary of State under this Act shall be payable subject to such conditions as to records, certificates, audit or otherwise as the Secretary of State may, with the approval of the Treasury, impose.

128.—(1) Any power of the Secretary of State to make an Orders. order under any provision of this Act shall be exercisable by statutory instrument.

(2) An order made by the Secretary of State under any provision of this Act may be varied or revoked by a subsequent order made under that provision.

(3) Subject to subsection (4) below, a statutory instrument containing an order made under any of the preceding provisions

PART IX of this Act shall be subject to annulment in pursuance of a resolution of either House of Parliament.

(4) Subsection (3) above shall not apply to an order made under any of sections 7, 46, 59, 64 or 78 of this Act.

Interpretation. **129.**—(1) In the application of this Act in England and Wales—

" the Corporation " means the Housing Corporation ;

" dwelling " means a building or part of a building occupied or intended to be occupied as a separate dwelling, together with any yard, garden, outhouses and appurtenances belonging to or usually enjoyed with that building or part ;

" hostel " means a building wherein is provided, for persons generally or for a class or classes of persons, residential accommodation (otherwise than in separate and self-contained sets of premises) and either board or facilities for the preparation of food adequate to the needs of those persons, or both ;

" house in multiple occupation " means a house which is occupied by persons who do not form a single household, exclusive of any part thereof which is occupied as a separate dwelling by persons who do form a single household ;

1957 c. 56. " housing association " has the meaning assigned to it by section 189(1) of the Housing Act 1957 ;

" improvement grant " and " intermediate grant " have the meanings assigned to them by section 56(2) of this Act ;

" operative date " means 1st April 1975 or such later date as may be specified under, and for the purposes of, section 17(1) of this Act ;

" registered ", except in the expression " registered charity " means registered in the register of housing associations established under section 13 of this Act, and " registration " and " unregistered " shall be construed accordingly ;

1960 c. 58. " registered charity " means a charity of which particulars are entered in the register of charities established under section 4 of the Charities Act 1960 ;

" repairs grant " and " special grant " have the meanings assigned to them by section 56(2) above.

(2) In the application of this Act in Scotland—

" charge " includes a heritable security ;

" the Corporation " means the Housing Corporation ;

" dwelling " means a house within the meaning of section
208(1) of the Housing (Scotland) Act 1966 ;   1966 c. 49.

" heritable security " has the meaning assigned to it by
section 12 of this Act ;

" hostel " has the same meaning as in section 21(4) of
the Housing (Financial Provisions) (Scotland) Act 1968 c. 31.
1968 ;

" housing association " has the meaning assigned to it by
section 208(1) of the Housing (Scotland) Act 1966 ;

" local authority " has the meaning assigned to it by section
1 of the Housing (Scotland) Act 1966 ;

" mortgage " means a heritable security and " mortgagee "
means the creditor in such a security ;

" operative date " has the same meaning as in subsection
(1) above ;

" registered " means registered in the register of housing
associations established under section 13 of this Act,
and " registration " and " unregistered " shall be construed accordingly.

(3) For the purposes of this Act a person is a member of
another's family if that person is—

(a) the other's wife or husband ; or

(b) a son or daughter or a son-in-law or daughter-in-law
of the other, or of the other's wife or husband ; or

(c) the father or mother of the other, or of the other's
wife or husband.

(4) In paragraph (b) of subsection (3) above any reference to
a person's son or daughter includes a reference to any step-son
or step-daughter, any illegitimate son or daughter, and any
adopted son or daughter of that person, and " son-in-law "
and " daughter-in-law " shall be construed accordingly.

(5) Any reference in this Act to any other enactment shall
be construed as referring to that enactment as amended by or
under any other enactment, including this Act.

PART IX
Amendments,
transitional
provisions,
savings and
repeals.
1973 c. 26.
1973 c. 56.

130.—(1) Schedule 13 to this Act, which contains minor amendments and amendments consequential on the provisions of this Act, shall have effect.

(2) In Schedule 13 to this Act, the amendments of the Land Compensation Act 1973 and the Land Compensation (Scotland) Act 1973 shall have effect in the case of persons displaced on or after the date of the passing of this Act.

(3) The transitional provisions and savings in Schedule 14 to this Act shall have effect.

(4) The enactments specified in Schedule 15 to this Act are hereby repealed to the extent specified in the third column of that Schedule.

Short title,
citation,
commence-
ment and
extent.

131.—(1) This Act may be cited as the Housing Act 1974.

(2) This Act and the Housing Acts 1957 to 1973 may be cited together as the Housing Acts 1957 to 1974.

(3) Except in so far as any provision of this Act otherwise provides, this Act shall come into operation on such day as the Secretary of State may by order appoint, and different days may be so appointed for different provisions and for different purposes.

(4) Without prejudice to any express saving contained in Schedule 14 to this Act, an order under subsection (3) above appointing a day for the coming into operation of any provision of Schedule 13 or Schedule 15 to this Act may contain such savings with respect to the operation of that provision as appear to the Secretary of State to be appropriate.

(5) Parts IV, V, VI, VII, and VIII and, in Part IX, sections 105, 106, 108, 118, 124, 125 and 126 of this Act extend to England and Wales only.

(6) Section 107 of this Act extends to Scotland only.

(7) This Act does not extend to Northern Ireland.

SCHEDULES

SCHEDULE 1

AMENDMENTS TO CONSTITUTION ETC. OF HOUSING CORPORATION

1. In sub-paragraph (1) of paragraph 2 of Schedule 1 to the 1964 Act (number of members of Corporation not to exceed nine) for the word " nine " there shall be substituted the word " fifteen ".

2. At the end of the said paragraph 2 there shall be inserted the following paragraph—

" 2A.—(1) Before appointing a person to be a member of the Corporation the Ministers shall satisfy themselves that that person will have no such financial or other interest as is likely to affect prejudicially the exercise of his functions as a member, and the Ministers shall also satisfy themselves from time to time with respect to every member of the Corporation that he has no such interest ; and any person who is, or whom the Ministers propose to appoint, a member of the Corporation shall, whenever requested by them to do so, furnish them with such information as the Ministers consider necessary for the performance of their duties under this paragraph.

(2) A member of the Corporation who is any way directly or indirectly interested in a contract made or proposed to be made by the Corporation shall disclose the nature of his interest at a meeting of the Corporation, and the disclosure shall be recorded in the minutes of the Corporation ; and the member shall not take part in any decision of the Corporation with respect to that contract.

(3) For the purposes of sub-paragraph (2) above a general notice given at a meeting of the Corporation by a member of the Corporation to the effect that he is a member of a specified company or firm and is to be regarded as interested in any contract which may, after the date of the notice, be made with the company or firm shall be regarded as a sufficient disclosure of his interest in relation to any contract so made.

(4) A member of the Corporation need not attend in person at a meeting of the Corporation in order to make any disclosure which he is required to make under this paragraph if he takes reasonable steps to secure that the disclosure is made by a notice which is brought up and read at the meeting.

(5) In sub-paragraph (1) above ' the Ministers ' means the persons by whom members of the Corporation are appointed under paragraph 2(1) above."

3. In paragraph 5 of that Schedule after the words " this Act " there shall be inserted the words " or the Housing Act 1974 ".

4. At the end of paragraph 5 of that Schedule there shall be added the following paragraph—

" 6. The Corporation shall be a public body for the purposes of the Prevention of Corruption Acts 1889 to 1916."

SCHEDULE 2

GRANT-AIDED LAND

1. For the purposes of section 2 of this Act " grant-aided land " means land—

   (a) in respect of which any such payment as is specified in paragraph 2 below falls or fell to be made in respect of a period ending after 24th January 1974 ; or

   (b) on which is or has been secured a loan which is of a description specified in paragraph 3 below and in respect of which any repayment (whether by way of principal or interest or both) falls or fell to be made after that date.

2. The payments referred to in paragraph 1(a) above are payments—

1949 c. 60.

1949 c. 61.
1950 c. 34.

   (a) by way of annual grants under section 31(3) of the Housing Act 1949 or by way of exchequer contributions under section 19(3) of the Housing (Scotland) Act 1949 or under section 121(3) of the Housing (Scotland) Act 1950 (arrangements by local authorities for improvement of housing accommodation) ;

1958 c. 42.

1962 c. 28.

1968 c. 31.

   (b) by way of annual grants under section 12(1) or section 15 of the Housing (Financial Provisions) Act 1958 or by way of exchequer contributions under section 89(1) of the Housing (Scotland) Act 1950 or under section 12 of the Housing (Scotland) Act 1962 or under section 21 of the Housing (Financial Provisions) (Scotland) Act 1968 (contributions for dwellings improved under arrangements with local authorities and grants for hostels) ;

1967 c. 29.

1964 c. 56.

   (c) by way of annual grant under section 12(6) of the Housing Subsidies Act 1967 or by way of exchequer contributions under section 121 of the Housing (Scotland) Act 1950 or under section 62 of the Housing Act 1964 or under section 17 of the Housing (Financial Provisions) (Scotland) Act 1968 (subsidies for conversions or improvements by housing associations) ;

1969 c. 33.

   (d) by way of annual grant under section 21(8) of the Housing Act 1969 (contributions for dwellings provided or improved by housing associations under arrangements with local authorities) ;

   (e) by way of basic residual subsidy, special residual subsidy or new building subsidy under section 72 ; section 73 or section 75 of the Housing Finance Act 1972 or by way of hostel subsidy under section 92 of that Act ; and

1972 c. 47.

1972 c. 46.

   (f) by way of basic residual subsidy, special residual subsidy, new building subsidy or improvement subsidy under section 52, section 53, section 55 or section 57 of the Housing (Financial Provisions) (Scotland) Act 1972.

3. The loans referred to in paragraph 1(b) above are—

1957 c. 56.
1966 c. 49.

   (a) loans under section 119 of the Housing Act 1957 or under section 152 of the Housing (Scotland) Act 1966 (power of certain local authorities to promote and assist housing associations) ;

(b) loans to housing associations under section 47 of the Housing (Financial Provisions) Act 1958 or under section 78 of the Housing (Scotland) Act 1950 or under section 24 of the Housing (Financial Provisions) (Scotland) Act 1968 (loans by Public Works Loan Commissioners to certain bodies) ;

(c) advances made under section 7 of the Housing Act 1961 or under section 11 of the Housing (Scotland) Act 1962 or under section 23 of the Housing (Financial Provisions) (Scotland) Act 1968 (advances to housing associations providing housing accommodation for letting) ; and

(d) loans made by the Corporation under section 2 of the Housing Act 1964.

SCHEDULE 3
Housing Association Tenancies
Part I
Interim Protection of Housing Association Tenants

1.—(1) The provisions of this Part of this Schedule apply where,—

(a) before the passing of this Act, any premises have been let on a tenancy (in this Part of this Schedule referred to as " the former tenancy ") ; and

(b) by reason only of section 5(5) of the Rent Act 1968 or of section 5(4) of the Rent (Scotland) Act 1971 (exclusion of housing association tenancies from protection) the former tenancy was not a protected tenancy on the relevant day ; and

(c) the former tenancy has come to an end before the passing of this Act or comes to an end after the passing of this Act but before the operative date ; and

(d) at any time after the passing of this Act or the termination of the former tenancy, whichever is the later, any of the persons specified in sub-paragraph (3) below remains in occupation of the premises or part of them and in residence therein.

(2) In this Part of this Schedule " the relevant day ", in relation to a tenancy, means,—

(a) in the case of a tenancy which expired before the passing of this Act, the day on which it expired ; and

(b) in any other case, the day immediately preceding that on which this Act was passed.

(3) The persons referred to in sub-paragraph (1)(d) above are—

(a) the tenant under the former tenancy ;

(b) any person to whom the premises or any part thereof has been lawfully sublet as a dwelling ; and

(c) where any such person as is mentioned in paragraph (a) or paragraph (b) above has died, any person who, if the deceased had been the original tenant, within the meaning of Schedule 1 to the Rent Act 1968, or to the Rent (Scotland) Act 1971, of the premises or part would have been the first successor, within the meaning of that Schedule, or would have become the statutory tenant on the death of that first successor.

2.—(1) In this paragraph " the occupier ", in relation to any premises, means the person remaining in occupation and in residence as mentioned in paragraph 1(1)(*d*) above and " the owner ", in relation to any premises, means the person who, as against the occupier, is entitled to possession thereof ; and the following provisions of this paragraph shall have effect subject to paragraph 3 below.

(2) Without prejudice to any power of the court apart from this Part of this Schedule to postpone the operation or suspend the execution of an order for possession, if in proceedings by the owner against the occupier of any premises the court makes, or has before the passing of this Act made, an order for possession the court may suspend the execution of the order for such period, not exceeding 12 months from the date of the order, as the court thinks reasonable.

(3) Where the court by virtue of this paragraph suspends the execution of an order for possession of any premises it may authorise the withdrawal from the occupier of any specified services or furniture and impose such terms and conditions, including conditions as to the payment by the occupier of arrears of rent, rent or mesne profits and otherwise, as the court thinks reasonable.

(4) The court may from time to time vary the period of suspension or terminate it and may vary any terms or conditions imposed by virtue of this paragraph, but shall not extend the period of suspension beyond the end of 12 months from the date of the order for possession.

(5) In considering whether or how to exercise its powers under this paragraph the court shall have regard to all the circumstances and, in particular, to the following, namely,—

(*a*) whether the occupier has failed (whether before or after the termination of the former tenancy) to observe any terms or conditions thereof ;

(*b*) whether he has unreasonably refused an offer of a tenancy of the premises or part of them for a reasonable term ; and

(*c*) whether greater hardship would be caused by the suspension of the execution of the order for possession than by its execution without suspension or further suspension.

(6) Where in proceedings for the recovery of possession of any premises the court makes an order for possession but suspends the execution of the order by virtue of sub-paragraph (2) above it shall make no order for costs, unless it appears to the court, having regard to the conduct of the owner or of the occupier, that there are special reasons for making such an order.

(7) In the application of this paragraph to Scotland—

(*a*) for any reference to an order for possession there shall be substituted a reference to a decree of removing or warrant of ejection,

(*b*) for the reference to mesne profits there shall be substituted ScH. 3
a reference to damages arising from unlawful possession,
and

(*c*) for the reference to costs there shall be substituted a
reference to expenses.

3.—(1) If at any time before the operative date the interest which,
on the relevant day, was the interest of the landlord under the former
tenancy (in this paragraph referred to as " the landlord's interest ")
becomes vested in one of the bodies specified in section 5(2) of the
Rent Act 1968 or of the Rent (Scotland) Act 1971 (bodies whose 1968 c. 23.
tenancies are excluded from protection under that Act) the court 1971 c. 28.
may not, in exercise of its power under paragraph 2(4) above, vary
the period of suspension otherwise than by shortening it.

(2) If on the operative date the landlord's interest belongs to a
housing association then, without prejudice to the provisions of Parts
II and III below and to the continued operation of any provision
made before that date by virtue of paragraph 2 above, the powers
of the court under that paragraph shall on that date cease to be
exercisable.

4.—(1) In this Part of this Schedule " the court ",—

(*a*) in relation to premises in England or Wales, means the
county court ; and

(*b*) in relation to premises in Scotland, means the sheriff.

(2) Any powers of a county court in proceedings for the recovery
of possession of any premises in circumstances where the powers
conferred by this Part of this Schedule are or may be exercisable
may be exercised by any registrar of the court, except in so far as
rules of court otherwise provide.

(3) Except in so far as the context otherwise requires, expressions
to which a meaning is assigned by section 113 of the Rent Act
1968 or, in Scotland, section 133 of the Rent (Scotland) Act 1971
have the same meanings in this Part of this Schedule.

PART II

APPLICATION OF RENT ACT 1968

5.—(1) The provisions of this paragraph apply on and after the
operative date in any case where—

(*a*) a tenancy of a dwelling-house under which the interest of
the landlord belonged to a housing association has come
to an end at a time before the operative date (whether
before or after the passing of this Act), and

(*b*) on the date when it came to an end, the tenancy was one
to which Part VIII of the 1972 Act applied, and

(*c*) if the tenancy had come to an end after the operative date
it would, by virtue of section 18(1) of this Act, have then
been a protected tenancy.

(2) No order for possession of the dwelling-house shall be made which would not be made if the tenancy had been a protected tenancy at the time it came to an end.

(3) Where a court has made an order for possession of the dwelling-house before the operative date, but the order has not been executed, the court, if of opinion that the order would not have been made if the tenancy had been a protected tenancy when it came to an end may, on the application of the person against whom it was made, rescind or vary it in such manner as the court thinks fit for the purpose of enabling him to continue in possession.

(4) If on the operative date the person who was the tenant under the tenancy which has come to an end duly retains possession of the dwelling-house, he shall be deemed to do so as a statutory tenant under a regulated tenancy and as a person who became a statutory tenant on the termination of a protected tenancy under which he was the tenant.

(5) If on the operative date a person duly retains possession of the dwelling-house as being a person who, in the circumstances described in paragraph 1(3)(c) above, would have been the first successor, within the meaning of Schedule 1 to the Rent Act 1968, he shall be deemed to do so as the statutory tenant under a regulated tenancy and as a person who became a statutory tenant by virtue of paragraph 2 or paragraph 3 of that Schedule.

(6) If on the operative date a person duly retains possession of the dwelling-house as being a person who, in the circumstances described in paragraph 1(3)(c) above, would have become the statutory tenant on the death of a first successor, he shall be deemed to do so as the statutory tenant under a regulated tenancy and as a person who became a statutory tenant by virtue of paragraph 6 or paragraph 7 of Schedule 1 to the Rent Act 1968.

(7) References in the preceding provisions of this paragraph to a person duly retaining possession of a dwelling-house are references to his retaining possession without any order for possession having been made or, where such an order has been made,—

(a) during any period while its operation is postponed or its execution is suspended ; or

(b) after it has been rescinded.

(8) Subject to sub-paragraph (9) below, the tenancy referred to in sub-paragraph (1) above shall be treated as the original contract of tenancy for the purposes of section 12 of the Rent Act 1968 (terms and conditions of statutory tenancies) in relation to a statutory tenancy imposed by any of sub-paragraphs (4) to (6) above.

(9) The High Court or the county court may by order vary all or any of the terms of a statutory tenancy imposed by any of sub-paragraphs (4) to (6) above in any way appearing to the court to be just and equitable (and whether or not in a way authorised by the provisions of sections 23 and 24 of the Rent Act 1968).

6.—(1) If, in a case where either a tenancy becomes a protected Sch. 3
tenancy by virtue of section 18(1) of this Act or a statutory tenancy
is imposed by virtue of paragraph 5 above,—

    (*a*) a rent was registered for the dwelling-house at a time when
Part VIII of the 1972 Act applied to that tenancy or, as
the case may be, to the tenancy referred to in paragraph 5(1)
above, and

    (*b*) a rent is subsequently registered for the dwelling-house under
Part IV of the Rent Act 1968 but the rent so registered is 1968 c. 23.
less than the rent registered as mentioned in paragraph (*a*)
above,

then, subject to paragraph 8 below, until such time as a rent is registered under Part IV of the Rent Act 1968 which is higher than the
rent registered as mentioned in paragraph (*a*) above, the contractual
rent limit, or, as the case may be, the maximum rent recoverable
during any statutory period of the regulated tenancy concerned shall be
the rent registered as mentioned in paragraph (*a*) above.

(2) If, in a case falling within sub-paragraph (1) above, the Secretary
of State has, in a direction under section 85 of the 1972 Act, specified
a rent limit for the dwelling-house higher than the rent registered as
mentioned in sub-paragraph (1)(*a*) above, then, during the period for
which that direction has effect as mentioned in that section, sub-
paragraph (1) above shall have effect with the substitution for any
reference to the rent registered as mentioned in paragraph (*a*) of
that sub-paragraph of a reference to the rent limit so specified.

(3) Nothing in the preceding provisions of this paragraph shall affect
the operation of section 48A of the Rent Act 1968 (cancellation of
registration of rent) and, accordingly, where the registration of a
rent is cancelled in accordance with that section sub-paragraph (1)
above shall cease to apply in relation to the rent of the dwelling-house
concerned.

7.—(1) This paragraph applies for the purposes of the application
of Part III of the Rent Act 1968 (rents under regulated tenancies) in
relation to—

    (*a*) a tenancy which becomes a protected tenancy by virtue of
section 18(1) of this Act,

    (*b*) a statutory tenancy arising on the termination of such a
tenancy, and

    (*c*) a statutory tenancy imposed by virtue of paragraph 5 above,

in any case where, at the time when Part VIII of the 1972 Act last
applied to the tenancy referred to in paragraph (*a*) above or, as the
case may require, paragraph 5(1) above, subsection (3) of section 83
of the 1972 Act applied (rent limit where no rent is registered).

(2) Where this paragraph applies, the rent limit applicable to the
tenancy or statutory tenancy referred to in sub-paragraph (1) above
shall be deemed to be (or, as the case may be, to have been) the
contractual rent limit under the relevant tenancy, but without prejudice
to the subsequent registration of a rent for the dwelling-house under

Part IV of the Rent Act 1968 or (during the currency of a protected tenancy) the making of an agreement under section 43 of the 1972 Act increasing the rent payable.

(3) Sub-paragraph (2) above shall have effect notwithstanding the repeal by the 1972 Act of section 20(3) of the Rent Act 1968 (contractual rent limit before registration), but nothing in this paragraph shall be taken as applying any provision of section 83 of the 1972 Act to a tenancy at a time when it is a protected tenancy.

(4) In this paragraph " the relevant tenancy " means—

    (a) in the case of a tenancy falling within sub-paragraph (1)(a) above, that tenancy ;

    (b) in the case of a statutory tenancy falling within sub-paragraph (1)(b) above, the tenancy referred to in sub-paragraph (1)(a) above ; and

    (c) in the case of a statutory tenancy falling within sub-paragraph (1)(c) above, the protected tenancy referred to in sub-paragraph (4) of paragraph 5 above or, in a case where sub-paragraph (5) or sub-paragraph (6) of that paragraph applies, a notional protected tenancy which, by virtue of section 7(4) of the Rent Act 1968, would be treated for the purposes of that Act as constituting one regulated tenancy when taken together with the statutory tenancy.

8.—(1) The provisions of this paragraph apply where—

    (a) a tenancy of a dwelling-house becomes a protected tenancy by virtue of section 18(1) of this Act or a statutory tenancy is imposed by virtue of paragraph 5 above ; and

    (b) immediately before the tenancy became a protected tenancy or, as the case may require, immediately before the tenancy referred to in paragraph 5(1) above came to an end, section 84 of the 1972 Act (phasing of progression to registered rent) applied to the rent of the dwelling-house let on that tenancy.

(2) In the following provisions of this paragraph " the regulated tenancy " means the regulated tenancy consisting of the protected or statutory tenancy referred to in sub-paragraph (1)(a) above, together with any subsequent statutory tenancy which, when taken with that regulated tenancy is by virtue of section 7(4) of the Rent Act 1968 treated for the purposes of that Act as constituting one regulated tenancy.

(3) Subject to the following provisions of this paragraph, section 84 of the 1972 Act shall continue to apply or, as the case may require, shall apply to the rent of a dwelling-house subject to the regulated tenancy.

(4) Section 84 of the 1972 Act shall cease to apply by virtue of this paragraph to the rent of a dwelling-house—

    (a) on the date on which a rent is registered for the dwelling-house under Part IV of the Rent Act 1968 if the date of

registration, within the meaning of Part VIII of the 1972 Sᴄʜ. 3
Act, is after the operative date ; or

(b) on the date on which a new regulated tenancy of the
dwelling-house is granted to a person who is neither the
tenant under the regulated tenancy nor a person who might
succeed him as a statutory tenant.

(5) If and so long as, by virtue of this paragraph, subsection (2)
of section 84 of the 1972 Act imposes for any rental period of a
tenancy or statutory tenancy a rent limit below the rent registered
for the dwelling-house as mentioned in subsection (1) of that
section,—

(a) the contractual rent limit shall be the rent limit so imposed
and not the registered rent (as provided by section 20(2) of
the Rent Act 1968) and section 87 of the 1972 Act (increase 1968 c. 23.
of rent without notice to quit) shall apply in relation to the
tenancy as if it were one to which Part VIII of that Act
applied ; and

(b) a notice of increase under section 22(2)(b) of the Rent Act
1968 (increase of rent for statutory periods) may not increase
the rent for any statutory period above the rent limit so
imposed, and any such notice which purports to increase it
further shall have effect to increase it to that limit but no
further.

(6) For the purposes of the application on and after the operative
date of section 84 of the 1972 Act to the rent of a dwelling-house
subject to a regulated tenancy consisting of or beginning with a
statutory tenancy which is imposed by virtue of paragraph 5 above,
that section shall be deemed to have continued to apply throughout
the period between the termination of the tenancy referred to in sub-
paragraph (1) of that paragraph and the operative date ; but nothing
in this paragraph shall affect the rent recoverable for that dwelling-
house at any time during that period.

9.—(1) This paragraph shall have effect with respect to the application of Schedule 6 to the 1972 Act (restriction on rent increases) in
relation to a regulated tenancy consisting of—

(a) a tenancy which becomes a protected tenancy by virtue of
section 18(1) of this Act, or

(b) a statutory tenancy imposed by virtue of paragraph 5 above,

together with any subsequent statutory tenancy which, when taken
with that regulated tenancy, is by virtue of section 7(4) of the Rent
Act 1968 treated for the purposes of that Act as constituting one
regulated tenancy.

(2) For the purposes of paragraph 1(1)(b) of the said Schedule 6
(application of paragraph 1 to the first registration of rent after
completion, during the existence of the regulated tenancy, of certain
works), a tenancy falling within sub-paragraph (1)(a) above shall be
deemed to have been a regulated tenancy throughout the period
when Part VIII of the 1972 Act applied to it.

SCH. 3   (3) In the case of a regulated tenancy falling within sub-paragraph (1)(*b*) above, paragraph 1(1)(*b*) of the said Schedule 6 shall have effect as if the reference to the completion of works during the existence of the regulated tenancy included a reference to their completion during the period beginning on the day on which Part VIII of the 1972 Act first applied to the tenancy referred to in paragraph 5(1) above and ending on the day on which the regulated tenancy came into existence.

1968 c. 23.   (4) The references in paragraph 3(1) of the said Schedule 6 to notices of increase authorised by the Rent Act 1968 shall include a reference to notices of increase under section 87 of the 1972 Act.

10. In the application of section 25 of the Rent Act 1968 (increase, on account of improvements, of recoverable rent for statutory periods before registration) in relation to a statutory tenancy arising on the termination of a tenancy which becomes a protected tenancy by virtue of section 18(1) of this Act and a statutory tenancy imposed by virtue of paragraph 5 above, for the reference to 7th December 1965 (the date after which the improvement must be completed) there shall be substituted a reference to the operative date.

11. In the application of section 46 of the Rent Act 1968 in relation to a tenancy which becomes a protected tenancy by virtue of section 18(1) of this Act or a statutory tenancy which is imposed by virtue of paragraph 5 above, the reference in subsection (3) to a failure to comply with any terms of a regulated tenancy or to carrying out an improvement includes a reference to a failure occurring or an improvement carried out before the tenancy became a regulated tenancy or, as the case may be, before the statutory tenancy was imposed.

1972 c. 47.   12. In this Part of this Schedule " the 1972 Act " means the Housing Finance Act 1972 and sections 38(1) and 113(1) of the Rent Act 1968 (interpretation) shall have effect for the purposes of this Schedule as they have effect for the purposes of Part III or, as the case may be, the whole of that Act.

PART III

1971 c. 28.   APPLICATION OF RENT (SCOTLAND) ACT 1971

13.—(1) The provisions of this paragraph apply on and after the operative date in any case where—

(*a*) a tenancy of a dwelling-house under which the interest of the landlord belonged to a housing association has come to an end at a time before the operative date (whether before or after the passing of this Act), and

(*b*) on the date when it came to an end, the tenancy was one to which sections 60 to 66 of the 1972 Act applied, and

(*c*) if the tenancy had come to an end after the operative date it would, by virtue of section 18(1) of this Act, have then been a protected tenancy.

(2) No order for possession of the dwelling-house shall be made which would not be made if the tenancy had been a protected tenancy at the time it came to an end.

(3) Where a court has made an order for possession of the dwelling-house before the operative date, but the order has not been executed, the court, if of opinion that the order would not have been made if the tenancy had been a protected tenancy when it came to an end may, on the application of the person against whom it was made, rescind or vary it in such manner as the court thinks fit for the purpose of enabling him to continue in possession.

(4) If on the operative date the person who was the tenant under the tenancy which has come to an end duly retains possession of the dwelling-house, he shall be deemed to do so as a statutory tenant under a regulated tenancy and as a person who became a statutory tenant on the termination of a protected tenancy under which he was the tenant.

(5) If on the operative date a person duly retains possession of the dwelling-house as being a person who, in the circumstances described in paragraph 1(3)(c) above, would have been the first successor, within the meaning of Schedule 1 to the 1971 Act he shall be deemed to do so as the statutory tenant under a regulated tenancy and as a person who became a statutory tenant by virtue of paragraph 2 or paragraph 3 of that Schedule.

(6) If on the operative date a person duly retains possession of the dwelling-house as being a person who, in the circumstances described in paragraph 1(3)(c) above, would have become the statutory tenant on the death of a first successor, he shall be deemed to do so as the statutory tenant under a regulated tenancy and as a person who became a statutory tenant by virtue of paragraph 6 or paragraph 7 of Schedule 1 to the 1971 Act.

(7) References in the preceding provisions of this paragraph to a person duly retaining possession of a dwelling-house are references to his retaining possession without any order for possession having been made or, where such an order has been made,—

(a) during any period while its operation is postponed or its execution is suspended ; or

(b) after it has been rescinded.

(8) Subject to sub-paragraph (9) below, the tenancy referred to in sub-paragraph (1) above shall be treated as the original contract of tenancy for the purposes of section 12 of the 1971 Act (terms and conditions of statutory tenancies) in relation to a statutory tenancy imposed by any of sub-paragraphs (4) to (6) above.

(9) The court may by order vary all or any of the terms of a statutory tenancy imposed by any of sub-paragraphs (4) to (6) above in any way appearing to the court to be just and equitable (and whether or not in a way authorised by the provisions of sections 22 and 23 of the 1971 Act).

14.—(1) This paragraph applies to—

(a) a tenancy which becomes a protected tenancy by virtue of section 18(1) of this Act ;

(*b*) a statutory tenancy which is deemed to arise under paragraph 13 above ; and

(*c*) a statutory tenancy arising on the termination of any such tenancy as is referred to in head (*a*) or (*b*) of this sub-paragraph.

(2) The contractual rent limit for any contractual period of a tenancy to which this paragraph applies or the limit of rent recoverable for any statutory period of that tenancy shall be determined as follows—

(*a*) where no rent has been registered for the dwelling-house under the previous housing association tenancy, the limit for the purposes of section 19(1) or, subject to sections 22 to 24, of section 21(1) of the 1971 Act, shall be the rent recoverable for the last rental period of that tenancy determined in accordance with section 62(3) of the 1972 Act, until either—

    (i) a rent is registered for the dwelling-house under Part IV of the 1971 Act, or

    (ii) a rent agreement with a tenant having security of tenure is entered into with respect to the dwelling-house ;

(*b*) where a rent has been registered for the dwelling-house under the previous housing association tenancy and the rent recoverable for the last rental period of that tenancy was that registered rent, the limit, for the purposes of section 19(2) or section 21(2) of the 1971 Act, but subject to the provisions of those sections, shall be the registered rent until either—

    (i) a new rent is registered for the dwelling-house under Part IV of the 1971 Act, or

    (ii) the rent registered for the dwelling-house is cancelled in terms of section 44A of the 1971 Act ;

(*c*) where a rent has been registered for the dwelling-house under the previous housing association tenancy and the rent recoverable for the last rental period of that tenancy was determined in accordance with section 63 of the 1972 Act, the limit, for the purposes of section 19(2) or of section 21(2) of the 1971 Act, shall be the rent limit as determined in accordance with the said section 63 of the 1972 Act and, for this purpose, that registration and the provisions of sections 62(4), 63(2) to (4) and 67 of that Act shall subject to the provisions of sub-paragraph (3) of this paragraph, continue to apply or, as the case may require, shall apply to the rent of a dwelling-house under a tenancy to which this paragraph applies as if that tenancy had been a tenancy to which sections 60 to 66 of the 1972 Act applied, until either—

    (i) a new rent is registered for the dwelling-house under Part IV of the 1971 Act, or

    (ii) the rent registered for the dwelling-house is cancelled in terms of section 44A of the 1971 Act ;

(*d*) where a rent has been registered for the dwelling-house
and the Secretary of State has given a direction under
section 64(4) of the 1972 Act, specifying the rent limit for
the dwelling-house under the previous housing association
tenancy, the limit, for the purposes of section 19(2) or of
section 21(2) of the 1971 Act, shall be the rent limit
specified in the direction and, for this purpose, the provisions of sections 62(1), (2), (4) and (5), 64 and 67
of the 1972 Act shall continue to apply or, as the case
may require, shall apply to the rent of a dwelling-house
under a tenancy to which this paragraph applies as if
that tenancy had been a tenancy to which sections 60 to
66 of the 1972 Act applies, until—

  (i) the direction ceases to have effect (whether because
  any condition included in the direction is not complied
  with or because the period for which the direction has
  effect ends), or

  (ii) a new rent is registered for the dwelling-house
  under Part IV of the 1971 Act (whether or not the new
  rent exceeds the rent provisionally registered or the rent
  specified in the direction) ;

and where any of the events specified in the foregoing provisions
of this sub-paragraph take place the said limits shall be determined
in accordance with the provisions of the Rent (Scotland) Acts 1971
and 1972.

(3) In the application, by virtue of sub-paragraph (2)(*c*) of this
paragraph, of subsection (2) of section 63 of the 1972 Act to the
rent of a dwelling-house subject to a statutory tenancy which is
deemed to arise under paragraph 13 above, that subsection shall
be deemed to have continued to apply throughout the period between
the termination of the tenancy referred to in paragraph 13(1)(*a*)
above and the operative date ; but nothing in this sub-paragraph
shall affect the rent recoverable for that dwelling-house at any time
during that period.

(4) In the case where sub-paragraph (2)(*c*) of this paragraph
applies, and the rent limit therein referred to is the rent limit as
determined in accordance with section 63 of the 1972 Act, any
notice of increase under section 21(2)(*b*) of the 1971 Act shall not
increase the rent for any statutory period of a tenancy to which
this paragraph applies above the rent limit as so determined, and
any such notice which purports to increase it further shall have
effect to increase it to that limit but no further.

(5) In the application of section 24(1) of the 1971 Act (increase
of rent for improvements) to a tenancy to which this paragraph
applies, for the reference to 8th December 1965 (the date after
which the improvement must be completed) there shall be substituted a reference to the operative date.

(6) Section 42 of the 1971 Act (determination of fair rent) shall
apply in relation to a tenancy to which this paragraph applies as if

SCH. 3

the reference in subsection (3) of the said section 42 to the tenant under the regulated tenancy included references to the tenant under the previous housing association tenancy.

(7) Any right conferred upon a tenant by section 31 of the 1971 Act, as applied by section 62(5) of the 1972 Act, to recover any amount by deducting it from rent should be exercisable by deducting it from rent for any rental period beginning after the tenancy has become a tenancy to which this paragraph applies to the same extent as the right would have been exercisable if the tenancy had not become such a tenancy.

(8) The fact that the tenancy has become a tenancy to which this paragraph applies should not be taken as affecting any court proceedings which are pending under section 67(3) of the 1972 Act at the time when the tenancy becomes such a tenancy and a decision on which may affect the recoverable rent for any period before that time or the rent under the tenancy to which this paragraph applies so far as that depends upon the recoverable rent before that time.

15. The sheriff shall have jurisdiction, either in the course of any proceedings relating to a dwelling-house or on an application made for the purpose by the landlord or the tenant, to determine any question—

(*a*) as to the application of this Part of this Schedule to any tenancy or as to any matter which is or may become material for determining any such question, or

(*b*) as to the amount of rent recoverable under a tenancy to which paragraph 13 above applies ;

and section 123(1) of the 1971 Act shall apply to any application to the sheriff under this paragraph as it applies to any application under any of the provisions mentioned in section 123(3) of that Act.

16. In this Part of this Schedule—

1971 c. 28.

" the 1971 Act " means the Rent (Scotland) Act 1971 ;

1972 c. 46.

" the 1972 Act " means the Housing (Financial Provisions) (Scotland) Act 1972 ;

" the court " means " the sheriff " ;

" the previous housing association tenancy ", in relation to a tenancy to which paragraph 14 above applies, means the tenancy to which sections 60 to 66 of the 1972 Act applied which either became the protected tenancy by virtue of section 18(1) of this Act or came to an end as mentioned in paragraph 13(1)(*a*) above ; and

other expressions used in this Part of this Schedule which are also used in the Rent (Scotland) Acts 1971 and 1972 shall have the same meanings in this Part as they have in those Acts.

Section 47.

SCHEDULE 4

NOTIFICATION PROCEDURE

1. Where, by virtue of the principal section, a person is under an obligation to notify a local authority of any matter, the obligation shall be fulfilled by furnishing to the local authority a notification in writing containing the information specified in the following provisions of this Schedule.

2.—(1) Every such notification shall contain—

(a) the name and address of the person by whom it is furnished ;

(b) the address of, and any further information necessary to identify, the land to which the notification relates ; and

(c) the estate or interest in that land which the person by whom the notification is furnished has at the time it is furnished.

(2) The reference in sub-paragraph (1)(a) above to a person's address is a reference to his place of abode or his place of business or, in the case of a company, its registered office.

(3) To the extent that it is capable of being so given, the information required by sub-paragraph (1)(b) above may be given by reference to a plan accompanying the notification.

3.—(1) A notification given in compliance with subsection (1) or subsection (2) of the principal section shall also specify—

(a) whether the tenancy concerned is periodic or for a term certain ;

(b) the duration of the period or term ; and

(c) the date on which the tenancy will come to an end (by virtue of the service of the notice to quit or by effluxion of time).

(2) If the landlord considers it appropriate, he may also, in a notification given in compliance with subsection (1) of the principal section, give his reason for serving the notice to quit.

4. A notification given in compliance with subsection (3) of the principal section shall also specify whether, at the time the notification is furnished, the person furnishing it intends to retain any estate or interest in the land specified in the notification in accordance with paragraph 2(1)(b) above and, if he does, the nature of that estate or interest and the land in which he intends that it should subsist.

5. In this Schedule " the principal section " means section 47 of this Act.

SCHEDULE 5

General Improvement Areas

Part I

Sections to be Substituted for Housing Act 1969, Section 28

28.—(1) Where a report with respect to a predominantly residential area within the district of a local authority is submitted to them by a person or persons appearing to the authority to be suitably qualified (whether or not that person is or those persons include an officer of the authority) and it appears to the authority, upon consideration of the report and of any other information in their possession, that living conditions in the area can most appropriately be improved by the improvement of the amenities of the area or dwellings therein or both and that such an improvement may be effected or assisted by the exercise of their powers under this Act, the authority may cause the area to be defined on a map and by a resolution (in this section referred to as a " preliminary resolution ") declare their intention that the area should become a general improvement area in accordance with the provisions of this section.

(2) If a local authority have passed a preliminary resolution with respect to any area, they may, subject to the following provisions of this section, proceed by a further resolution (in this section referred to as a " confirmatory resolution ") to confirm the preliminary resolution and to declare the area to be a general improvement area ; and in relation to a confirmatory resolution or a proposed confirmatory resolution, " the relevant preliminary resolution " means the preliminary resolution confirmed or, as the case may be, proposed to be confirmed, by the confirmatory resolution.

(3) A local authority may not proceed to pass a confirmatory resolution with respect to the area to which the relevant preliminary resolution relates (in the following provisions of this section referred to as " the proposed general improvement area ") unless, within the period of six months beginning with the date on which the relevant preliminary resolution was passed, they notify the Secretary of State in writing of their intention to do so and send to him—

(a) a copy of the relevant preliminary resolution ;

(b) a copy of the map defining the proposed general improvement area ;

(c) a copy of the report referred to in subsection (1) above, the consideration of which led to the passing of the relevant preliminary resolution ; and

(d) such other information and documents as the Secretary of State may direct with respect to general improvement areas generally.

(4) On receipt of a notification or of any other document or information sent to him under subsection (3) above with respect to a proposed general improvement area, the Secretary of State shall send a written acknowledgment to the authority by whom the notification or other document was sent and, if it appears to him to be appropriate to do so, he may, at any time within the appropriate period, send a notification to the authority—

(a) that they may not pass a confirmatory resolution with respect to the proposed general improvement area ; or

(b) that he requires more time to consider the proposed declaration of that area as a general improvement area.

(5) Where the Secretary of State notifies a local authority as mentioned in subsection (4)(b) above, he shall, on completion of his consideration of the matter, send a further notification to the authority—

(a) that they may not pass a confirmatory resolution with respect to the proposed general improvement area ; or

(b) that they are at liberty to proceed to pass such a resolution.

(6) Without prejudice to subsection (3) above, if—

(a) a local authority have notified the Secretary of State as mentioned in that subsection with respect to a proposed general improvement area but are not yet able to proceed to pass a confirmatory resolution with respect to it, and

(b) the Secretary of State, by a direction given with respect to that particular area, so requires,

the local authority shall send to him such other information and documents with respect to that area as may be specified in the direction.

(7) In this section " the appropriate period ", in relation to the proposed general improvement area to which a preliminary resolution relates, means the period—

(a) of 28 days or such longer period as the Secretary of State may by order made by statutory instrument specify for the purposes of this subsection, and

(b) beginning on the date on which the acknowledgment or, as the case may be, the last acknowledgment of any document or information with respect to that proposed general improvement area was sent to the local authority concerned under subsection (4) above.

(8) In any case where a local authority have passed a preliminary resolution and, in accordance with subsection (3) above, have sent to the Secretary of State a notification and other documents relating to the proposed general improvement area, they may not proceed to pass a confirmatory resolution with respect to that area—

(a) before the expiry of the appropriate period, and

(b) if the Secretary of State notifies them as mentioned in subsection (4)(b) above, unless and until they are notified as mentioned in subsection (5)(b) above,

but if the authority are notified as mentioned in subsection (4)(a) or subsection (5)(a) above, no resolution confirming that preliminary resolution may be passed with respect to the proposed general improvement area.

28A. As soon as may be after the passing of a confirmatory resolution, within the meaning of section 28 of this Act, declaring an area to be a general improvement area, the local authority shall—

(a) publish in two or more newspapers circulating in the locality (of which one at least shall, if practicable, be a local newspaper) a notice of the resolution identifying the area and naming a place or places where a copy of the resolution, of the map on which the area is defined and of the report mentioned in section 28(1) of this Act may be inspected at all reasonable times ;

(b) take such further steps as may appear to them best designed to secure that the resolution is brought to the attention of persons residing or owning property within the area and that those persons are informed of the name and address of the person to whom any enquiries and representations concerning any action to be taken in the exercise of the local authority's powers under this Part of this Act should be addressed ; and

(c) send to the Secretary of State a copy of the resolution and a statement of the number of dwellings in the area.

PART II

OTHER AMENDMENTS OF PART II OF HOUSING ACT 1969

1. After section 29 of the Housing Act 1969 there shall be inserted the following sections:—

" Housing action areas excluded from general improvement areas.

29A. A general improvement area shall not be so defined as to include (but may be so defined as to surround) any land which is for the time being comprised in a housing action area declared under Part IV of the Housing Act 1974.

Incorporation of priority neighbourhoods into general improvement areas.

29B.—(1) If a local authority propose, by a preliminary resolution under section 28(1) of this Act, to declare their intention that an area should become a general improvement area and that area consists of or includes land which, immediately prior to the declaration, is comprised in a priority neighbourhood declared under Part VI of the Housing Act 1974, they shall indicate on the map referred to in the said section 28(1) the land which is so comprised (in this section referred to as " priority land ").

(2) If a local authority, by a confirmatory resolution under section 28(2) of this Act, confirm a preliminary resolution and declare as a general improvement area an area which, immediately prior to the declaration, consists of or includes priority land, then, with effect from the date on which the confirmatory resolution is passed, the priority land shall be deemed, as the case may require, either—

(a) to have ceased to be a priority neighbourhood by virtue of a resolution passed on that date under section 39(3) of the Housing Act 1974 (as it applies in relation to such a neighbourhood by virtue of section 54 of that Act) ; or

(b) to have been excluded from the priority neighbourhood concerned by virtue of a resolution passed on that date under section 40(1) of that Act (as it applies in relation to such a neighbourhood by virtue of the said section 54)."

2.—(1) In section 30 of that Act (changes with respect to general improvement area) after subsection (1) there shall be inserted the following subsection:—

" (1A) In any case where, by virtue of a resolution under subsection (1) above, any land is excluded from a general improvement area or, as the case may be, an area ceases to be a general improvement area, the resolution shall not affect the continued operation of this Part of this Act and of any other provision relating to general improvement areas in relation to any works which have been begun before the date on which the resolution takes effect, but, subject thereto, the exclusion or cessation shall apply with respect to the approval before that date of any expenditure in respect of works which have not been begun before that date."

(2) Subsections (2) and (3) of that section (power of local authority by resolution to include land adjoining a general improvement area in that area) shall cease to have effect.

3. In section 32 of that Act (general powers exercisable by local authority in general improvement area) in subsection (5) (nothing in section 32 to enable a local authority to make any grant where such a grant might be made under Part I of that Act) for the words " Part I of this Act " there shall be substituted the words " Part VII of the Housing Act 1974 ".

4.—(1) After subsection (5) of section 37 of that Act (power of Secretary of State by order to alter the maximum of the aggregate expenditure of local authorities which can be approved for the purposes of his contribution in respect of a general improvement area) there shall be inserted the following subsection:—

" (5A) Without prejudice to subsection (5) above, the Secretary of State may direct that, in the case of a particular general improvement area or any description of general improvement area, subsection (4) above shall have effect as if for the amount of £100 mentioned in that subsection, or such other amount as may for the time being be substituted for that amount under subsection (5) above, there were substituted a greater amount."

(2) In subsection (7) of that section (for purposes of contributions by Secretary of State to local authorities towards expenditure in general improvement areas, certain expenditure by housing association to be treated as that of local authority) there shall be inserted before the words " housing association ", in the first and third places where they occur, the word " registered " and at the end of that subsection there shall be added the following subsection:—

" (8) In subsection (7) of this section ' registered housing association ' means a housing association registered in the register of housing associations established under section 13 of the Housing Act 1974 ".

5. In subsection (2) of section 40 of that Act (in relation to land in a general improvement area declared by them, the Greater London Council is to be deemed to be the local authority for certain purposes and certain functions are to be exerciseable by other authorities only after consultation with the Greater London Council) in paragraph

F

SCH. 5 (*a*), for the words " sections 17 to 22 and 74 of this Act ", there shall be substituted the words " section 74 of this Act and section 79 of the Housing Act 1974 ", the words " Part I of this Act other than sections 17 to 22 " shall be omitted and for the words " and Part II of the Act of 1957 " there shall be substituted the words " Part II of the Act of 1957 and Part VII of the Housing Act 1974 other than section 79 " ; and in paragraph (*b*), for the words from " section 19 " to " that Act " there shall be substituted the words " or Part IV of the Housing Act 1964 ".

Sections 58, 68 and 70.

SCHEDULE 6

STANDARD AMENITIES

PART I

LIST OF AMENITIES AND MAXIMUM ELIGIBLE AMOUNTS

Description of Amenity	Maximum eligible amount £
A fixed bath or shower	100
A hot and cold water supply at a fixed bath or shower...	140
A wash-hand basin	50
A hot and cold water supply at a wash-hand basin ...	70
A sink	100
A hot and cold water supply at a sink	90
A water closet	150

PART II

PROVISIONS APPLICABLE TO CERTAIN AMENITIES

1. Except as provided by paragraph 2 below, a fixed bath or shower must be in a bathroom.

2. If it is not reasonably practicable for the fixed bath or shower to be in a bathroom but it is reasonably practicable for it to be provided with a hot and cold water supply it need not be in a bathroom but may be in any part of the dwelling which is not a bedroom.

3. The water closet must, if reasonably practicable, be in, and accessible from within, the dwelling or, where the dwelling is part of a larger building, in such a position in that building as to be readily accessible from the dwelling.

Section 106.

1972 c. 47.

SCHEDULE 7

LODGING-HOUSES AND HOSTELS: AMENDMENTS OF SCHEDULE 1 TO HOUSING FINANCE ACT 1972

1. In Part I (credits and debits) in paragraph 1(1)(*a*) after the word " rents ", in the first place where it occurs, there shall be inserted the words " and charges " and after the word " rents ", in

the second place where it occurs, there shall be inserted the words
" or charges ".

2. In Part II (rate fund contributions to the Housing Revenue Account) after paragraph 9 there shall be added the following paragraph:—

" Charges for lodging-houses and hostels

9A.—(1) If for any year the amount received by the local authority by way of charges in respect of lodging-houses (that is to say, houses not occupied as separate dwellings) and hostels within the account is less than the amount which would have been received if those charges had been equal to the reckonable charges, the local authority shall make a rate fund contribution for that year of an amount equal to the deficiency.

(2) In this paragraph " the reckonable charges ", in relation to any such lodging-houses or hostels, means such charges as, in the opinion of the Secretary of State, are reasonable and appropriate, having regard to all the circumstances.

(3) For the purposes of this paragraph the amount of any charges shall be calculated in such manner as the Secretary of State may from time to time determine, either generally or with respect to a particular authority or authorities or in any particular case.

(4) Before making a general determination under sub-paragraph (3) above, the Secretary of State shall consult with such associations of housing authorities as appear to him to be concerned and with any housing authority with whom consultation appears to him to be desirable."

3. In Part III (limitation of certain subsidies and rate fund contributions) in head E of the Table in paragraph 11, for the words " and 9 " there shall be substituted the words " 9 and 9A ".

SCHEDULE 8

REDUCTION OF RATEABLE VALUE IN CASE OF CERTAIN IMPROVEMENTS

1.—(1) Where the tenant, or any previous tenant, has made or contributed to the cost of an improvement on the premises comprised in the tenancy and the improvement is one to which this Schedule applies, then, if the tenant serves on the landlord a notice in the prescribed form requiring him to agree to a reduction under this Schedule, their rateable value as ascertained for the purposes of subsection (1) of section 1 of this Act shall be reduced by such amount, if any, as may be agreed or determined in accordance with the following provisions of this Schedule.

(2) This Schedule applies to any improvement made by the execution of works amounting to structural alteration, extension or addition.

2.—(1) The amount of any such reduction may at any time be agreed in writing between the landlord and the tenant.

(2) Where, at the expiration of a period of six weeks from the service of a notice under paragraph 1 of this Schedule any of the following matters has not been agreed in writing between the landlord and the tenant, that is to say,—

(*a*) whether the improvement specified in the notice is an improvement to which this Schedule applies ;

(*b*) what works were involved in it ;

(*c*) whether the tenant or a previous tenant under the tenancy has made it or contributed to its cost ; and

(*d*) what proportion his contribution, if any, bears to the whole cost ;

the county court may on the application of the tenant determine that matter, and any such determination shall be final and conclusive.

(3) An application under the last foregoing sub-paragraph must be made within six weeks from the expiration of the period mentioned therein or such longer time as the court may allow.

3.—(1) Where, after the service of a notice under paragraph 1 of this Schedule, it is agreed in writing between the landlord and tenant or determined by the county court—

(*a*) that the improvement specified in the notice is one to which this Schedule applies, and what works were involved in it, and

(*b*) that the tenant or a previous tenant under the tenancy has made it or contributed to its cost, and, in the latter case, what proportion his contribution bears to the whole cost, then if, at the expiration of a period of two weeks from the agreement or determination, it has not been agreed in writing between the landlord and the tenant whether any or what reduction is to be made under this Schedule, and the tenant, within four weeks from the expiration of that period, makes an application to the valuation officer for a certificate under the next following sub-paragraph, that question shall be determined in accordance with the certificate unless the landlord and the tenant otherwise agree in writing.

(2) On any such application the valuation officer shall certify—

(*a*) whether or not the improvement has affected the rateable value on the 1st April, 1973 (as ascertained for the purposes of subsection (1) of section 1 of this Act), of the hereditament of which the premises consist or, as the case may be, in which they are wholly or partly comprised, and

(*b*) if it has, the amount by which the rateable value would have been less if the improvement had not been made.

(3) An application for such a certificate shall be in the prescribed form and shall state the name and address of the landlord, and the Valuation Officer shall send a copy of the certificate to the landlord.

(4) Where the amount of the reduction under this Schedule falls to be determined in accordance with such a certificate, it shall be equal to the amount specified in pursuance of head (*b*) of subparagraph (2) of this paragraph, but proportionately reduced in any case where a proportion only of the cost was contributed by the tenant or a previous tenant under the tenancy.

(5) Where at the time of an application for a certificate under this paragraph a proposal for an alteration in the valuation list relating to the hereditament is pending and the alteration would have effect from a date earlier than the 2nd April, 1973, the Valuation Officer shall not issue the certificate until the proposal is settled.

FORM . . .

Leasehold Reform Act 1967

Notice by Tenant to Landlord of Tenant's Improvements affecting Rateable Value

Date ....

To .... landlord of ....

1 [I] [A previous tenant of the above mentioned premises under the tenancy] [made] [contributed to the cost of] the improvement[s] to the above mentioned premises particulars of which are set out in the First Schedule hereto (Note 1).

2 I hereby require you to agree to a reduction in the rateable value of the premises for the purposes of the Leasehold Reform Act 1967.

3 I propose that the rateable value shall be reduced to £ . . . (Note 2).

4 If you do not agree to this reduction (Note 3), do you agree that—

> (*a*) the improvement[s] [is] [are] [an] improvement[s] made by the execution of works amounting to the structural alteration or extension of the premises or a structural addition thereto ;
>
> (*b*) the works set out in the Second Schedule hereto were involved in the making of the improvement[s] ;
>
> (*c*) [I] [A previous tenant under the tenancy] [made the improvement[s]] [contributed to the cost of the improvement[s]] ;
>
> (*d*) the proportion of the cost borne by me or a previous tenant is . . . .

Signature of tenant ....

First Schedule

Description of Improvement(s)

Second Schedule

Description of Works

Strike out words in square brackets if inapplicable.

Note 1

The improvement must be one made by the execution of works amounting to the structural alteration or extension of the premises or a structural addition thereto, e.g. the erection of a garage in the grounds.

Note 2

If the amount of the reduction is agreed in writing between the landlord and the tenant, the amount of the reduced rateable value as so agreed will be substituted for the purposes of the Leasehold Reform Act 1967, for the rateable value on 1st April, 1973.

Note 3

If the amount of the reduction is not agreed in writing between the landlord and the tenant, the Valuation Officer will have to decide whether the improvement has affected the rateable value of the premises, and if so, what that value would have been had the improvement not been made. The name and address of the Valuation Officer can be obtained from the local authority. Before, however, an application is made to the Valuation Officer, the landlord and the tenant must try to agree in writing on the items mentioned at (*a*) to (*d*) of this paragraph, or such of those items as are material. If at the end of a period of six weeks after the service of this notice any of these items have not been agreed, the tenant may, within a further six weeks or so much longer time as the court may allow, apply to the county court to settle the matter.

If it has either been agreed or determined by the county court that there has been an improvement of the kind described in Note 1 involving specified works, and that the improvement was carried out by the tenant or a previous tenant, or that the tenant or a previous tenant contributed to its cost, and in the latter case what proportion the contribution bears to the whole cost of the works, then, if within a period of two weeks after the agreement or determination of the county court the landlord and the tenant have still not agreed in writing whether any or what reduction is to be made, the tenant has a further four weeks in which to make an application in the statutory form to the Valuation Officer for a certificate as to whether or not the improvement has affected the rateable value, and if so, the amount by which that value would have been less if the improvement had not been made.

FORM . . .

Leasehold Reform Act 1967

Application by Tenant to Valuation Officer for Certificate as to Reduction for the purposes of the Leasehold Reform Act 1967, in the Rateable Value of premises on account of Tenant's Improvements

Date ....

To the Valuation Officer.

1   I am the tenant of   , and my landlord is
        of   .

2   It has been [agreed in writing between me and my landlord] [determined by the county court] that the improvement[s] specified in the First Schedule hereto [is an improvement] [are improvements] to which Schedule Seven to the Leasehold Reform Act 1967 applies, and that I or a previous tenant under the tenancy made the improvement[s] or contributed to [its] [their] cost, and that the works specified in the Second Schedule hereto were involved in the improvement[s].

3   It has not been agreed between me and my landlord whether any or what reduction is to be made under said Schedule Seven in the rateable value of the premises for the purposes of the Leasehold Reform Act 1967, and I hereby make application to you for a certificate under paragraph 3(2) of the said Schedule Seven (Note 4).

Signature of Tenant ....

First Schedule

Description of Improvement(s)

Second Schedule

Description of Works

Strike out words in square brackets if inapplicable.

Note 4

> If the Valuation Officer certifies that the rateable value would have been less but for the improvement by the amounts mentioned in the certificate, the rateable value will be reduced by those amounts for the purposes of the Leasehold Reform Act 1967 except in the case where a proportion only of the cost was contributed by the tenant, in which case the amounts of the reductions will be proportionately reduced accordingly.

SCHEDULE 9   Section 108.

PROVISIONS TO BE SUBSTITUTED FOR SUBSECTION (1) OF SECTION 60 OF THE HOUSING ACT 1957   1957 c. 56.

(1) Where a house is made the subject of a compulsory purchase order under this Part of this Act as being unfit for human habitation

SCH. 9

or is made the subject of a clearance order, then not later than the date or, if there is more than one, the last date on which they served a notice of the effect of the order under paragraph 2(1)(*b*) of Schedule 3 or, as the case may be, paragraph 3(1)(*b*) of Schedule 5 to this Act, the local authority shall—

(*a*) serve on every owner, lessee, mortgagee and occupier of the house, so far as it is reasonably practicable to ascertain those persons, a notification under subsection (1A) of this section with respect to the house ; and

1969 c. 33.

(*b*) in the case of a house falling within subsection (2) of section 67 of the Housing Act 1969 (houses comprising more than one dwelling or occupied partly for the purposes of a dwelling and partly for other purposes), serve on every owner, lessee, mortgagee and occupier of each dwelling in the house, so far as it is reasonably practicable to ascertain those persons, a notification under subsection (1A) of this section with respect to that dwelling.

(1A) The notification referred to in subsection (1) of this section shall be in the prescribed form and shall state that the local authority are satisfied—

(*a*) that, in the case of a house which does not fall within subsection (1) or subsection (2) of section 67 of the Housing Act 1969 (payments in respect of partially well maintained houses or parts of buildings), both the interior and the exterior of the house have been well maintained ; or

(*b*) that, in the case of a house which, apart from section 67 of the Housing Act 1969, would not be treated as well maintained for the purposes of this section, either the exterior or the interior of the house has been well maintained ; or

(*c*) that, in the case of a house falling within subsection (2) of the said section 67, the exterior, as defined in that subsection, has been well maintained ; or

(*d*) that, in the case of any such dwelling as falls within subsection (2) of the said section 67, the interior of the dwelling has been well maintained ; or

(*e*) that no part of the house or dwelling in respect of which a payment might otherwise be made under this section has been well maintained.

(1B) Any notification stating that a local authority are satisfied—

(*a*) as mentioned in paragraph (*b*) of subsection (1A) of this section shall also state the reasons why the local authority are not satisfied that the interior or, as the case may be, the exterior of the house concerned has been well maintained ;

(*b*) as mentioned in paragraph (*e*) of that subsection shall also state the reasons why the local authority are satisfied that no part of the house or dwelling in respect of which a payment might otherwise be made under this section has been well maintained.

(1C) Where a local authority have served a notification under subsection (1A) above, other than a notification falling within paragraph (*e*) thereof, and the house or dwelling to which the notification relates is included in the compulsory purchase order or clearance order as confirmed by the Secretary of State and, in the case of a compulsory purchase order, is so included as being unfit for human habitation, then, according to the nature of the notification, the local authority shall make a payment under this section in respect of the house or dwelling, namely—

(*a*) in the case of a notification falling within paragraph (*a*) of that subsection, a payment of such amount, if any, as is ascertained in accordance with Part I of Schedule 2 to this Act ; and

(*b*) in the case of any other notification, a payment of one-half of the amount, if any, so ascertained.

(1D) If, in the case of a notification to which subsection (1B) of this section applies, any owner, lessee, mortgagee or occupier of the house or dwelling to which the notification relates is aggrieved at the decision of the local authority that they are not satisfied as mentioned in paragraph (*a*) or paragraph (*b*) of that subsection and makes written representation to that effect to the Secretary of State—

(*a*) in the prescribed manner, and

(*b*) within the period within which an objection may be made to the compulsory purchase order or clearance order concerned,

the Secretary of State may, if he thinks it appropriate to do so and (if he considers it necessary) after causing the house or dwelling concerned to be inspected by an officer of his department, give directions for the making by the local authority of a payment (or, as the case may be, a further payment) in respect of the house or dwelling concerned of such amount, if any, as is ascertained in accordance with Part I of Schedule 2 to this Act or, as the case may require, of one-half of that amount.

SCHEDULE 10

Rehabilitation Orders

General

1.—(1) A rehabilitation order may, in addition to applying to any building to which section 114 of this Act applies, be made to apply to—

(*a*) any other building comprised in the clearance area,

(*b*) any land or building which is not comprised in the clearance area but which is subject to the same compulsory purchase order or, as the case may be, has (since being included in the clearance area) been acquired by the authority by agreement under section 43(2) of the Act of 1957, and

(*c*) any land or building to which the provisions of Part III of the Act of 1957 apply by virtue of section 49 of that Act.

G

Sch. 10

(2) Where, by virtue of this Schedule, a local authority are freed from the duty to demolish a house which was included in a clearance area as being unfit for human habitation, the authority shall take such steps as are necessary—

(a) to bring the building up to the full standard, or

(b) where the building is not vested in the authority, to ensure that it is brought up to that standard.

(3) A local authority may, for the purpose of section 114 of this Act, accept undertakings from the owner of a building, or any other person who has or will have an interest in the building, and in particular undertakings concerning the works to be carried out to bring the building up to the full standard, and the time within which the works are to be carried out.

2.—(1) A local authority shall not make a rehabilitation order relating to land subject to a compulsory purchase order unless they are satisfied that, after the rehabilitation order comes into force, they can effectively fulfil their duties under Part III of the Act of 1957 as regards the remaining land subject to the compulsory purchase order.

(2) Subject to sub-paragraph (1) above, a rehabilitation order may be made notwithstanding that the effect of the order in excluding any building from a clearance area is to sever that area into two or more separate and distinct areas, and in any such case the provisions of Part III of the Act of 1957 relating to the effect of a compulsory purchase order when confirmed, and to the proceedings to be taken after confirmation of the order, shall apply as if those areas formed one clearance area.

(3) In exercising his power under this Schedule of confirming a rehabilitation order subject to modifications, the Secretary of State shall have regard to the considerations in sub-paragraphs (1) and (2) above.

3.—(1) This paragraph shall have effect in relation to any land or building in respect of which a local authority have made a rehabilitation order which has been confirmed in accordance with the provisions of this Schedule ; and in this Schedule " relevant date " means the date on which the rehabilitation order was confirmed or, as the case may be, on which confirmation was refused.

(2) If, at the relevant date (in the case of any land or building subject to a compulsory purchase order)—

(a) no interest in the land or building has, after the date on which the compulsory purchase order concerned was made, vested in the authority, and

1965 c. 56.

(b) no notice to treat has been served by the authority under section 5 of the Compulsory Purchase Act 1965, in respect of any interest in the land or building,

the compulsory purchase order shall cease to have effect and, where applicable, the building shall cease to be comprised in a clearance area.

(3) Where sub-paragraph (2) above does not apply, the authority shall, where applicable, cease to be subject to the duty, imposed by

Part III of the Act of 1957, to demolish the building, and in relation   SCH. 10
to any interest in the land or building which at the relevant date
has not vested in the authority (being land or a building subject
to a compulsory purchase order) the compulsory purchase order
shall have effect as if—

(*a*) in the case of a house, it had been made and confirmed
under Part V of the Act of 1957, and

(*b*) in any other case, it had been made and confirmed under
Part VI of the Act of 1971.

(4) If the land or building, or any interest therein, was vested
in the authority at the relevant date it shall be treated—

(*a*) in the case of a house, as appropriated to the purposes of
Part V of the Act of 1957, and

(*b*) in any other case, as appropriated to the purposes of Part VI
of the Act of 1971.

(5) Where a local authority have made a rehabilitation order they
shall not—

(*a*) serve notice to treat under section 5 of the Compulsory 1965 c. 56.
Purchase Act 1965 in respect of any land or building
subject to the relevant compulsory purchase order, or

(*b*) demolish any such building,

until after the relevant date.

(6) Where the owner of any building in respect of which a
rehabilitation order could be made applies to the local authority
concerned for such an order to be made in respect of the building,
and the authority refuse to make the order, they shall give their
reasons for so refusing in writing to the owner.

(7) Where a rehabilitation order is confirmed in accordance with
this Schedule and the effect of the order is to exclude from a
clearance area any land adjoining a general improvement area in
England and Wales (within the meaning of Part II of the Housing 1969 c. 33.
Act 1969), that land shall, unless the Secretary of State otherwise
directs, be included in the general improvement area.

Procedure for making and confirming rehabilitation orders

4. A rehabilitation order shall be made in the prescribed form
and shall describe, by reference to a map—

(*a*) the land and buildings to which it applies,

(*b*) the boundaries of the clearance area to which it applies,

(*c*) the boundaries of the land comprised in any relevant compulsory purchase order, and

(*d*) the parts (if any) of the land to which the rehabilitation
order applies which will remain subject to a compulsory
purchase order.

5.—(1) Before submitting the rehabilitation order to the Secretary
of State the local authority shall—

(*a*) publish in one or more newspapers circulating within their
district a notice in the prescribed form stating that an order

has been made and describing the land and buildings to which it applies and naming a place where a copy of the order and its accompanying map may be seen at all reasonable hours, and

(b) serve—

(i) on every person on whom notice of the making of any relevant compulsory purchase order was served, or

(ii) on the person from whom the land or building was purchased by agreement, as the case may be, or

(iii) on their successors in title, where appropriate,

a notice in the prescribed form stating the effect of the rehabilitation order and that it is about to be submitted to the Secretary of State for confirmation and specifying the time within, and the manner in which, objections thereto can be made.

(2) A notice which is to be served on any person under this paragraph shall be served in accordance with the provisions of section 169 of the Act of 1957; and any notice served in accordance with this paragraph shall be accompanied by a statement of the grounds on which the authority are seeking confirmation of the rehabilitation order.

6.—(1) If no objection is duly made by any of the persons on whom notices are required to be served in accordance with paragraph 5 above, or if all objections so made are withdrawn, then, subject to the provisions of this Schedule, the Secretary of State may if he thinks fit confirm the order with or without modifications.

(2) If any objection duly made is not withdrawn, the Secretary of State shall, before confirming the order, either cause a public local inquiry to be held or afford to a person by whom an objection has been duly made and not withdrawn an opportunity of appearing before and being heard by a person appointed by the Secretary of State for the purpose.

(3) After considering any objection not withdrawn and the report of the person who held the inquiry or of the person appointed under sub-paragraph (2) above, the Secretary of State may, subject to the provisions of this Schedule, confirm the order with or without modifications.

(4) Notwithstanding anything in the provisions of this paragraph, the Secretary of State may require any person who has made an objection to state in writing the grounds thereof and may disregard the objection for the purposes of this paragraph if he is satisfied that the objection relates exclusively to matters which can be dealt with by the tribunal by whom the compensation is to be assessed.

(5) The Secretary of State may modify a rehabilitation order by extending its application to any other land or building to which the order could have been made to apply by the authority making it, but shall not do so unless—

(a) he is satisfied that any unfit house which he proposes to include in the rehabilitation order should be improved to the full standard, instead of being demolished, (*b*) he is satisfied, in respect of any land or building which he proposes to include in the rehabilitation order (being land or a building which is not comprised in the clearance area concerned) that its acquisition by the local authority is unnecessary, and

(*c*) he has served on every owner, lessee and occupier (except tenants for a month or a lesser period than a month) and, so far as it is reasonably practicable to ascertain such persons, on every mortgagee, of the land or building a notice in the prescribed form stating the effect of his proposals and has afforded them an opportunity to make their views known.

7.—(1) The provisions of Schedule 4 to the Act of 1957 shall have effect, subject to the necessary modifications, in relation to the validity and date of operation of a rehabilitation order as they have effect in relation to the validity and date of operation of a compulsory purchase order made under section 43 of that Act.

(2) The modifications subject to which the provisions of Schedule 4 are to have effect by virtue of this paragraph shall include the addition, at the end of paragraph 1, of the words—

" and every person on whom the Secretary of State served notice under paragraph 6(5)(*c*) of Schedule 10 to the Housing Act 1974."

8.—(1) In this Schedule " prescribed " means prescribed by order made by the Secretary of State for the purposes of this Schedule ; and " full standard " has the same meaning as in section 114(3) of this Act.

(2) An order under this paragraph shall be contained in a statutory instrument which shall be subject to annulment in pursuance of a resolution of either House of Parliament.

(3) In the application of this Schedule to Scotland the words " as being unfit for human habitation " shall be omitted.

SCHEDULE 11

OPTION MORTGAGES : AMENDMENTS OF PART II OF
HOUSING SUBSIDIES ACT 1967

1.—(1) In section 24 (right to opt for subsidy for certain loans in connection with dwellings) at the end of subsection (1) there shall be added the words " and

(*d*) the loan is not one to which a direction under subsection (3A) of this section for the time being applies ".

(2) In paragraph (*c*) of subsection (3) of that section (declaration by borrower as to use of land, etc.),—

(*a*) for the words " and the land " there shall be substituted the words " that the amount of the loan will not exceed the appropriate limit determined under section 24A of this Act and that, before the expiry of the period of 12 months beginning on the date referred to in paragraph (*b*) of this subsection, the land " ; and

G 3

(*b*) for the words from " being the borrower " to " one of them) ", in the second place where those words occur, there shall be substituted the words " or persons in such circumstances that the residence condition in section 24B of this Act is fulfilled " ;

and at the end of that paragraph there shall be added the words " and

(*d*) in a case where the specified person or persons named in a declaration under paragraph (*c*) above is, are or include the borrower or all or any of the joint borrowers, that, if the borrower or, in the case of joint borrowers, any of them is married and is not treated for income tax purposes as living apart from his spouse, the borrower or, as the case may be, each of those joint borrowers and (in either case) his spouse have signed and delivered to the lender a declaration either that there is no existing loan—

(i) the whole or any part of the interest on which is payable (whether alone or jointly with any other person) by the spouse, and

(ii) in respect of which an option notice for the time being has effect or in respect of which a claim for relief has been or is to be made under section 75 of the Finance Act 1972 (relief for payment of interest), and

(iii) which relates to, or was made with a view to the repayment of a previous loan which related to, land used wholly or mainly for the purposes of a dwelling (not being the dwelling to which the declaration under paragraph (*c*) above relates) which is that spouse's only or main residence or a caravan so used,

or that such a loan does exist but the spouse intends that, within the period of 12 months beginning on the date referred to in paragraph (*b*) above, the dwelling referred to in sub-paragraph (iii) above will cease to be the spouse's only or main residence ".

(3) At the end of subsection (3) of that section there shall be added the following paragraphs—

" (viii) the taking effect of a direction under subsection (3A) of this section with respect to the loan ;

(ix) if subsection (5) of section 24B of this Act applies, the expiry of the period of one month beginning with the date on which the lender receives a notification (or, if he receives more than one notification, the first notification) under that subsection or, if he does not receive such a notification, the date on which the lender first becomes aware that the residence condition is not fulfilled as mentioned in that subsection ;

(x) if subsection (6) of section 24B of this Act applies and the lender receives a notification in accordance with that subsection, the expiry of the period of twelve months beginning with the date specified in that notification, and if that subsection applies but the lender does not receive such a

notification, the expiry of the period of one month beginning
with the date on which the lender first becomes aware that
the residence condition is not fulfilled as mentioned in that
subsection ;

(xi) if the lender becomes aware that a declaration under paragraph (c) or paragraph (d) of this subsection is false in a
material particular, the expiry of the period of one month
beginning with the date on which the lender first becomes so
aware."

(4) After subsection (3) of that section there shall be inserted
the following subsections :—

" (3A) The Secretary of State may, after consultation with
such qualifying lenders or bodies representative of qualifying
lenders of any description as may appear to him appropriate,
direct that subsidy in accordance with this Part of this Act
shall not be available in the case of any loan to which the direction applies, being a loan falling within subsection (3B) below.

(3B) A loan is one in respect of which a direction may be
made under subsection (3A) above if the terms of the repayment
contract (as originally entered into or as subsequently varied)
are such that the amount due from the borrower for any period
by way of interest under the repayment contract is less than
the total of the interest which accrues in respect of that period,
so that part of the interest is treated as an addition to the
capital outstanding or is otherwise carried forward.

(3C) In considering whether to make a direction under subsection (3A) above with respect to any loan, the Secretary of
State shall follow such principles, and take account of such
matters, as he may from time to time decide after the like
consultation as is specified in that subsection.

(3D) A direction under subsection (3A) above may be made
with respect to a particular loan or loans or any description
of loans, and, in so far as the direction relates to a loan in
respect of which an option notice has already been given,
the direction shall specify a date (being a date after the
giving of the direction) with effect from which the direction
is to take effect with respect to any such loan.

(3E) Any provision of subsection (3A) or subsection (3C)
above which imposes on the Secretary of State a duty to consult
any persons or bodies appearing to him to be appropriate shall
not be taken as implying that further consultation is required by
the provision where the Secretary of State is satisfied that there
was consultation before the coming into force of that subsection
and in his opinion that consultation was sufficient for the
purpose ".

(5) In subsection (4) of that section for the words from " conditions
specified in subsection (3)(c) " to the end of the subsection there
shall be substituted the words " conditions specified in paragraphs (c)
and (d) of subsection (3) of this section there are satisfied such other
conditions as may be specified in the direction ; and where any such
direction has effect in relation to an option notice, the provisions of

SCH. 11   subsections (5) and (6) of section 24B of this Act shall apply as if the reference therein to the residence condition were a reference to such a condition as may be so specified ".

(6) After subsection (5) of that section there shall be inserted the following subsection:—

" (5A) In the case of an option notice to which a direction under subsection (5) of this section applies, paragraph (c) of subsection (3) of this section shall have effect as if for the words from " before the expiry " to " to be occupied " there were substituted the words " the land in question is being and will continue to be used wholly or partly for the purposes of a dwelling occupied ".

2. After section 24 there shall be inserted the following sections:—

"The appropriate limit for loans.   24A.—(1) In relation to a loan in respect of which an option notice has been signed (in this section referred to as " the relevant loan ") the appropriate limit referred to in paragraph (c) of subsection (3) of section 24 of this Act is £25,000 reduced by the amount or, as the case may require, the aggregate amount outstanding by way of capital on the date referred to in paragraph (b) of that subsection in respect of every loan—

(a) the whole or any part of the interest on which is payable (whether alone or jointly with any other person) by the borrower who signed the declaration under the said paragraph (c) or, in the case of joint borrowers, by any of the borrowers who signed that declaration or, where that borrower or any of those joint borrowers is married and is not treated for income tax purposes as living apart from his spouse, that spouse ; and

(b) which falls to be taken into account by virtue of subsection (2) below and is not to be disregarded by virtue of subsection (4) below.

(2) Subject to subsections (3) and (4) below, a loan falls to be taken into account under subsection (1) above if—

(a) it is a loan in respect of which an option notice for the time being has effect ; or

(b) it is a loan to which Part I of Schedule 9 to the Finance Act 1972 (loans for purchase or improvement of land on which interest is eligible for relief in full) for the time being applies (either in respect of the whole loan or subject to any limit of amount), and the land or caravan referred to in that Part is not used in such circumstances that it falls within paragraph 4(1)(b) of Schedule 1 to the Finance Act 1974 (commercial lettings).

(3) Without prejudice to section 34(2) of this Act, the reference in subsection (2)(b) above to Schedule 9 to the

Finance Act 1972 is a reference to that Schedule either
as amended by Schedule 1 to the Finance Act 1974
(restrictions on relief for interest) or (if interest on the
loan is excepted from section 19(3) of that Act) as originally enacted ; and in the case of a loan to which the said
Schedule 9 applies as originally enacted, the reference in
subsection (2)(*b*) above to the use of land or a caravan in
circumstances falling within paragraph 4(1)(*b*) of the said
Schedule 1 shall be construed as a reference to use which
would fall within that paragraph if that Schedule applied
in relation to interest on the loan in question.

(4) Notwithstanding anything in subsection (2) above,
a loan (in this subsection referred to as a " previous
loan ") which falls within paragraph (*a*) or paragraph (*b*)
of that subsection shall be disregarded in determining
the appropriate limit in relation to the relevant loan
if—

    (*a*) the relevant loan is made with a view to the
repayment by means of the relevant loan of the
amount outstanding on the previous loan ; or

    (*b*) the previous loan is an existing loan which is
specified in a declaration made for the purpose
of satisfying, in relation to the relevant loan,
the condition in section 24(3)(*d*) of this Act ;
or

    (*c*) the previous loan was in connection with the
only or main residence of a person who is,
or is a qualifying relative of, the borrower or
any of the joint borrowers under the relevant
loan and the relevant loan is made for or in
connection with any one or more of the purposes specified in section 24(1)(*b*) of this Act in
such circumstances that the dwelling referred to
in that section is to be used instead as that
person's only or main residence.

(5) In any case where the option notice in respect
of the relevant loan is one to which a direction under
section 24(5) of this Act applies, the preceding provisions of this section shall have effect subject to such
modifications as may be prescribed.

The
residence
condition.

24B.—(1) For the purposes of this Part of this Act,
the residence condition is fulfilled with respect to a
dwelling to which a declaration under section 24(3)(*c*) of
this Act relates if and so long as—

    (*a*) the dwelling is occupied wholly or partly as his
only or main residence by the borrower him-
self or, in the case of joint borrowers, by each
of them ; or

    (*b*) at any time when the borrower or any joint
borrower does not occupy the dwelling as men-

tioned in paragraph (*a*) above, the dwelling is so occupied by a qualifying relative of his.

(2) For the purposes of this Part of this Act a person is a qualifying relative of a borrower (or a joint borrower) if he or she is—

(*a*) the borrower's spouse and is living apart from the borrower ;

(*b*) the borrower's former spouse ;

(*c*) the mother of either the borrower or his spouse and is widowed or living apart from her husband or, in consequence of dissolution or annulment of marriage, is a single woman ; or

(*d*) such a relative of the borrower or his spouse as is specified in subsection (3) below and is either over the age of 65 or incapacitated by infirmity from maintaining himself, in whole or in part.

(3) The relatives referred to in subsection (2)(*d*) above are—

(*a*) a parent or grandparent ;

(*b*) a brother or sister who is over the age of 16 ; and

(*c*) a child or grandchild (in either case whether legitimate, adopted or illegitimate) who is over the age of 16.

(4) A person shall be treated for the purposes of this section as living apart from his or her spouse if he or she would be so treated for income tax purposes.

(5) If, after the delivery of a declaration under paragraph (*c*) of subsection (3) of section 24 of this Act (other than a declaration delivered in respect of an option notice to which a direction under subsection (5) of that section applies), the residence condition is not, within the period of 12 months specified in that paragraph, fulfilled with respect to the dwelling concerned, then, within the period of one month beginning on the day following the expiry of that period of 12 months, the borrower or, in the case of joint borrowers, each of them shall notify the lender in writing to that effect.

(6) If, at any time after—

(*a*) the delivery of a declaration under paragraph (*c*) of section 24(3) of this Act, and

(*b*) the residence condition has been fulfilled with respect to the dwelling concerned,

the residence condition ceases to be so fulfilled, then, within the period of one month beginning on the date on which that condition first ceased to be so fulfilled, the borrower or, in the case of joint borrowers, each of them shall notify the lender in writing of the date on which

the condition ceased, and of the fact that it has ceased,   Sᴄʜ. 11
to be so fulfilled.

(7) Any person who knowingly fails to notify the
lender as required by subsection (5) or subsection (6)
above shall, on conviction on indictment, be liable to
imprisonment for a term not exceeding 2 years ".

3.—(1) In section 26 (extension of right to opt for subsidy to
certain other cases) in subsection (2)(*b*) after the words " this section "
there shall be inserted the words " and to such modifications as may
be prescribed ".

(2) After subsection (4) of that section there shall be inserted the
following subsection:—

" (4A) In relation to a case where a self-build society, within
the meaning of Part I of the Housing Act 1974, which is for the
time being approved for the purposes of section 341A of the
Income and Corporation Taxes Act 1970 borrows or has
borrowed from a qualifying lender on the security of a freehold
or leasehold estate of that society in Great Britain, the Secretary
of State shall by regulations provide that this Part of this Act
shall have effect with such adaptations and modifications of the
provisions thereof (other than section 24(2)(*b*) and (*c*)), appearing
to him to be appropriate or expedient, and subject to such special
conditions appearing to him to be necessary or expedient, as
may be prescribed by the regulations ; and in relation to such a
society, the said section 24(2)(*b*) shall have effect as if—

    (*a*) the reference therein to the Income Tax Acts included a
       reference to the Corporation Tax Acts ; and

    (*b*) in sub-paragraph (ii) thereof, for the reference to income
       tax there were substituted a reference to corporation
       tax."

4. In subsection (1) of section 27 (qualifying lenders) at the end of
paragraph (*e*) there shall be inserted the following paragraph:—

    " (*f*) the Housing Corporation " ;

and the words from " and for the purposes " to the end of the subsection shall be omitted.

5.—(1) In paragraph (*a*) of subsection (1) of section 28 (calculation of the aggregate amount which, apart from Part II of the
Housing Subsidies Act 1967, would have become due from the 1967 c. 29.
borrower) after the words " the aggregate sum which " there shall
be inserted the words " taking account of subsection (1A) of this
section but otherwise ".

(2) After subsection (1) of that section there shall be inserted
the following subsection:—

" (1A) In any case where, under the terms of a repayment
contract (as originally entered into or as subsequently varied)
the amount due from the borrower for any period by way
of interest under the repayment contract is less than the total
of the interest which accrues in respect of that period so that
part of the interest is treated as an addition to the capital

SCH. 11

outstanding or is otherwise carried forward then, for the purpose of determining the aggregate amount of the subsidy in respect of the loan, there shall be treated as becoming due from the borrower in any period the whole of the interest which accrues in that period."

6. After section 28 there shall be inserted the following section:—

"Recovery of subsidy in certain cases.

28A.—(1) If a declaration under paragraph (c) or paragraph (d) of subsection (3) of section 24 of this Act is false in a material particular, the Secretary of State may recover from the borrower or, as the case may be, jointly and severally from the borrowers an amount equal to the total of the payments received by the lender by virtue of subsection (2)(a)(ii) of that section in relation to the loan in respect of which the declaration was made.

(2) If, in a case where subsection (5) of section 24B of this Act applies, the lender does not receive a notification under that subsection, the Secretary of State may recover from the borrower or, as the case may be, jointly and severally from the borrowers, an amount equal to the total of the payments received by the lender as mentioned in subsection (1) above after the expiry of the period of 2 months beginning on the day following the expiry of the period of 12 months specified in the said subsection (5).

(3) If, in a case where subsection (6) of section 24B of this Act applies, the lender does not receive a notification under that subsection, the Secretary of State may recover from the borrower or, as the case may be, jointly and severally from the borrowers, an amount equal to the total of the payments received by the lender as mentioned in subsection (1) above after the expiry of the period of 2 months beginning with the date on which the condition specified in the said subsection (6) first ceased to be fulfilled."

7. At the end of section 32(1) (interpretation) there shall be inserted the following definition:—

" 'prescribed' means prescribed by regulations made by statutory instrument by the Secretary of State ; and a statutory instrument containing any such regulations shall be subject to annulment in pursuance of a resolution of either House of Parliament ".

Section 124.

1972 c. 47.

SCHEDULE 12

SERVICE CHARGES: AMENDMENTS OF SECTIONS 90 AND 91 OF HOUSING FINANCE ACT 1972

1. After section 90(1) there shall be inserted:—

" (1A) A qualified accountant shall have a right of access to such accounts, receipts and other documents, and shall be entitled to require from the landlord such information and explanation,

as appear to him to be necessary to enable him to decide
whether to give a certificate under subsection (1) above."

2. After section 90(10) there shall be inserted: —

" (10A) Where an offence under subsection (10) above which
has been committed by a body corporate is proved to have been
committed with the consent or connivance of, or to be attributable to any neglect on the part of, a director, manager, secretary
or other similar officer of the body corporate, or any person who
was purporting to act in any such capacity, he, as well as the
body corporate, shall be guilty of that offence and be liable to
be proceeded against and punished accordingly.

(10B) Where the affairs of a body corporate are managed by
its members, subsection (10A) above shall apply in relation to
the acts and defaults of a member in connection with his functions of management as if he were a director of the body
corporate."

3. In section 90(12): —

(a) in the definition of " landlord ", after that word there shall
be inserted " includes any person who has a right to
enforce payment of a service charge, and also " ;

(b) in the definition of " qualified accountant ", after " excludes "
there shall be inserted " any person mentioned in subsection
(12A) below, and also ".

4. After section 90(12) there shall be inserted: —

" (12A) None of the following persons is a qualified
accountant—

(a) an officer or employee of the landlord or, where the
landlord is a company, of a company which is the
landlord's holding company or subsidiary, or a subsidiary of the landlord's holding company ;

(b) a person who is a partner or employee of any such
officer or employee ;

and in this subsection " holding company " and " subsidiary "
have the meanings given to them by section 154 of the
Companies Act 1948."

5. Paragraph 2 above shall not have effect in relation to an offence
committed before the coming into operation of section 124 of this
Act and paragraphs 3 and 4 above shall not have effect in relation
to an accounting year (within the meaning of section 90(12) of the
Housing Finance Act 1972) ending before 1st August 1974.   1972 c. 47.

SCHEDULE 13

MINOR AND CONSEQUENTIAL AMENDMENTS

The Sheriff Courts (Scotland) Act 1907   1907 c. 51.

1. In the Sheriff Courts (Scotland) Act 1907, after section 38
there shall be inserted the following section—

SCH. 13

"Notice of termination in respect of dwelling-houses.

38A. Any notice of termination of tenancy or notice of removal given under section 37 or 38 above in respect of a dwelling-house, on or after the date of the coming into operation of section 123 of the Housing Act 1974, shall be in writing and shall contain such information as may be prescribed by virtue of section 131 of the Rent (Scotland) Act 1971, and Rule 112 of Schedule 1 to this Act shall no longer apply to any such notice under section 37 above."

1952 c. 55.

The Magistrates' Courts Act 1952

2. In Schedule 1 to the Magistrates' Courts Act 1952 (indictable offences by adults which may be dealt with summarily with consent of accused) the following paragraph shall be inserted after paragraph 14:—

"14A. Offences under section 24B(7) of the Housing Subsidies Act 1967".

1957 c. 56.

The Housing Act 1957

3. In section 70 of the Housing Act 1957 (provisions as to re-development, improvement or structural alteration by owners not to have effect in certain cases) in subsection (1) for the words from " clearance order " to " so confirmed " there shall be substituted the words " compulsory purchase order confirmed by the Minister ".

4. In section 105 of that Act (local authority's powers of dealing with land acquired for provision of housing accommodation) after subsection (4) there shall be inserted the following subsection:—

" (4A) Where a local authority acquire a house or building which may be made suitable as a house (or an estate or interest therein) and, in the case of such a building, themselves carry out any necessary work as mentioned in the last foregoing subsection, they shall, as soon as practicable after the acquisition or, as the case may be, after the completion of the necessary work, secure that the house or building is used as housing accommodation."

5. Section 121 of that Act (arrangements with housing associations for improvement of housing) shall cease to have effect, but without prejudice to the continuation of any arrangements made before the day appointed for the coming into operation of this paragraph.

6. In section 189(1) of that Act, in the definition of " housing association " after the words " those of " there shall be inserted the word " providing " and after the word " houses " there shall be inserted the words " or hostels, as defined in section 129(1) of the Housing Act 1974 ".

7. In Schedule 2 to that Act (payments in respect of unfit houses) in the proviso to paragraph 4(4) for the words " demolition or closing order or clearance order " there shall be substituted the words " or demolition or closing order " and in paragraph 5(1)(*b*) for the words " closing order or clearance order " there shall be substituted the words " or closing order ".

The Land Compensation Act 1961

8.—(1) In Schedule 2 to the Land Compensation Act 1961 (acquisi- tion of houses as being unfit for human habitation) in sub-paragraph (2) of paragraph 2 (application of certain provisions of Housing Act 1957) for the words " sections sixty and sixty-one of that Act, and " there shall be substituted the words " section 61 of that Act, and Part II of " and for the words " that Schedule " there shall be substituted the words " that Part of that Schedule ".

(2) After the said sub-paragraph (2) there shall be inserted the following sub-paragraphs:—

" (2A) Where the local authority make and submit an order under sub-paragraph (2) of this paragraph in relation to a house, the provisions of section 60 of the Act of 1957 and Part I of Schedule 2 thereto shall apply, subject to sub-paragraph (2B) of this paragraph, as if—

(a) the house had been made the subject of a compulsory purchase order under Part III of that Act as being unfit for human habitation ; and

(b) any reference in those provisions to a local authority, other than a provision requiring, or enabling the Secretary of State to direct, a local authority to make a payment, were a reference to the appropriate local authority.

(2B) In the application of section 60 of the Act of 1957 by virtue of sub-paragraph (2A) of this paragraph—

(a) for the reference in subsection (1) to a notice under paragraph 2(1)(b) of Schedule 3 or, as the case may be, paragraph 3(1)(b) of Schedule 5 to that Act there shall be substituted a reference to a notice under sub-paragraph (3) of this paragraph ;

(b) in so far as any provision of subsection (1C) or subsection (1D) of that section requires, or enables the Secretary of State to direct, a local authority to make a payment, the reference to a local authority shall be construed as a reference to the acquiring authority ;

(c) the reference in subsection (1C) of that section to the compulsory purchase order being confirmed by the Secretary of State shall be construed as a reference to the condition in either paragraph (a) or paragraph (b) of sub-paragraph (2) of this paragraph being fulfilled ; and

(d) for the reference in subsection (1D)(b) of that section to the compulsory purchase order or clearance order concerned there shall be substituted a reference to the order under sub-paragraph (2) of this paragraph."

(3) The amendments effected by sub-paragraphs (1) and (2) above shall have effect with respect to orders under paragraph 2(2) of Schedule 2 to the Land Compensation Act 1961 made on or after the day on which section 108 of this Act comes into operation.

The Landlord and Tenant Act 1962

9. At the end of section 6 of the Landlord and Tenant Act 1962 (interpretation) there shall be added the following subsection:—

" (2) Any reference in section 2(1)(*a*) or section 3(1) of this Act to a person's address is a reference to his place of abode or his place of business or, in the case of a company, its registered office."

The Housing Act 1964

10.—(1) In section 5(1) of the Housing Act 1964 (schemes for Corporation to provide housing accommodation in place of housing society) after the words " housing society ", in the first place where they occur, there shall be inserted the words " which is not a registered housing association, within the meaning of the Housing Act 1974, and to which a loan has been made under section 2 of this Act before the operative date ".

(2) In section 8 of that Act (building society advances to housing societies to which Corporation have made loans) for the words " housing society " or " housing societies ", in each place where they occur, there shall be substituted respectively the words " housing association " or " housing associations ".

(3) In section 10(4) of that Act (account to be prepared of certain sums advanced to and repaid by the Corporation) after the words " this Act " there shall be inserted the words " or Part I of the Housing Act 1974 ".

(4) In subsection (1) of section 11 of that Act (power of Corporation to authorise Scottish Special Housing Association to act in Scotland as Corporation's agents for certain purposes) the words " section 3 " and " section 6 " shall be omitted and at the end of that subsection there shall be added the words " or under section 3(1), section 4 or section 5 of the Housing Act 1974 ".

(5) Section 72 of that Act (restriction on recovery of possession after making of compulsory purchase order) shall be amended as follows:—

(*a*) in subsection (1) in the definition of " the relevant period " the words " of twelve months ", in each case where they occur, shall be omitted and after the words " making of the said order " there shall be inserted the words " and ending on the third anniversary of the date on which the order becomes operative " ;

(*b*) in subsection (2) in paragraph (*a*) for the words from " not exceeding " to " said compulsory purchase order " there shall be substituted the words " not extending beyond the end of the period of three years beginning on the relevant date " and in paragraph (*b*) for the words " twelve months " there shall be substituted the words " three years " ; and

(*c*) after subsection (2) there shall be inserted the following subsection:—

" (2A) for the purposes of subsection (2) above " the relevant date " means—

(*a*) if the compulsory purchase order concerned has
become operative before the date on which the
court exercises its power under that subsection,
the date on which the order became operative ;
and

(*b*) in any other case the date on which the court
exercises or, as the case may be, exercised its
power under paragraph (*a*) of that subsection in
relation to the order for possession in question."

The Housing (Slum Clearance Compensation) Act 1965 1965 c. 81.

11. In section 2 of the Housing (Slum Clearance Compensation)
Act 1965 (money borrowed by owner-occupier to purchase unfit
house or on security of an unfit house) in subsection (2) for the
words " closing order or clearance order " there shall be substituted
the words " or closing order ".

The Housing (Scotland) Act 1966 1966 c. 49.

12. In section 135 of the Housing (Scotland) Act 1966, the same
amendments shall be made as are set out in paragraph 10(5) above
with the substitution for the reference to an order for possession of
a reference to a decree of removing or warrant of ejection or other
like order.

13. Sections 153 to 155 and 159 of the Housing (Scotland) Act
1966 shall cease to have effect.

14. In section 175 of that Act (compulsory purchase of land by
Scottish Special Housing Association) in subsection (2) (power of
Association to acquire land compulsorily for selling it or leasing
it to a housing society) for the words from " section 4(1) of the
Housing Act 1964 " to the end of the subsection there shall be
substituted the words " section 3(5) of the Housing Act 1974, acquire
land compulsorily " and in subsection (3) (application of Acquisition
of Land (Authorisation Procedure) (Scotland) Act 1947) after the
word " and ", in the second place where it occurs, there shall be
inserted the words " in relation to the exercise of the Association's
powers under subsection (1) of this section ".

15. In section 208(1) of that Act, in the definition of " housing
association " after the words " those of " there shall be inserted
the word " providing " and after the words " housing accommodation "
there shall be inserted the words " including hostels, as defined in
section 21(4) of the Housing (Financial Provisions) (Scotland) Act 1968 c. 31.
1968 ".

The Rent Act 1968 1968 c. 23.

16. In section 5(6) of the Rent Act 1968 (conditions for a housing
association tenancy to be excluded from that Act) after paragraph
(*cc*) there shall be inserted the following paragraph : —

" (*ccc*) that the dwelling was comprised in a housing project
approved for the purposes of section 29 of the Housing
Act 1974 ".

Sch. 13   17.—(1) In section 57 of that Act (grant-aided improvements, etc.) in paragraph (*a*) of subsection (1) (amount of certain grants to be disregarded in increasing rent limit) after the words " (improvement grants and standard grants) " there shall be inserted the words " section 61 or section 65 of the Housing Act 1974 (improvement grants and intermediate grants) ".

(2) In subsection (2) of that section (amount of certain grants obtainable but not obtained to be disregarded in increasing rent limit) after the words " the Housing Act 1964 " there shall be inserted the words " or an improvement notice within the meaning of Part VIII of the Housing Act 1974 ", for the words " that Part of that Act " there shall be substituted the words " either of those Parts ", after the words " the Housing Act 1969 " there shall be inserted the words " or an intermediate grant under section 65 of the Housing Act 1974 " and after the words " the standard grant " there shall be inserted the words " or intermediate grant ".

18.—(1) Sections 16 and 17 of the Housing (Financial Provisions) (Scotland) Act 1968 shall cease to have effect.

(2) In section 18(1) of that Act (local authority to furnish certain particulars to Secretary of State for purpose of determining the amount of certain Exchequer contributions) the words from " or any such " to " section 16 of this Act " and the words " or arrangements " shall be omitted.

1957 c. 56.   19. In section 69 of the Housing Act 1969 (repayment of certain payments made under the Housing Act 1957 or that Act), for the words " closing order or clearance order " there shall be substituted the words " or closing order ".

20.—(1) In section 75 of that Act (power of local authority to carry out works of improvement by agreement with and at expense of owner, etc.) in subsection (1) for the words " Part I of this Act ", in the first place where they occur, there shall be substituted the words " Part VII of the Housing Act 1974 " and for the words " Part I of this Act ", in the second place where they occur, there shall be substituted the words " that Part ".

(2) In subsection (2) of that section, paragraph (*b*) shall be omitted and, in paragraph (*c*), for the words " section 27 of this Act " there shall be substituted the words " section 84 of the Housing Act 1974 ".

21. In Schedule 5 to that Act (payments to owner-occupiers and others in respect of unfit houses purchased or demolished) in paragraph 1(1) for the words " a closing order under section 17 of that Act or a clearance order " there shall be substituted the words " or a closing order under section 17 of that Act ".

The Rent (Scotland) Act 1971

22. In section 5(5) of the Rent (Scotland) Act 1971 (conditions 1971 c. 28. for a housing association tenancy to be excluded from that Act) after paragraph (*f*) there shall be inserted the following paragraph:—

" (*g*) that the dwelling-house was comprised in a housing project approved for the purposes of section 29 of the Housing Act 1974 ".

The Housing (Financial Provisions) (Scotland) Act 1972   1972 c. 46.

23.—(1) In section 23(3)(*a*) of the Housing (Financial Provisions) (Scotland) Act 1972 (certain buildings not to be included among those in respect of which local authority are required to keep a housing revenue account) after the words " the Act of 1968 " there shall be inserted the words " or section 107 of the Housing Act 1974 ".

(2) In section 52 of that Act (the basic residual subsidy), at the beginning of subsection (8) (the withdrawal factor for years subsequent to 1972-73) there shall be inserted the words " Subject to subsection (9) below " and after that subsection there shall be added the following subsection:—

" (9) For the year 1974-75, the withdrawal factor is zero.".

(3) In section 53 of that Act (the special residual subsidy), at the beginning of subsection (9) (the reduction factor for houses completed during any specified year) there shall be inserted the words " Subject to subsection (10) below " and after that subsection there shall be added the following subsection:—

" (10) For the purposes of subsections (6)(*b*) and (7) above the reduction factor for houses completed during the year 1972-73 or, as the case may be, 1973-74 is zero."

(4) In sections 54(1) and 55(12) of that Act (power of Secretary of State to modify basis of calculation of certain subsidies where a housing association's income for any year will be inadequate to meet the expenditure which it would be reasonable for them to incur in that year in exercise of their housing functions) after the words " will be " there shall be inserted the words " or was " and after the words " would be " there shall be inserted the words " or, as the case may be, was ".

(5) In section 61(2) of that Act (rents to be registrable under Part IV of the Rent (Scotland) Act 1971) after the words " the Act of 1971 " there shall be inserted the words " (and no other provisions of that Act) shall apply to a tenancy to which the said sections 60 to 66 apply and in their application to such tenancies ".

(6) After subsection (3) of section 62 of that Act (rent limit where no rent is registered) there shall be inserted the following subsection—

" (3A) The reference in paragraph (*b*) of subsection (3) above to another tenancy includes, in addition to a tenancy to which sections 62 to 66 of this Act apply, a regulated tenancy within the meaning of the Act of 1971—

(*a*) which subsisted at any time after the operative date, within the meaning of the Housing Act 1974 ; and

(*b*) under which, immediately before it came to an end, the interest of the landlord belonged to a housing association ".

(7) In section 66 of that Act (increase of rent without notice to quit) the reference to a housing association shall, on and after the operative date, be construed as not extending to an unregistered housing association unless the provisions of section 18(1)(*b*) or (*c*) of this Act apply to that association.

The Housing Finance Act 1972

24. In the Housing Finance Act 1972 (in this Schedule referred to as " the 1972 Act "), in paragraph (*e*) of section 12(1) (with the consent of the Secretary of State, a local authority may include in their Housing Revenue Account income and expenditure in respect of houses and buildings not specifically referred to in paragraphs (*a*) to (*d*) of that section) after the word " such " there shall be inserted the word " land " and at the end of that paragraph there shall be added the words " and any consent given by the Secretary of State for the purposes of this paragraph may be given either generally to local authorities or to any local authority or description of local authority or in any particular case ".

25.—(1) In section 28 of the 1972 Act (application for qualification certificate) in subsection (1) (application may be combined with application for a grant under Part I of the Housing Act 1969) for the words " Part I of the Housing Act 1969 " there shall be substituted the words " Part VII of the Housing Act 1974 ".

(2) In subsection (4) of that section (local authority need not serve notice on tenant where they approved an application for a grant under section 2(1) or section 9(1) of the Housing Act 1969 and work has been carried out) after the words " section 2(1) or section 9(1) of the Housing Act 1969 " there shall be inserted the words " or section 61(1) or section 65(1) of the Housing Act 1974 ".

26.—(1) In section 33 of the 1972 Act (if one of two conditions is satisfied, county court may by order empower landlord to carry out certain works to which tenant does not consent) in subsection (2)(*a*) (one of the conditions is that the works were specified in an application for a grant under Part I of the Housing Act 1969 and the application has been approved) after the words " Part I of the Housing Act 1969 " there shall be inserted the words " or Part VII of the Housing Act 1974 ".

(2) At the end of subsection (3) of that section (order under subsection (1) may impose conditions as to time for carrying out works) there shall be added the words " or section 82(1) of the Housing Act 1974 ".

27. In section 34(3) of the 1972 Act (definitions for purposes of
Part III of the Act: " standard amenities " has the meaning assigned
to it by section 7 of the Housing Act 1969) for the words " section 7
of the Housing Act 1969 " there shall be substituted the words
" section 58 of the Housing Act 1974 ".

28. In section 38(2) of the 1972 Act (section 25(1) of the Rent Act
1968, which provides for increase in recoverable rent for improvements, not to apply to improvements with respect to which a grant
under Part I of the Housing Act 1969 is payable or has been paid)
after the words " Part I of the Housing Act 1969 " there shall be
inserted the words " or Part VII of the Housing Act 1974 ".

29. In section 45 of the 1972 Act (protection of tenant with security
of tenure where grant-aided improvement is carried out) in subsection (1) after the words " Part I of the Housing Act 1969 " there
shall be inserted the words " or Part VII of the Housing Act 1974 ".

30. In section 72 of the 1972 Act (the basic residual subsidy) at the
beginning of subsection (9) (the withdrawal factor for years subsequent to 1972-73) there shall be inserted the words " Subject to
subsection (10) below " and after that subsection there shall be added
the following subsection: —

" (10) For the year 1974-75, the withdrawal factor is zero ".

31. In section 73 of the 1972 Act (the special residual subsidy) at
the beginning of subsection (7) (the reduction factor for dwellings
completed during any specified year) there shall be inserted the words
" Subject to subsection (8) below " and after that subsection there
shall be added the following subsection: —

" (8) For the purposes of subsections (4)(*b*) and (5) above, the
reduction factor for dwellings completed during the year 1972-73
or, as the case may be, 1973-74 is zero ".

32. In sections 74(1) and 75(12) of the 1972 Act (power of
Secretary of State to modify basis of calculation of certain subsidies
where a housing association's income for any year will be inadequate
to meet the expenditure which it would be reasonable for them
to incur in that year in exercise of their housing functions) after
the words " will be " there shall be inserted the words " or was "
and after the words " would be " there shall be inserted the words
" or, as the case may be, was ".

33.—(1) In subsection (2) of section 82 of the 1972 Act (application
of certain provisions of Part IV of Rent Act 1968 in relation to
tenancies to which Part VIII of the 1972 Act applies),—

(*a*) after the words " the following " there shall be inserted
the words " and no other " ; and

(*b*) after the word " shall " there shall be inserted the words
" apply in relation to tenancies to which this Part of this
Act applies, and in their application to such tenancies
shall ".

(2) If, pursuant to an application by a local authority under
section 44A of the Rent Act 1968, a rent has, at any time before

SCH. 13

the appointed day, been registered in the part of the register under Part IV of that Act which is provided for by subsection (1) of section 82 of the 1972 Act, that registration—

1968 c. 23.

    (*a*) shall be as valid as if section 44A of the Rent Act 1968 had, before the appointed day, been specified in subsection (2) of section 82 of the 1972 Act ; and

    (*b*) shall be treated on and after the appointed day as if it had been effected pursuant to an application under section 44 of the Rent Act 1968.

(3) In this paragraph "the appointed day" means the day appointed for the coming into operation of this paragraph.

34. After subsection (3) of section 83 of the 1972 Act (rent limit where no rent is registered) there shall be inserted the following subsection—

"(3A) The reference in paragraph (*b*) of subsection (3) above to another tenancy includes, in addition to a tenancy to which this Part of this Act applies, a regulated tenancy, within the meaning of the Rent Act 1968—

    (*a*) which subsisted at any time after the operative date, within the meaning of the Housing Act 1974 ; and

    (*b*) under which, immediately before it came to an end, the interest of the landlord belonged to a housing association ".

35.—(1) In section 91(1) of the 1972 Act (exceptions from duty to give information about service charges) at the end of paragraph (*d*) there shall be added the words "which either is registered under section 13 of the Housing Act 1974 or falls within any of paragraphs (*a*) to (*c*) of section 18(1) of that Act."

(2) This paragraph shall come into operation on the operative date.

36. In Schedule 1 to the 1972 Act (the Housing Revenue Account) in paragraph (*d*) of paragraph 1(1) (amounts to be carried to the credit of the account to include contributions towards costs of improvements and conversions) the word " or " at the end of sub-paragraph (iii) shall be omitted and, after sub-paragraph (iv), there shall be inserted the words " or

    (*v*) section 79 of the Housing Act 1974 ".

37. In Schedule 6 to the 1972 Act (restriction on rent increases) in paragraph 1(1) and, in paragraph 2, in Case F in the Table, after the words " Part I of the Housing Act 1969 " there shall be inserted the words " or Part VII of the Housing Act 1974 ".

1973 c. 26.

The Land Compensation Act 1973

38.—(1) In the Land Compensation Act 1973 (in this Schedule referred to as " the 1973 Act "), in section 29 (right to home loss payment where person displaced from dwelling) subsection (1) shall be amended as follows :—

    (*a*) at the end of paragraph (*b*) there shall be added the words " or the service of an improvement notice, within the meaning of Part VIII of the Housing Act 1974, in respect of the dwelling ";

(b) in paragraph (c) after the words " the carrying out of " there shall be inserted the words "any improvement to the dwelling or of " and at the end of that paragraph there shall be added the following paragraph : —

" (d) where the land has previously been acquired by a registered housing association, within the meaning of the Housing Act 1974, or by an unregistered housing association which falls within section 18(1)(a) of that Act, the carrying out by that association of any improvement to the dwelling or of redevelopment on the land " ; and

(c) for the words from " the acquiring authority " to the end of the subsection there shall be substituted the following paragraphs : —

" (i) where paragraph (a) above applies, the acquiring authority ;

(ii) where paragraph (b) above applies, the authority who made the order, passed the resolution, accepted the undertaking or served the notice ;

(iii) where paragraph (c) above applies, the authority carrying out the improvement or redevelopment ; and

(iv) where paragraph (d) above applies, the housing association carrying out the improvement or redevelopment.

(2) After subsection (3) of that section there shall be inserted the following subsection : —

" (3A) For the purposes of this section a person shall not be treated as displaced from a dwelling in consequence of the acceptance of an undertaking, of the service of such an improvement notice as is mentioned in subsection (1)(b) above or of the carrying out of any improvement to the dwelling unless he is permanently displaced from it in consequence of the carrying out of the works specified in the undertaking or notice or, as the case may be, of the improvement in question ".

(3) In subsection (7) of that section for the words " or section 15(4)(i) of the said Act of 1966 " there shall be substituted the words " secton 15(4)(i) of the said Act of 1966 or section 87 of the Housing Act 1974 ", the words " and ' redevelopment ' includes a change of use " shall be omitted and at the end of that subsection there shall be inserted the following subsection : —

" (7A) In this section—

' improvement ' includes alteration and enlargement ; and ' redevelopment ' includes a change of use."

39.—(1) In section 37 of the 1973 Act (disturbance payments for persons without compensatable interests) subsection (1) shall be amended—

(a) by adding, at the end of paragraph (b), the words " or the service of an improvement notice, within the meaning of

Part VIII of the Housing Act 1974, in respect of a house on the land " ;

(b) by inserting, in paragraph (c), after the words " the carrying out of " the words " any improvement to a house or building on the land or of " ;

(c) by adding, at the end of paragraph (c) the following paragraph : —

" (d) where the land has previously been acquired by a registered housing association, within the meaning of the Housing Act 1974, or by an unregistered housing association which falls within section 18(1)(a) of that Act, the carrying out by that association of any improvement to a house or building on the land or of redevelopment on that land " ; and

(d) by making the like amendments as are specified, in relation to section 29(1) of that Act, in paragraph 38(1)(c) above.

(2) Subsection (3) of that section shall be amended as follows : —

(a) for the words " or redevelopment as is mentioned in paragraph (a) or (c) " there shall be substituted the words " improvement or redevelopment as is mentioned in paragraph (a), (c) or (d) " ;

(b) for the words " or undertaking " there shall be substituted the words " undertaking or improvement notice " ;

(c) for the words " or the undertaking was accepted " there shall be substituted the words " the undertaking was accepted or the notice was served ".

(3) After subsecton (3) of that section there shall be inserted the following subsection : —

" (3A) For the purposes of subsection (1) above a person shall not be treated as displaced in consequence of the acceptance of an undertaking, of the service of such an improvement notice as is mentioned in paragraph (b) of that subsection or of the carrying out of any improvement to a house or building unless he is permanently displaced in consequence of the carrying out of the works specified in the undertaking or notice or, as the case may be, of the improvement in question."

(4) In subsection (9) of that section after the word " undertaking " there shall be inserted the word " ' improvement ' ".

40.—(1) In section 39 of the 1973 Act (duty to rehouse residential occupiers) in paragraph (c) of subsection (1) after the words " the carrying out of " there shall be inserted the words " any improvement to a house or building on the land or of " and at the end of that paragraph there shall be added the following paragraph : —

" (d) the service of an improvement notice, within the meaning of Part VIII of the Housing Act 1974, in respect of premises in which that accommodation is situated ".

(2) In subsection (3) of that section after the word "demolition" there shall be added the words "or improvement".

(3) In subsection (6) of that section after the words "such acquisition" there shall be inserted the word "improvement", after the words "paragraph (*b*) of that subsection" there shall be inserted the words "or of such an improvement notice as is mentioned in paragraph (*d*) of that subsection" and for the words "or the undertaking was accepted" there shall be substituted the words "the undertaking was accepted or the notice was served".

(4) After subsection (6) of that section there shall be inserted the following subsection:—

"(6A) For the purposes of subsection (1) above a person shall not be treated as displaced in consequence of the acceptance of an undertaking, of the carrying out of any improvement to a house or building or of the service of such an improvement notice as is mentioned in paragraph (*d*) of that subsection unless he is permanently displaced from the residential accommodation in question in consequence of the carrying out of the works specified in the undertaking, the carrying out of the improvement or, as the case may be, the carrying out of the works specified in the notice."

(5) In subsection (7) of that section for the words "subsection (8)" there shall be substituted the words "subsections (8) and (8A)".

(6) After subsection (8) there shall be inserted the following subsection:—

"(8A) In a case where subsection (1) above applies in consequence of the acceptance of an undertaking under section 87 of the Housing Act 1974 or the service of an improvement notice within the meaning of Part VIII of that Act, the relevant authority for the purposes of this section is the authority which is the local authority, within the meaning of Part VII of that Act, in relation to the premises in which the residential accommodation is situated".

(7) In subsection (9) of that section after the word "undertaking" there shall be inserted the word "' improvement '".

41.—(1) In section 43 of the 1973 Act (power to defray expenses in connection with acquisition of new dwellings) in subsection (1),—

(*a*) for the words "any such acquisition as is mentioned in section 39(1)(*a*) above", there shall be substituted the words "any of the events specified in paragraphs (*a*) to (*d*) of section 39(1) above; and

(*b*) for the words "the acquiring authority" there shall be substituted the words "then, according to the nature of the event in consequence of which he was displaced, the acquiring authority, the authority who made the order, passed the resolution, accepted the undertaking or served the notice or the authority carrying out the improvement or redevelopment".

(2) In subsection (4) of that section for the words " and (6) " there shall be substituted the words " (6) and (6A) " and for the words " subsection (1)(*a*) " there shall be substituted the words " any provision of subsection (1) ".

The Land Compensation (Scotland) Act 1973

42.—(1) In section 27 of the Land Compensation (Scotland) Act 1973 (right to home loss payment where person displaced from dwelling), subsection (1) shall be amended as follows:—

(*a*) in paragraph (*c*) after the words " the carrying out of " there shall be inserted the words " any improvement to the dwelling or of " and at the end of that paragraph there shall be added the following paragraph:—

" (*d*) where the land has previously been acquired by a registered housing association, within the meaning of the Housing Act 1974, the carrying out by that association of any improvement to the dwelling or of redevelopment on the land " ; and

(*b*) for the words from " the acquiring authority " to the end of the subsection there shall be substituted the following paragraphs:—

" (i) where paragraph (*a*) above applies, the acquiring authority ;

(ii) where paragraph (*b*) above applies, the authority who made the order, passed the resolution or accepted the undertaking ;

(iii) where paragraph (*c*) above applies, the authority carrying out the improvement or redevelopment ; and

(iv) where paragraph (*d*) above applies, the housing association carrying out the improvement or redevelopment."

(2) After subsection (3) of that section there shall be inserted the following subsection:—

" (3A) For the purposes of this section a person shall not be treated as displaced from a dwelling in consequence of the carrying out of any improvement to the dwelling unless he is permanently displaced from it in consequence of the carrying out of the improvement in question."

(3) In subsection (7) of that section the words " and ' redevelopment ' includes a change of use " shall be omitted and at the end of that subsection there shall be inserted the following subsection:—

" (7A) In this section
' improvement ' includes alteration and enlargement ; and
' redevelopment ' includes a change of use ".

43.—(1) In section 34 of that Act (disturbance payments for persons without compensatable interests), subsection (1) shall be amended—

(*a*) by inserting, in paragraph (*c*), after the words " the carrying

out of ", the words "any improvement to a house or
building on the land or of " ;

(b) by adding, at the end of paragraph (c), the following
paragraph : —

"(d) where the land has previously been acquired by
a registered housing association, within the meaning of
the Housing Act 1974, the carrying out by that association of any improvement to a house or building
on the land or of redevelopment on that land " ; and

(c) by making the like amendments as are specified, in relation
to section 27(1) of that Act, in paragraph 42(1)(b) above.

(2) In subsection (3) of that section for the words " or redevelopment as is mentioned in paragraph (a) or (c) " there shall be substituted the words " improvement or redevelopment as is mentioned
in paragraph (a), (c) or (d) ".

(3) After subsection (3) of that section, there shall be inserted the
following subsection : —

"(3) For the purposes of subsection (1) above a person shall
not be treated as displaced in consequence of the carrying out
of any improvement to a house or building unless he is permanently displaced in consequence of the carrying out of the
improvement in question ".

(4) In subsection (8) of that section after the word " undertaking "
there shall be inserted the word " ' improvement ' ".

44.—(1) In section 36 of that Act (duty to rehouse residential
occupiers) in paragraph (c) of subsection (1) after the words " the
carrying out of " there shall be inserted the words " any improvement
to a house or building on the land or of ".

(2) In subsection (3) of that section after the word " demolition "
there shall be added the words " or improvement ".

(3) In subsection (6) of that section after the words " such acquisition " there shall be inserted the word " improvement ".

(4) In subsection (9) of that section after the word " undertaking "
there shall be inserted the word " ' improvement ' ".

45.—(1) In section 40 of that Act (power to defray expenses in
connection with acquisition of new dwellings) in subsection (1)—

(a) for the words " any such acquisition as is mentioned in
section 36(1)(a) above ", there shall be substituted the words
" any of the events specified in paragraphs (a) to (c) of
section 36(1) above " ; and

(b) for the words " the acquiring authority " there shall be
substituted the words " then, according to the nature of the
event in consequence of which he was displaced, the acquiring authority, the authority who made the order, passed
the resolution or accepted the undertaking or the
authority carrying out the improvement or re-development ".

(2) In subsection (4) of that section for the words " subsection
(1)(a) " there shall be substituted the words " any provision of subsection (1) ".

Local Government (Scotland) Act 1973

46.—(1) Section 131(3) shall cease to have effect.

(2) In Schedule 12, in paragraph 6, in the substituted section 1 for the words " sections 152 and 153 " there shall be substituted the words " section 152 " ; and paragraph 11 shall be omitted.

Section 130.

SCHEDULE 14

TRANSITIONAL PROVISIONS AND SAVINGS

Transitional provisions

1. Notwithstanding the repeals effected by this Act, in any case where—

1964 c. 56.

    (a) the Housing Corporation have before the operative date made a loan under section 2 of the Housing Act 1964, and

    (b) under a mortgage or heritable security, entered into by the body to whom the loan was made, to secure the loan the Housing Corporation have an interest as mortgagee or, as the case may be, as creditor in any land belonging to that body,

1972 c. 47.

then, whether or not that body becomes a registered housing association on or after the operative date, subsections (3) and (4) of that section, as amended by section 77(2) of the Housing Finance Act 1972, shall continue to apply in relation to that land as if those provisions had not been repealed.

2. In any case where—

    (a) before the operative date, the Corporation agreed to make a loan to a housing association under section 2 of the Housing Act 1964 but no such loan was made before the repeal of that section by this Act took effect, and

    (b) that loan was to be made for the purpose of assisting the association in connection with any of the matters specified in paragraphs (a) to (c) of subsection (4) of section 17 of this Act,

section 9 of this Act shall have effect as if subsection (1) of that section permitted the Corporation to make to the association, at a time when they are an unregistered association, a loan of the same amount and for the same purpose as the loan referred to in paragraphs (a) and (b) above.

3. Before the operative date, sections 36(4)(d) and 74(3) of this Act shall have effect as if the word " registered " in each place where it occurs, were omitted.

4.—(1) Without prejudice to section 99(2)(d) of this Act, no provisional notice or improvement notice may be served in respect of a dwelling before the operative date if the person having control of the dwelling is a housing association and the dwelling is a dwelling-house falling within any of paragraphs (a) to (d) of subsection (6) of section 5 of the Rent Act 1968 (tenancies of certain dwelling houses excluded from protection under that Act).

1968 c. 23.

SCH. 14

(2) If, after a provisional notice or an improvement notice has been served in respect of any dwelling but before the operative date, a housing association becomes the person having control of the dwelling and, by virtue of sub-paragraph (1) above, no such notice could then be served in respect of the dwelling, any such notice with respect to the dwelling and any undertaking accepted under Part VIII of this Act with respect to the dwelling shall cease to have effect.

(3) In this paragraph " provisional notice ", " improvement notice " and " person having control " have the same meanings as in Part VIII of this Act.

Savings

5.—(1) The repeal by this Act of sections 17 to 20 of the Housing Act 1969 shall not apply in any case where an application for an improvement contribution or a standard contribution has been approved before the day appointed for the coming into operation of that repeal.

1969 c. 33.

(2) In sub-paragraph (1) above " improvement contribution " and " standard contribution " have the same meanings as in sections 18 to 20 of the Housing Act 1969.

6. Subject to section 35(7) of this Act, the repeal by this Act of section 21 of the Housing Act 1969 or, as the case may be, section 16 or section 17 of the Housing (Financial Provisions) (Scotland) Act 1968 shall not affect the continued operation of that section in relation to any such arrangements as are referred to in subsection (1) of that section if, before the day appointed for the coming into operation of that repeal, approval has been given in accordance with subsection (2) of the said section 21 or, in Scotland, section 14 of the said Act of 1968 as applied by section 17(1)(ii) of that Act to the making and terms of those arrangements.

1968 c. 31.

7.—(1) Subject to sub-paragraph (2) below, the repeal by this Act of any provision of Part I of the Housing Act 1969 shall not affect the continued operation of that Part in relation to any case where an application for a grant under that Part has been made (whether or not it has been approved) before the day appointed for the coming into operation of that repeal.

(2) For the purpose of allowing an application for a grant under Part VII of this Act to be made notwithstanding that all or some of the works in respect of which that grant is to be sought were specified in an application, made before the day appointed as mentioned in sub-paragraph (1) above, for a grant under Part I of the Housing Act 1969, the local authority to whom that application was made shall allow it to be withdrawn (whether or not it has been approved) unless they are satisfied that the works specified in the application have been begun.

SCHEDULE 15

ENACTMENTS REPEALED

Chapter	Short Title	Extent of Repeal
5 & 6 Eliz. II. c. 56.	The Housing Act 1957.	In section 43(1) the words from " in one or other " to " (b) ". Sections 44 to 46. In section 50 the words from " (a) " to " vested in the authority ". Section 51. Sections 53 and 54. In section 60(1) the word " (a) " and the words from " or " to " order ". In section 67(1) the words " a clearance order, or in ". In section 70(2) the words " clearance or ", " clearance order or " and " as the case may be ". Section 121. In section 159 paragraph (b)(iv). In section 162(1) the words " or a clearance order ". In section 163(1) the words " or a clearance order ". In section 166(1) the words " any clearance order ". In Schedule 2, in paragraph 4(1), paragraph (c) and the word " or " immediately preceding it, in paragraph 6(1) the words " (a) " and " or (b) a clearance order ", and in paragraph 7(2) the words " clearance order ". In Schedule 4 in paragraph 1 the words " or a clearance order " and in paragraph 5 the words " or fifty-one " and " or a clearance order ". Schedule 5.
9 & 10 Eliz. II. c. 64.	The Public Health Act 1961.	In section 29(4)(b) the words " or clearance order ", in both places where they occur.
9 & 10 Eliz. II. c. 65.	The Housing Act 1961.	Section 24. Schedule 3.
1964 c. 56.	The Housing Act 1964.	In section 1, in subsection (1) the words from " whose general duty " to the end of the subsection and subsection (1A). Sections 2 to 4. Section 6. In section 8 subsections (6), (7) and (9). Section 9.

Chapter	Short Title	Extent of Repeal
1964 c. 56— *cont.*	The Housing Act 1964— *cont.*	In section 11(1) the words " section 3 " and " section 6 ". In section 12, in subsection (1) the definition of " local auth- ority " and subsection (2). Part II. Sections 57 and 59. In section 72(1) the words " of twelve months " in each place where they occur.
1965 c. 56.	The Compulsory Purchase Act 1965.	Section 35.
1965 c. 75.	The Rent Act 1965.	In section 35(5) the words " 45(3) ". In Schedule 6, in paragraph 10(2), the words " 45(3) ".
1965 c. 81.	The Housing (Slum Clearance Compensa- tion) Act 1965.	In section 1(1) the words " or clearance orders ".
1966 c. 49.	The Housing (Scotland) Act 1966.	Sections 153 to 155. Section 159.
1967 c. 29.	The Housing Subsidies Act 1967.	Section 14. In section 27, in subsection (1) the words from " and for the purposes " to the end of the subsection. Schedule 2.
1968 c. 13.	The National Loans Act 1968.	In Schedule 1 the entries relating to subsections (1), (3) and (5) of section 9 of the Housing Act 1964.
1968 c. 23.	The Rent Act 1968.	In Schedule 15 in the entry relating to the Housing Act 1957 the words " 45(6) " and in the entry relating to the Housing Act 1964, the amend- ments of section 44(2)(*a*) and Schedule 2.
1968 c. 31.	The Housing (Financial Provisions) (Scotland) Act 1968.	Sections 16 and 17. In section 18(1) the words from " or any such " to " section 16 of this Act "; and the words " or arrange- ments ".
1969 c. 33.	The Housing Act 1969.	Part I (including Schedule 1). In section 29(2) the words " or a clearance order under Schedule 5 to that Act ". In section 30, subsections (2) and (3). Section 36. In section 37(4), paragraph (*b*) and the word " or " immedi- ately preceding it. In section 40(2)(*a*) the words " Part I of this Act other than sections 17 to 22 ".

SCH. 15

Chapter	Short Title	Extent of Repeal
1969 c. 33— *cont.*	The Housing Act 1969— *cont.*	Section 41. In section 69 paragraph (*c*) and the word " or " immediately preceding it. In section 70 the words " section 20 or ". Section 75(2)(*b*). Sections 76 and 77. In section 88(1) the words " Part I ". In Schedule 5, in each of paragraphs 3(1) and 5(2), the words " clearance order ". In Schedule 8 paragraphs 25 to 28 and 31.
1971 c. 76.	The Housing Act 1971.	In section 2, subsections (1) to (3) and (5). In section 3, subsections (1) to (3) and (5).
1972 c. 47.	The Housing Finance Act 1972.	In section 11(7) the words " sections 53 and 54 (clearance orders made before 30th August 1954) and other than ". In section 36, in subsection (1), paragraph (*c*) and, in subsection (2), in paragraph (*c*) the words " or clearance order " and " or 44 ". Section 77. In Schedule 1, in paragraph 1(1)(*d*), the word " or " at the end of sub-paragraph (iii). In Schedule 8, paragraph 9(2).
1972 c. 70.	The Local Government Act 1972.	In section 171(1) the words " section 6(4) of the Housing Act 1969 ". In Schedule 22, in paragraph 24 the words " 26 ".
1973 c. 5.	The Housing (Amendment) Act 1973.	In section 1, subsections (2) to (4).
1973 c. 26.	The Land Compensation Act 1973.	In section 29(7) the words " and ' redevelopment ' includes a change of use ". Section 73(2).
1973 c. 56.	The Land Compensation (Scotland) Act 1973.	In section 27(7) the words " and ' redevelopment ' includes a change of use ".
1973 c. 65.	The Local Government (Scotland) Act 1973.	Section 131(3). In Schedule 12, paragraph 11.

PRINTED IN ENGLAND BY HAROLD GLOVER
Controller of Her Majesty's Stationery Office and Queen's Printer of Acts of Parliament
(384607)